MILL'S
*THE SUBJECTION
OF WOMEN*

Critical Essays on the Classics

Series Editor: Steven M. Cahn

The volumes in this series offer insightful and accessible essays that shed light on the classics of philosophy. Each of the distinguished editors has selected outstanding work in recent scholarship to provide today's readers with a deepened understanding of the most timely issues raised in these important texts.

MILL'S
THE SUBJECTION
OF WOMEN

Edited by
Maria H. Morales

ROWMAN & LITTLEFIELD PUBLISHERS, INC.
Lanham • Boulder • New York • Toronto • Oxford

ROWMAN & LITTLEFIELD PUBLISHERS, INC.

Published in the United States of America
by Rowman & Littlefield Publishers, Inc.
A wholly owned subsidary of The Rowman & Littlefield Publishing Group, Inc.
4501 Forbes Boulevard, Suite 200, Lanham, Maryland 20706
www.rowmanlittlefield.com

PO Box 317
Oxford
OX2 9RU, UK

British Library Cataloguing in Publication Information Available

Library of Congress Cataloging-in-Publication Data

Mill's The subjection of women / edited by Maria H. Morales.
    p. cm. — (Critical essays on the classics)
    Includes bibliographical references and index.
    ISBN 0-7425-3517-7 (cloth : alk. paper) — ISBN 0-7425-3518-5
(pbk. : alk. paper)
    1. Mill, John Stuart, 1806–1873 Subjection of women. 2. Feminism—Great
Britain I. Morales, Maria H. II. Series
HQ1596.J64 2004
305.42'0941—dc22

                                                              2004013907

Printed in the United States of America

♾™ The paper used in this publication meets the minimum requirements of
American National Standard for Information Sciences—Permanence of Paper
for Printed Library Materials, ANSI/NISO Z39.48-1992.

Being about, if I am so happy to obtain her consent, to enter into the marriage relation with the only woman I have ever known, with whom I would have entered into that state; and the whole character of the marriage relation as constituted by law being such as both she and I entirely and conscientiously disapprove, for this among other reasons, that it confers upon one of the parties to the contract, legal power and control over the person, property, and freedom of action of the other party, independent of her own wishes and will; I having no means of legally divesting myself of these odious powers (as I most assuredly would do if an engagement to that effect could be made legally binding on me) feel it my duty to put on record a formal protest against the existing law of marriage, in so far as conferring such powers; and a solemn promise never in any case or under any circumstance to use them. And in the event of marriage between Mrs. Taylor and me I declare it to be my will and intention, and the condition of the engagement between us, that she retains in all respects whatever the same absolute freedom of action and freedom of disposal of herself and of all that does or may at any time belong to her, as if no such marriage had taken place; and I absolutely disclaim and repudiate all pretension to have acquired any rights whatever by virtue of such marriage.

John Stuart Mill, 1851

Contents

Acknowledgments

THE EDITOR AND PUBLISHER WISH TO THANK the following authors and publishers for permission to reprint their work in this volume:

Chapter 1, Wendy Donner's "John Stuart Mill's Liberal Feminism," originally appeared in *Philosophical Studies* 69 (1993): 155-66. Here reprinted with permission from Kluwer Academic Publishers.

Chapter 2, John Howes's "Mill on Women and Human Development," originally appeared in *The Australasian Journal of Philosophy*, supplement to volume 64 (1986): 66–74.

Chapter 3, Susan Moller Okin's "John Stuart Mill's Feminism: The Subjection of Women and the Improvement of Mankind," originally appeared in *The New Zealand Journal of History* 7 (1973): 105-27.

Chapter 4, Julia Annas's "Mill and The Subjection of Women," originally appeared in *Philosophy* 52 (1977): 179-94. Here reprinted with permission from Cambridge University Press.

Chapter 5, Keith Burgess-Jackson's "John Stuart Mill, Radical Feminist," originally appeared in *Social Theory and Practice* 21 (1995): 369–396.

Chapter 6, Maria H. Morales's "The Corrupting Influence of Power," originally appeared in *Philosophical Perspectives on Power and Domination*, edited by Laura Duhan-Kaplan and Lawrence Bove (Amsterdam: Rodopi Press, 1997).

Chapter 7, Mary Lyndon Shanley's "Marital Slavery and Friendship: John Stuart Mill's *The Subjection of Women*," originally appeared in *Political Theory* 9 (1981): 229-47.

Chapter 8, Susan Mendus's "The Marriage of True Minds: The Ideal of Marriage in the Philosophy of John Stuart Mill" originally appeared in *Sexuality and Subordination: Interdisciplinary Studies of Gender in the Nineteenth Century,* edited by Susan Mendus and Jane Rendall. (London: Routledge, 1989.) Here reprinted with permission from Routledge.

Chapter 9, Nadia Urbinati's "John Stuart Mill on Androgyny and Ideal Marriage," originally appeared in *Political Theory* 19 (1991): 626–648.

I wish to thank David Lyons and Dale Miller for their prompt responses to my request for feedback concerning the selections included in this volume. The responsibility for the finished product, however, is mine. I also thank Karen Foulke and Whitney Mutch for their hands-on help. Finally, but not less importantly, I thank Eve DeVaro and Tessa Fallon at Rowman and Littlefield for their patience and understanding in the face of unanticipated delays with the project.

Introduction

Maria H. Morales

The moral training of mankind will never be adapted to the conditions of the life for which all other human progress is a preparation, until they practise in the family the same moral rule which is adapted to the normal constitution of human society.

John Stuart Mill, 1861

JOHN STUART MILL'S *THE SUBJECTION OF WOMEN* IS a landmark work both in the long history of women's struggles for political, legal, economic, and personal equality, and in the shorter history of rigorous intellectual analyses of women's subordination. As an instance of the former, it is inextricably tied to Mill's life and intellectual development. As an instance of the latter, *The Subjection of Women* (1869) occupies a critical place in the history of early feminist theory. In importance for the development of feminist arguments for women's political and legal rights it is only matched by an earlier work, Mary Wollestonecraft's *A Vindication of the Rights of Woman* (1792). Yet Mill's work also was among the first to tackle the even more difficult questions of women's social and personal subordination. In this vein, it shares a great deal with such more radical, and lesser known, works as the Owenite William Godwin's *Enquiry Concerning Political Justice* (1793) and the utilitarian William Thompson's *Appeal of One Half the Human Race, Women* (1825).

In the first paragraph of *The Subjection of Women* Mill explains that his concern is to examine the grounds of one of his earliest opinions, which "the progress of reflection and the experience of life" had only served to strengthen. This opinion is that

> the principle which regulates the existing *social* relations between the two sexes—the legal subordination of one sex to the other—is *wrong in itself* and one of the chief hindrances to human improvement; and that it ought to be replaced by *a principle of perfect equality*, admitting no power or privilege on the one side, nor disability on the other. (*The Subjection of Women, Collected Works of John Stuart Mill*, vol. xxi, chap. 1, 261, my emphasis)

Mill's claim is that legal subordination regulates a power differential in social relations between women and men and that a principle of "perfect equality" should serve that regulative function instead. As contemporary readers, we may fail to appreciate the magnitude and breadth of Mill's enterprise. We live in a world quite different from Mill's, where women have a legal personality. We can vote, can attain high levels of education, can own property, can initiate divorces and be granted custody of our own children upon divorce, and can have other recourses via the legal system to right wrongs inflicted upon us. Today, we can pursue a variety of professions: we are lawyers, doctors, professors, scientists, artists, religious leaders, and even astronauts. We can earn our own wages and manage our money, and we can travel without supervision. We can demand (though we might not always receive) equality in the distribution of domestic labor without seeming mad, and we can even choose to remain single without (though not in all cases) risking economic and social disaster. In the 1860s, Mill, against the tide of a powerful philosophical and social tradition, had to *argue* that women are persons before he could even argue that we are legal persons, let alone that we should be treated as persons in all aspects of our lives.

Mill's impassioned pleas in *The Subjection of Women*, however, are not simply aids to our understanding of the long historical plight for women's rights. Even in the political, legal, and economic arena women today are not yet living Mill's ideal of full personhood. Women are scrutinized in their public lives to a much larger degree than their male counterparts, and their wages are not always comparable. Many women still live in a condition of economic dependency, especially (but not exclusively) if we analyze women's situation from a global point of view. In addition, women and men are still socialized according to old gender stereotypes and norms, which often affect women differentially—for example, by reinforcing primary caretaking and nurturing roles. And despite a century and a half of argument and struggle, the "private" realm is *assumed* to be just (if not beyond the scope of the "public" virtue of justice). One of the lasting legacies of Mill's *The Subjection of Women* is its careful argument for the need for justice at *both* the "public" and the "private" levels. In fact, Mill understood that much more is required for "perfect equality" than legal reforms, and that the structure of the *domestic* realm, rooted as it is in harmful socialization practices, must change dramatically for this ideal to become a reality. Such change is radical indeed, even at the dawn of the twenty-first century.

Mill wrote the first draft of *The Subjection of Women* between 1860 and 1861 in his home near Avignon, rewriting it often to improve it (he claimed), and waiting to publish it until such time as it should seem likely to be most useful. The final revision of the manuscript took place in England in 1868, and the book was published in 1869 amidst much criticism on the part of his contemporaries. Mill expected hostility, and wanted to delay publication of this work until the political atmosphere surrounding debates in Parliament over women's suffrage and property rights was more auspicious. (It did not turn out to be "auspicious" for quite some time.) Mill was constantly ridiculed in Parliament for his views on women, and it is doubtful that his concern was with not being *more* abused. (Newspapers and periodicals routinely carried cartoons of Mill "with the ladies," and there are various reports of the vociferous objections to Mill's arguments in Parliament.) The fact is that Mill was actively involved in these causes and did not want to hurt them with the publication of a work calling for much more than political and legal equality for women, notably social equality and equality within marriage. These more radical arguments would give those who opposed even the political and legal gains being sought in Parliament ammunition to dismiss all of it as a big chimera.

The negative reception of *The Subjection of Women* even among Mill's fellow utilitarians can be explained in part by their skewed belief that the views expressed in the work were not Mill's, but Harriet Taylor's, his long-time friend and, eventually, his wife. Mill was quite isolated while writing this work and knew of his colleagues' judgment that *The Subjection of Women* would be "his greatest error as a scientific thinker." (Alexander Bain, *John Stuart Mill*, 146) Interestingly, his contemporaries' adverse judgment of his philosophical work on gender became

standard among Mill scholars until the first wave of "revisionary" scholarship in the 1960s. The received view was that *The Subjection of Women*
was at best ancillary to Mill's "central" doctrines, at worst the ramblings
of a man who was himself "subjected" to the domineering will of a cold,
ruthless "woman." The many *ad hominem* attacks on Harriet Taylor's
character and standing as an intellectual themselves lend support to
Mill's contention in *The Subjection of Women* that men have not been
able to face even the *idea* of living with women as equals.

The views expressed in *The Subjection of Women* were not the exclusive
intellectual patrimony of Mill *or* of Taylor. In his *Autobiography*, Mill himself denied that he simply adopted Harriet Taylor's views on gender equality. (A 253n) This denial was unnecessary. A commitment to gender equality was very much alive in the intellectual circles within which Mill moved.
Mill did not meet Taylor until 1830, and he explained that her influence on
his views was "one among many" at a critical point in his intellectual development, namely the 1820s and 1830s, when he was revising the nature
of his commitment to utilitarianism. At this time, Mill's influences were
mainly the utopian socialists of the period, especially the St. Simonians,
whom he praised for their progressive views on economic and gender
equality. Taylor's egalitarianism, Mill maintained, did not "alter" his path,
but made him bolder in some respects and reinforced his practical sense of
the harms of women's inequality. It would be a mistake to attribute his
"strong convictions on the complete equality [of women and men] in all
legal, political, social, and domestic relations" to Taylor. (*Autobiography, Collected Works of John Stuart Mill*, vol. I, 253n, my emphasis)

In addition, some of Mill's early publications demonstrate that the genesis of his commitment to perfect equality predates his acquaintance with
Taylor. In 1824, for example, Mill wrote a scathing criticism of the conservative *Edinburgh Review*, which he accused of perpetuating the "sham"
morality "usually chalked out for women." Forty years before the publication of *The Subjection of Women* Mill was condemning his society's attitudes toward women in strong terms:

> [A]ll who can or will be of any use, either to themselves or to the world,
> otherwise than as slaves and drudges of their husbands, are called mascu
> line, and other names intended to convey disapprobation. (*Periodical Lit
> erature: Edinburgh Review, Collected Works of John Stuart Mill*, vol. I, 312)

Further record of Mill's early convictions, which stood out in utilitarian
circles, appears in the *Autobiography*'s report of Lord Macauley's criti-

cism of James Mill's (John Stuart's father) *Essay on Government* (1820). The elder Mill argued that women's interests can be subsumed under men's, politically, and, of course, personally. John Stuart Mill praised Macauley's insistence that good government does not depend even primarily on the "identity of interests" between the governed, and he reports that he "most positively dissented" from his father's assumption that women's disenfranchisement and dependence are consistent with good government. Finally, Mill read with approval William Thompson's *Appeal* (1825), and many of the themes of this work reappear in Millian form in *The Subjection of Women*.

The issue of Mill's "collaboration" with Taylor is too large and complex to treat justly here. For a complete collection of their writings, I refer the reader to *Sexual Equality: Writings by John Stuart Mill, Harriet Taylor Mill, and Helen Taylor*, edited by Ann and John Robson. Mill and Taylor worked together a great deal, combining intellectual forces to change the lives of women. (Particularly powerful, and very little known, are their joint writings on cruelty against women and children, published in newspapers and periodicals of the time.) If anything, Mill should be commended for a rare gift indeed: in a world hostile to women's intellectual capacities, he lived what he preached. He treated Taylor as an equal, and publicly acknowledged having been *enriched*, as a thinker and a man, by her intellect and presence in his life. I do not know of any philosophers of Mill's status in the history of philosophy who come even close to him in this regard.

To illuminate this status, I will conclude with some brief facts about Mill's notorious life. He was born in England in 1806, and he died in Avignon, in a house near his wife's grave, in 1873. His father was a stern character who, together with the famous utilitarian Jeremy Bentham, his son's godfather, decided to train young John Stuart according to the rational principles of the orthodox utilitarian creed enjoining the maximization of pleasure over pain. John Stuart was reading classical languages when children today attend preschool and winning prizes for his knowledge of political economy when children today reach middle school. Yet this rigorous education, which emphasized the power of reason over sentiment, led the younger Mill to a serious mental and emotional crisis around 1826. During months of bleak depression, Mill lost faith in the creed that he inherited from his father and Bentham. He reported in his *Autobiography* that he asked himself one day whether success as a Benthamite reformer of the political and legal world would bring him happiness. His negative answer crumbled the edifice on which his intellectual world had been built. Mill lost all motivation to pursue the ends for which he had been trained, which he attributed to the neglect of his emotions. Aided in his despondency by romantic poetry and readings from traditions other than the received one, especially the utopian socialists, Mill set out to change utilitarianism so as to accommodate the culture of feeling and the importance of moral character formation for the improvement of society. He thus redefined the aim of utilitarianism to be the realization of "the permanent interests of man as a progressive being." (*On Liberty, Collected Works of John Stuart Mill*, vol. I, chap. 1, 224)

Mill was a prolific writer with a wide range of philosophical interests, from logic to gender equality! He worked full-time at the British East India Company from 1823 to 1858. He was elected to Parliament in 1865, where he was, as I noted earlier, an active advocate of social and political reforms. Not surprisingly, given his position on the pressing questions with which he was concerned, he was not reelected to a second term. In part for health reasons, he moved to Avignon in 1868, where he composed several of his late works. At the time of his death in 1873 he was working on *Chapters on Socialism*. He died years after Harriet Taylor Mill's death, whom he had married in 1851. His grave is next to hers.

* * *

Commentators long have debated whether Mill's philosophical commitments are consistent with one another. Indeed, we encounter in Mill scholarship as many "Mills" as we might encounter in his corpus. There is Mill the individualist, the classical liberal, the socialist, the classical utilitarian, the positivist, the elitist, the egalitarian, the pragmatic humanist, and the democrat bent on overthrowing privilege and oppression. The question whether these strands in Mill's thought harmonize has kept Mill scholarship alive and well for over a century now. This question is asked as much of Mill's overall corpus as of the arguments within one (or several) of his works. Critical scholarship on *The Subjection of Women* is not an exception. The papers collected in this critical edition represent a variety of interpretations both of the kind of feminism Mill represents and of the specific arguments he offers in *The Subjection of Women*, including their lexical ordering and relative merit. Although I have included several and different perspectives on Mill's work, inevitably I have had to *select* only some among many rich scholarly discussions. Also, I have selected literature that focuses *primarily* on *The Subjection of Women*, as opposed to literature that analyzes side by side Mill's and Taylor's respective views on questions of gender equality.

There are nine selections in this critical edition. I have ordered them roughly by theme—I say *roughly* because their content (for obvious reasons) overlaps and, to that extent, the order is artificial. The first three chapters present Mill as a liberal feminist, but emphasize different concepts as central to his feminism: self-development and sociability (chapter one, Donner), liberty and individuality (chapter two, Howes), and human improvement (chapter three, Moller Okin). Chapters four to six address the question whether Mill's feminism is "reformist" (chapter four, Annas) or "radical" (chapter five, Burgess-Jackson and chapter six, Morales). Finally the last three chapters focus on Mill's conception of marriage as a union of equals in friendship (chapter seven, Lyndon Shanley), as an intellectual union (chapter eight, Mendus), and as a form of egalitarian community based on the rejection of gender-specific natures.

Each selection is preceded by a brief summary of the author's position. This summary is meant primarily to assist the introductory student of Mill and/or of *The Subjection of Women* by indicating the nature and direction of the author's interpretation and arguments. For a richer understanding of Mill's *The Subjection of Women*, the student ought also to read at least Mill's other writings on gender equality, as well as *On Liberty, Utilitarianism*, and *Chapters on Socialism*. The amount of secondary literature on these other works is staggering, but the student can begin with the excellent critical essays on *Utlitiarianism* and *On Liberty* also published in this series.

1

John Stuart Mill's Liberal Feminism

Wendy Donner

Donner defends Mill's feminism as rooted in an egalitarian strand of liberal feminism. She argues that at the heart of Mill's liberal feminism is the value of self-development. This ideal, in her view, is tied to several theses that most feminists would accept: (1) an ethic of feeling, (2) the importance of human attachments, (3) a categorical rejection of materialism and domination, and (4) the value of autonomy as pivotal to maintaining independence and privacy. In Donner's view, Mill's feminist concerns are egalitarian, practical, and social, rather than individualist, abstract, and egoist. What renders his feminism "liberal" is his emphasis on the development of the internal culture of the individual, but not of "individuality" at the expense of social relations.

IN THIS PAPER I EXPLORE AND DEFEND some aspects of John Stuart Mill's liberal feminist political theory and its foundations in his moral philosophy.[1] Feminist ethics and political theory is rich and diverse. One important question in feminist debate is whether historical moral and political theories ought to be rejected entirely by feminists or whether at least some historical thinkers have valuable contributions to make to a feminist revisioning of the traditional canon. I contend that there is much in Mill's philosophy which is in harmony with feminist vision and thought.[2] While Mill's liberal feminism is complex, my focus in this paper is on his conceptions of value, of human nature and of the self, and I leave for another occasion an examination of the politics of his liberal feminism and his views on the sexual division of labor within the family.[3] Liberal feminist theories have been the subject of intense discussion and criticism in current debates among feminist scholars. While this examination has several facets, I concentrate here on some recent critiques which find fault with liberal feminism for its allegedly flawed values of individualism and its flawed conception of human nature and the relation of self to the community. I argue that Mill's conceptions of the self, individualism, and self-development meet many of the concerns raised by these critics whose concerns are more correctly focused on other models of liberalism.

Mill's moral theory and his views of human nature and of the good have important implications for his liberal political philosophy, shaping it into a form of radical egalitarianism. I argue that Mill's conception of value for humans essentially involves a notion of self-development. Let me begin by setting out the core values which shape Mill's liberal feminism. While some critiques of liberalism by both feminist and communitarian thinkers assume that there is one unified liberal theory, there are also several divergent streams of liberal thought. The correct target of these critiques is a liberalism built on core values of possessive and abstract individualism and a view of moral agents as rational egoists. For example, Alison Jaggar criticizes the alleged liberal commitment to abstract individualism. According to Jaggar, abstract individualism assumes that human beings are ontologically prior to and independent of society. "Logically if not empirically, human individuals could exit outside a social content; their essential characteristics, their needs and interests, their capacities and desires, are given independently of their social context and are not created or even fundamentally altered by that context."[4] She also points to the common liberal assumption of egoism which holds that "people typically seek to maximize their individual self-interest" although she concedes that Mill is not the worst offender in this case.[5] Jaggar claims that these views are fundamentally male and should not be accepted by feminists.[6] But Mill himself decisively rejects these views.

Mill is a utilitarian as well as a liberal and is thus committed to locating value in mental states of happiness or satisfaction. But he is a qualitative hedonist and claims that the quality or kind of happiness is important in assessing its value; moreover, the most valuable kinds of happiness are those that engage humans in developing and exercising certain capacities. Mill's core value of development and self-development is not a fixed unity, but an intricate balance of elements. To be more specific, the most valuable forms of happiness are those of engagement in the use of intellectual, affective and moral or caring capacities. Mill maintains that these are generic human capacities which our society has an obligation to nurture, and which members of our society have a right to have developed.[7]

The development of our intellectual, feeling and moral capacities is crucial to our well-being. Mill does not order these capacities hierarchically, but he holds that these aspects of our nature must balance each other. In addition, since these capacities can manifest and be promoted in diverse ways, this allows room for the different experiences of men and women to have equal play, but does not imply that women will seek to become like men. Mill's arguments for the development of our reasoning capacities are well known. What perhaps needs emphasis in the context of his feminist theory is his stress on the importance of the internal culture of the individual, or on the development of our feelings and our capacities of caring for others.[8] This resonates with some principles of a feminist ethic of care. As well he argues that in the process of moral development children must be socialized to feel connected to others and to take pleasure in their happiness and well-being. The deeper point is that Mill's utilitarian commitments require him to maintain that feelings are pivotal to morality and that if we are to take pleasure in intellectual pursuits or in the good of others we must be persons who feel deeply, who are in touch with our emotions, and who are motivated by our concern for others. Cultivation of sympathy with others is the foundation of moral development, and two widely held tenets of feminism—a stress on the importance of feelings and of sympathetic attachments to others—flow from this. Unselfish feelings are a basic element of human nature.[9] These feelings of sympathy, which must be cultivated, are the basis for both generalized moral feelings and social feelings or sociality. Our moral/social side and our intellectual/individualist side are both elements of our nature, and Mill's refusal to elevate the one above the other importantly affects both his concept of self-development and his egalitarian liberalism.

> But there *is* this basis of powerful natural sentiment. . . . This firm foundation is that of the social feelings of mankind; the desire to be in unity with our fellow creatures, which is already a powerful principle in human

nature, and happily one of those which tend to become stronger, even without express inculcation, from the influences of advancing civilization. The social state is at once so natural, so necessary, and so habitual to man, that, except in some unusual circumstances or by an effort of voluntary abstraction, he never conceives himself otherwise than as a member of a body. . . . In this way people grow up unable to conceive as possible to them a state of total disregard of other people's interests. . . .They are also familiar with the fact of cooperating with others, and proposing to themselves a collective, not an individual, interest, as the aim . . . of their actions. . . . He comes, as though instinctively, to be conscious of himself as a being who *of course* pays regard to others. The good of others becomes to him a thing naturally and necessarily to be attended to.[10]

This development of our generic human capacities in childhood socialization is the first part of the process and in the usual course of events, when we reach adulthood we take control of this process as individuals and continue it as one of self-development. In this continuation, we nurture the higher-order capacities of individuality, autonomy, and sociality. These capacities are also balanced holistically and sociality and cooperativeness are given equal play with autonomy and individuality. Mill does not compromise his conviction that autonomy and individuality are essential components of a happy human life. However, his conceptions of individuality and autonomy and his balancing of the various aspects of self-development make his theory responsive to feminism and its concerns.

Certain versions of liberal individualism—abstract and possessive individualism—have rightly borne the brunt of feminist criticism. Mill joins other feminists in this repudiation and his individualism is a reaction against what he sees as objectionable egoistic individualism. He rejects the view, pivotal in other brands of liberalism, that humans see their good as being bound up in the acquisition of material things and in the control and domination and power over others.[11] He rejects the notion that control or power over one's one life and destiny requires control and domination of others. This rejection is categorical, and he heaps outrage and derision upon those men who brutalize and tyrannize their wives. He claims that "the love of power and the love of liberty are in eternal antagonism. . . . The desire of power over others [is a] depraving agency among mankind."[12]

Mill's individualism and autonomy work together. Individualism is the process in which and the ability by means of which we discover our own endowment or balance of talents based on the generic capacities, for although all humans have these talents, the blend will vary and take many forms. This mix of talents is not a set essence, but is a range of possibilities from within which we can make choices and create and shape ourselves. Autonomy is the capacity to critically reflect upon and endorse our commitments, our character, and our lives and revise them if we want. The most worthwhile forms of human happiness and lives result from this discovery of possibilities and this choice of lifestyles and pursuits on its foundation. Mill believes that it is essential that women as well as men have genuine choices about the commitments and pursuits of their lives.

This conception of autonomy as self-determination and power over our lives is consistent with feminist vision. Many feminist writers eloquently elaborate upon the significance of empowerment and self-determination for women, and the harm done to women when they are denied these goods. Other writers are more ambivalent about the value of autonomy for women. However, bell Hooks movingly elucidates the hazards that can result from devaluing strength and self-affirmation for women.

> Sexist ideology teaches women that to be female is to be a victim. Rather than repudiate this . . . women's liberationists embraced it, making shared victimization the basis for woman bonding. . . . Bonding as victims created a situation in which assertive, self-affirming women were often seen as having no place in feminist movement. . . . Ironically, the women who were most eager to be seen as 'victims' . . . were more privileged and powerful than the vast majority of women in our society. An example of this tendency is some writing about violence against women. Women who are exploited and oppressed daily cannot afford to relinquish, the belief that they exercise some measure of control, however relative, over their lives. They cannot afford to see themselves solely as 'victims' because their survival depends on continued exercise of whatever personal powers they possess.[13]

Mill's individualism values social beings and does not celebrate isolated individuals lacking social connections.[14] His individualism regards the individual as the locus, source and evaluator of value. Value is located in each individual, and the value of groups flows from the value of its individual members. So while individuals are socially situated and embedded and have relations with others, it is the individual, and not the community as a whole, that bears value, and thus each individual must be treated with appropriate respect. Millian individuals are accustomed to making and carrying out choices and their lives are an expression of their particularity.[15] Mill highlights the spontaneity of the process: our character and commitments must flow from our inner being and not be imposed from without. While persons have the potential to grow if their social circumstance permit, the developmental path of each is unique and thus diversity of lifestyle and character is both desirable and inevitable.

Mill claims that the dualism set up by some critics between individuality and sociality is incorrect. These values are complementary, not contradictory, and development of individuality not only must be balanced by development of sociality, but it is essentially tied to it such that one of these values, properly understood, cannot be achieved without the other. They are two sides of the same coin, two aspects of one whole, a flourishing human being, and must grow together and balance each other at every stage.

To sum up: Mill's concepts of value, of the self, and of its relation to the community and of individualism are in accord with feminist theory. But this survey raises other questions to which I devote the remainder of this paper. One tendency in some feminist and communitarian thought denigrates, sometimes to the point of altogether denying, the worth of an independent self with strong boundaries and a zone of privacy, and consequently denies any place for the attendant values of individualism and autonomy. Such feminist and communitarian critique of the liberal self and individualism should properly address too strong an emphasis on the individual, an out of balance of the elements, rather than deny outright their importance. When these theories violate their own methodology by creating a dualism between ideals of individualism/autonomy and of sociality/caring, when they go further and claim a conflict between these ideals in which a stark choice must be made, they advance a position which is at odds with defensible views of human functioning. If each cluster of individualism/autonomy or sociality/caring is taken to an extreme without its appropriate balance of the other, what results is not health and well-being but deformity. Furthermore, these critiques also often err in equating individualism and self-love (or, more appropriately, love of self) with selfishness and egoism. Selfishness and egoism masquerade as self-love; they are impostors. A selfish person does not love herself; the very opposite. If she did love herself, her love would flow from her being beyond her boundaries. There is no other source for love of others. This points to a deeper problem with the dichotomous mapping of individualism/caring and the other dualisms directed at liberal feminists by these critics.

The criticisms are based upon the false assumption that there is just so much love, caring or concern to be divided up. If you love yourself, on this picture, you deplete the amount of love that is available to be directed at others or the community. Conversely, if you are involved deeply with others outside yourself, there is less love left for yourself. But this picture is mistaken, for love is not the sort of energy that lends itself to such divisions. It grows dynamically; the more that is expressed, the more that is created. Not only is it false that if you love yourself you have less for others, but the truth is that *unless* you love yourself, your ability to love others or involve yourself in community is hampered. One of the most difficult human projects is to engage in that process whereby you struggle to love and accept yourself. Yet until we do learn to love ourselves, and to follow through by discovering and creating a life in accord with our individuality and use our power of autonomous choice, we will engage in selfish substitutes to fill the void. However, there are still hazards if an appropriate balance between care for self and care for others (particularly dependent others such as children) is not maintained.[16]

The problem we must grapple with is how to balance the values of individualism and sociality. To try to get the right elements is tricky. As we attempt to strike the right balance, it is well to keep in mind some of the dangers of community that some feminist and communitarian theorists can overlook, the very dangers that a liberal theorist like Mill is at pains to argue against so eloquently. Some communitarians and feminists paint a highly romanticized picture of the community they seek.

According to mainstream communitarian theories such as those of Sandel and Taylor, the correct view of the self is not the independent, unencumbered, autonomous, reflective self of liberalism, who can question the values of the community, but the socially embedded self of communitarianism who is fully immersed in the "way of life" of the community and fully accepting of its values.[17] Will Kymlicka explains that,

> On the liberal view of the self, individuals are considered free to question their participation in existing social practices, and opt out of them, should

those practices seem no longer worth pursuing. As a result, individuals are not defined by their membership in any particular economic, religious, sexual, or recreational relationship, since they are free to question and reject any particular relationship. . . .

Communitarians believe that this is a false view of the self. It ignores the fact that the self is "embedded" or "situated" in existing social practices, that we cannot always stand back and opt out of them.[18]

According to communitarians, liberals fail to see that individuals require a social context to develop their human capacities. A shared culture and way of life is essential for the meaningful pursuit of life plans. Many of the arguments of communitarians can be disputed. But what are the special dangers here for feminist communitarians? One danger is that the more we move toward a view that individuals ought to be immersed in and share the way of life of the community, the more we risk shutting out or excluding those who are members of minorities, or who do not agree with the majority, and the more we risk such things as silencing or coercing those who are different or who do not agree. This danger is rather clear if we take the case of present day North American society as our community. In this case feminists must part company with mainstream upholders of community, for, as Kymlicka points out, "the problem of the exclusion of historically marginalized groups is endemic to the communitarian project."[19] North American culture is male-shaped culture, and women's perspectives and experiences are systematically excluded. Feminists must challenge, rather than accept or be immersed in, such a way of life. On Sandel's argument, "members of marginalized groups must adjust their personalities and practices so as to be inoffensive to the dominant values of the community."[20] This is obviously unacceptable.

However, those communitarian feminists who reject individualism do not have mainstream North American society in mind as their model of community. They envisage building a smaller community around feminist values in which they would live according to their principles. As Iris Young points out, the feminist idea of community relies on a "desire for closeness and mutual identification."[21] The feminist ideal often goes beyond shared values to shared understanding: community is seen as "a unification of particular persons through the sharing of subjectivities: Persons will cease to be opaque, other, not understood, and instead become fused, mutually sympathetic, understanding one another as they understand themselves." This is an "ideal of shared subjectivity, or the transparency of subjects to one another."[22]

However, several dangers apply to this model of feminist community. Young agues that "the desire for community relies on the same desire for social wholeness and identification that underlies racism and ethnic chauvinism on the one hand and political sectarianism on the other".[23] Even within this feminist community, any process that seeks to define the identity and values of the group will thereby exclude, marginalize or silence those who differ, and the temptation will exist to label as "not feminist" those in the minority. The last thirty years have illustrated the richness, power and diversity of feminist thought. There is no reason to expect a reduction in this diversity, and it is a challenge for feminist groups to accept and encourage it. Young puts well the pitfalls that may be encountered.

> The striving for mutual identification and shared understanding among those who seek to foster a radical and progressive politics, moreover, can and has led to denying or suppressing differences within political groups or movements. Many feminist groups, for example, have sought to foster relations of equality and reciprocity of understanding in such a way that disagreement, difference, or deviation have been interpreted as a breech of sisterhood, the destruction of personal relatedness and community. There has often been strong pressure within women's groups for members to share the same understanding of the world and the same lifestyle.[24]

Political groups or communities who ignore traditional liberal values of individuality, freedom of expression and diversity of lifestyle and push too strongly for common group understanding can enter into a dynamic in which agreement is forced or factions arise. Such groups can continue in these dynamics, thinking that if only they can reach the right understanding and get all group members to see it the factionalism will cease. But the solution is not to find the right common understanding, for it is the very process that creates the dynamic. Instead, the solution is to accept diversity and heterogeneity as part of the territory of feminism and to use the energy of diversity and debate to promote feminist vision.

Even in the case of a feminist community whose members are in substantial agreement on principles and values of the community, issues remain for which liberal values are the balance. Even within close-knit groups, issues of solitude, privacy and overlap can arise. Human beings are multi-aspected and multi-dimensional creatures, and even in this case of substantial agreement around feminist principles, many aspects and layers of their beings can escape from the boundaries and confines of group definition. Some members may desire both deep involvement in the community and a large measure of solitude. In a state of solitude one lives alone, or, more interestingly, one lives with oneself. It is possible, and indeed may be necessary for some, to combine a measure of solitude with a measure of community involvement. Janice Raymond explores solitude as a condition of female friendship: "Thinking is where I keep myself company, where I find my original friend, if you will. It is the solitude, as opposed to loneliness, where I am alone with, but not lonely in, the companionship of myself."[25]

Members of communities may also choose to combine their involvement with a measure of privacy, another traditional liberal value. They may choose not merely a physical separation of walls to secure privacy from the group, but they may also desire to remain opaque in certain respects, to shield parts of themselves from group contact and scrutiny and understanding. They may not want to be transparent to the others in all respects. They may have this desire not because of a wish for secrecy or because they want to hide something, but because they may simply desire to hold a part of themselves in reserve for themselves or for intimates.[26] The part of themselves that they share with intimates may be a different aspect of themselves than that shared with the community, or it may be a part that is in tension with community values. These separations and tensions may be chosen as part of an overall life which the community only partially glimpses.

Finally, a person may have layered or even conflicting aspects of themselves which lead to different commitments to different groups. Again, these aspects or commitments may form part of a meaningful life which is only partially shared with these different groups. For example, a woman may strongly identify with a community of radical feminists engaged in environmental activism. The values of the group may be entirely social and political. This woman may also strongly identify with a community of Buddhists on the path of the warrior, and may practice mediation in order to attain the state of peacefulness, balance and centeredness which is the foundation of her activist strength. Neither of these groups may be aware of the other, and perhaps if they were, few members of either could identify with the values of the other. Yet these values resonate with this woman's different aspects and commitments and she understands and has integrated both sets of values. The antidote for the dangers of too strong a reliance on community are certain principles of Mill's liberalism, especially his principles of tolerance, freedom of expression, respect for the dignity of all persons, and respect for idiosyncrasy and diversity of lifestyle. It is well to recall Mill's arguments in *On Liberty* for the importance of encouraging debate and expression of minority opinion and encouraging experiments in lifestyle. He expresses concerns that in the absence of ongoing debate truth will be suppressed and beliefs will be held as dead dogmas rather than living truths.[27] Mill argues that "diversity of opinion" is necessary to progress in understanding, and that a community is never justified in silencing its minority members.[28]

Notes

I am grateful to Laura Purdy, Mary Anne Waren, Ann Donchin, Catherine Hopwood and Ross Andaloro for comments and support.

1. In the first part of this paper I draw upon an interpretation of Mill's moral and political philosophy which I more fully develop and defend in my book *The Liberal Self: John Stuart Mill's Moral and Political Philosophy* (Ithaca: Cornell University Press, 1991).

2. For a useful guide to current views of feminist ethics, see *Feminist Ethics*, ed. Claudia Card (Lawrence, Kansas: University Press of Kansas, 1991), especially Alison Jaggar, "Feminist Ethics: Projects, Problems, Prospects", 78–104. Also see *Feminist Interpretations and Political Theory*, ed. Mary Lyndon Shanley and Carole Pateman (University Park, PA: Pennsylvania State University Press, 1991) for a helpful collection of feminist views of the canon.

3. John Stuart Mill, *The Subjection of Women*, in *Essays on Sex Equality*, ed. Alice Rossi (Chicago: University of Chicago Press, 1970), 125. See also Susan Moller Okin, *Women in Western Political Thought* (Princeton: Princeton University Press, 1979) and Susan Moller Okin, *Justice, Gender, and the Family* (Basic Books, 1989).

4. Alison Jaggar, *Feminist Politics and Human Nature* (Totowa, New Jersey: Rowman & Allanheld, 1983), 29.

5. *Ibid.*, 31.

6. *Ibid.*, 40–46.

7. Donner, 160–87.

8. Donner, 97–106; 112–17.

9. John Stuart Mill, "Sedgwick's Discourse", in *The Collected Works of John Stuart Mill* 33 vols., ed. John M. Robson (Toronto: University of Toronto Press, 1974–91) 10:60.

10. Mill, *Utilitarianism*, in *Collected Works* 10:231–32.

11. C. B. Macpherson, *The Political Theory of Possessive Individualism* (Oxford: Oxford University Press, 1962).

12. Mill, *The Subjection of Women*, in Rossi, 238.

13. Bell Hooks, "Sisterhood: Political Solidarity Between Women", in Janet Kourany, James Sterba and Rosemarie Tong, eds., *Feminist Philosophies* (Prentice Hall, 1992), 392. See also Janice Raymond, *A Passion for Friends* (Beacon Press, 1986), 192–99.

14. Mill, *Utilitarianism*, 10:216; Donner, 141–52.

15. Mill, *Oh Liberty*, in *Collected Works*, 18:264.

16. Sarah Lucia Hoagland, "Some Thoughts About 'Caring'", in Card, 256–7; Jean Grimshaw, *Philosophy and Feminist Thinking* (Minneapolis: University of Minnesota Press, 1986), 176–86.

17. Will Kymlicka, *Contemporary Political Philosophy* (Oxford: Oxford University Press, 1990), 206–207.

18. *Ibid.*, 207.

19. *Ibid.*, 227.

20. *Ibid.*, 228.

21. Iris Marion Young, "The Ideal of Community and the Politics of Difference", in *Feminism/Postmodernism*, ed. Linda Nicholson (New York: Routledge, 1990), 301. For a fuller statement of Young's politics of difference theory, see Iris Young, *Justice and the Politics of Difference* (Princeton: Princeton University Press, 1990). I am not here claiming that Young would accept my model of balance of different capacities and elements.

22. *Ibid.*, 309.

23. *Ibid.*, 302.

24. *Ibid.*, 312.

25. Raymond, 222.

26. Kymlicka, 257–62.

27. Mill, *On Liberty*, 243.

28. *Ibid.*, 229.

2

Mill on Women and Human Development

John Howes

Like Donner, Howes believes that Mill is a liberal. Yet Howes's construal of Mill's liberalism is quite different from Donner's. Howes maintains that what propels Mill's defense of women's equality is his staunch defense of liberty and individuality. On Howes's interpretation, these liberal values are rooted in Mill's view that women and men have the same nature. Hence, Mill's arguments for women's equality are ultimately pleas for recognizing women as human beings and for granting them the same freedom to cultivate their faculties and develop as autonomous individuals as men. Howes's analysis relies on a comparison of portions of The Subjection of Women *with chapter three of* On Liberty.

1. Britton's Quotation and Criticism

1.1 In his *John Stuart Mill* (1953), Karl Britton does a double service to those of his readers who value Mill as a feminist. He quotes from a letter of the young Mill to Carlyle, written in 1833:

> But the women, of all I have known, who possessed the highest measure of what are considered feminine qualities, have combined with them more of the highest *masculine* qualities than I have ever seen in any but one or two men, and those one or two men were also in many respects almost women. I suspect it is the second-rate people of the two sexes that are unlike . . . but then, in this respect, my position has been and is, . . . 'a peculiar one'.[1]

1.2 Britton also gives his view of Mill's position:

> From [Harriet Taylor] he derived the extreme feminism which led him to
> see no essential differences between the best masculine characters and the
> best feminine characters. . . . Mill held that a philosophy is to be judged by
> its conception of human nature: and it is somewhat disconcerting to find
> that his own conception suffered from this eccentric limitation. (p. 37f)

1.3 Was it an eccentric limitation, or is Mill right? Britton's criticism has
at least the merit of raising that question.

1.4 Thirty years later, we may well be more cautious. More sensitive
than was common in the 1950s to the ways in which women are ex-
ploited, we may now read Chapter I of *The Subjection of Women* and
wonder if any subsequent account of the oppressive male has been so
vivid and perceptive. Was Mill nevertheless quite mistaken, as Britton
holds, in considering that the best men and women have qualities substantially similar, including both of those sets traditionally thought of as
masculine and feminine?

1.5 I believe that Mill is right; and also that his view of the kind of
human development which is possible and desirable for both men and
women needs to be widely shared if we are to overcome that rancorous
divisiveness and suspicion which often besets both feminism and anti-
feminism.

1.6 If Mill's view is to be properly appreciated, however, it must be understood in relation to his general conception of human development
which is set out in *On Liberty* Chapter III. In this article, then, which is
primarily an expository and comparative one, I shall (sec. 2) exhibit Mill's
conception of human development as found in that chapter, and then
(sec. 3) show how similar it is to that found in *Subjection*. In sec. 4 I shall
show that Mill rightly presents the primary claim of women as that they
be regarded and treated as beings who share with men the same human
nature. Finally (sec. 5) I shall argue that he was substantially right to hold
that 'it is the second-rate people of the two sexes that are unlike'.

1.7 The theme of justice is even more fundamental in *Subjection* than
that of human development, and both it and Mill's insistence that the subjection of women is an anachronism are heard in the ringing sentence:

> We have had the morality of submission, and the morality of chivalry and
> generosity; the time is now come for the morality of justice. (II, p. 478ab)[2]

However, it was because women were not regarded as human beings capable of the same sort of development as men that so many men, and not a few women, supposed that their subjection was just; nor can the subjection be decisively overcome where Mill's vision of a human development embracing men and women alike is not shared.

2. Mill's Conception of Human Development (I) in On Liberty, Ch. III

2.1 Millicent Garrett Fawcett says the *Subjection* 'was first written in 1861, but not published till 1869'. (Introduction to the Oxford edition of 1912, p. xviic) *On Liberty*, written during the 'fifties was published in 1859'. So it is unsurprising that there is a considerable similarity of language, especially in respect of Ch. III of *On Liberty*, where Mill explains how essential to the maturity of human beings generally is that development of individuality which, as *Subjection* shows, has been so widely denied to women.

2.2 It is a serious mistake to regard the third chapter of *On Liberty* as, on the whole, a plea for eccentricity. Because at the time at which he is writing, there is such a 'tyranny of opinion' that 'so few now dare to be eccentric', Mill says that 'it is desirable, in order to break through that tyranny, that people should be eccentric'. (p. 83a)

The reader who wants to attain a just perspective on Ch. III (and its significance for education) should, however, read carefully from the second to the ninth paragraph. That the promotion of eccentricity is far from being Mill's main concern emerges clearly from this remark in the third paragraph in which he not only recognises that certain customs may be both valuable in general and suitable for a particular individual who looks at them critically, but also provides a criterion for assessing any instance of conformity (or nonconformity) to custom:

> . . . though the customs be both good as customs, and suitable to him, yet to conform to custom, merely *as* custom, does not educate or develop in him any of the qualities which are the distinctive endowment of a human being. (p. 72cd)

2.3 What Mill values is indeed the *development* of such qualities. His text is von Humboldt's doctrine that

the end of man . . . is the highest and most harmonious development of
his powers to a complete and consistent whole. (p. 71bc)

He follows von Humboldt in linking individuality with development: he
quotes him as saying that our object should be 'the individuality of power
and development', (p. 71c) and summarises his own doctrine thus:

> that Individuality is the same thing with development, and that it is only
> the cultivation of individuality which produces, or can produce well-
> developed human beings. . . . (p. 79a)

2.4 We might ask whether individuality can really be identified with development. Mill is not saying that 'individuality' and 'development' have
the same connotation. He is affirming that if and only if a person can
properly be said to have attained individuality, then he or she has engaged extensively and successfully in a spontaneous yet disciplined
process of development. Nothing deserves to count as individuality
which does not also deserve to count as the thorough development appropriate to human beings, and *vice versa*.

2.5 Though Mill recognises and insists upon the differences between
types of human character (pp. 72c, 83f), it is noteworthy that he does
not define individuality in terms of such differences. A person with individuality, for him, is not primarily one who differs markedly from others, but one who has thoroughly engaged in the process of development.
Writing in the fifth paragraph of human desire and impulses, he does
not depict these as essentially various and constituting individuality by
their variety. Rather, he stresses the need for *balance* (as well as the value
of strength and thus of energy). What matters is the individuality (of
which *autonomy* is an essential and prominent feature) which is only
possible through development:

> A person whose desires and impulses are his own—are the expression of his
> own nature, as it has been developed and modified by his own culture—is
> said to have a character. (p. 74e)

2.6 Mill's third and fourth paragraphs show him (by contrast with
Sartre) happy to talk about human nature, but not in the static, all-is-
given way which Sartre detested. Accompanying the recognition of diversity is an emphasis (with examples) on 'human faculties', 'mental and
moral [and muscular] powers', and the range of qualities required by

any person who, because he 'chooses his plan [of life] for himself', 'employs all his faculties'. Mill's commitment to an all-round ideal, and to development, is summed up in the sentence which uses his favoured kind of metaphor, the botanical:

> Human nature is not a machine to be built after a model . . ., but a tree, which requires to grow and develop itself on all sides, according to the tendency of the inward forces which make it a living thing.

These 'inward forces' exhibit variety, certainly, but also much similarity: what matters most about them is that they are inward rather than external.

2.7 Mill employs also such verbs closely related to 'develop' as 'exercise', 'unfold' and 'cultivate', not least in his appeal to theists in the eighth paragraph. (p. 77) We should note, too, the characteristic passive participles used by Mill of those people (or their capacities or types) who have not been developed: 'withered', 'starved', 'pinched', 'hidebound', 'cramped' and 'dwarfed' all occur on p. 76f.

2.8 Britton tells us that *On Liberty* 'expresses an inward, spiritual egotism—an egotism of the unworldly-minded. . . .' (p. 37)

Mill's conception of development is in fact both practical and related to the benefit of others:

> In proportion to the development of his individuality, each person becomes more valuable to himself, and is therefore capable of being more valuable to others. (p. 78)

3. Mill's Conception of Human Development (II) in The Subjection of Women

3.1

> [Women] have always hitherto been kept, as far as regards spontaneous development, in so unnatural a state, that their nature cannot but have been greatly distorted and disguised. . . . (*Subjection*, Ch. III, p. 494a)

The criterion of development is as in *On Liberty* Ch. III; the idea of spontaneity, i.e. of doing things *sponte sua*, of one's own will and decision, is prominent in that chapter's second paragraph; 'distorted' and 'disguised' complement the passive participles we have noted. (2.7) (The passage is reminiscent of Plato's *Republic* 611f, where the soul's true nature is said to be as difficult to discern as that of the sea-god Glaucus with all his seaweed and encrustations.)

3.2 Mill's propensity for botanical metaphor (2.6) is apparent in *Subjection*, in the devastating paragraph in Ch. I (p. 451f) which concludes that

> men . . . indolently believe that the tree ['what is now called the nature of women'] grows of itself in the way they have made it grow, and that it would die if one half of it were not kept in a vapour bath and the other half in the snow.

There is a similar passage in Ch. III, part of a long paragraph (pp. 498–501) on the supposed 'greater nervous susceptibility of women'. Mill draws attention to the value of nervous sensibility in both men and women, and says (cf. *On Liberty* Ch. III para. 6):

> Strong feeling is the instrument and element of strong self-control: but it requires to be cultivated in that direction. (p. 500bc)

3.3 In *On Liberty* Ch. III (paras. 7 and 8) Mill makes much of the contrast between a theory of human development and what he calls 'the Calvinistic theory', of which the essence is obedience and abnegation. Those two words recur in *Subjection* Ch. I: men want the obedience, and also the sentiments, of women, and women are brought up to believe that their duty and even their nature is 'to make complete abnegation of themselves'. (p. 443f) If there were equality of rights, says Mill in Ch. II then

> the exaggerated self-abnegation which is the present artificial ideal of feminine character

would be abated,

> and . . . a good woman would not be more self-sacrificing than the best man; but on the other hand, men would be much more unselfish and self-sacrificing than at present. . . . (p. 476c)

3.4 Mill would want to ask Britton whether the primary criteria for excellence in a woman really ought to be different from those for men. He would suggest that *both* the men *and* the women whom, on critical reflection, we should count as possessing *arête* or excellence (not in this or that particular respect alone, but as persons) are those who have both developed the faculties and sensibilities 'which are the distinctive endowment of a human being' (2.2) and learned to moderate their own desires in the interests of others as well as of themselves. Is that, in Mill, an 'eccentric limitation'?

3.5 In Ch. I (p. 457b) and Ch. III (p. 493d), Mill asserts that women in general are not allowed the same 'free development of originality' or 'freedom of development' as men. 'Originality', like 'individuality', is for Mill a word more closely akin to 'freedom' and 'spontaneity' than to 'diversity', though diversity will be involved. To be original is to develop one's own character autonomously and therefore, while learning from others, to be ready to make one's own decisions and follow one's own path.

3.6 Perhaps the passage which most fully and strikingly sets out Mill's conception of development is that in which he presents what he regards as the only *ideal* of marriage. (Ch. IV, p. 541) It would be easy and unfair to mock Mill by reading this passage aloud in an unctuous or pompous manner. Given the rigour and insight of *Subjection* as a whole, it should surely be read in a tone of serious delight. Mill is describing a strenuous and profoundly satisfying kind of marriage. At a time when so many marriages suffer from lack of communication, mutual disappointment and boredom, Mill deserves a hearing, but I quote the passage at length primarily because it throws such light on his view of human nature in both men and women and its possibility of development.

> What marriage may be in the case of two persons of cultivated faculties, identical in opinions and purposes, between whom there exists that best kind of equality, similarity of powers and capacities with reciprocal superiority in them—so that each can enjoy the luxury of looking up to the other, and can have alternatively the pleasure of leading and of being led in the path of development—I will not attempt to describe. To those who can conceive it, there is no need; to those who cannot, it would appear the dream of an enthusiast.

3.7 The two persons have simliar faculties, powers and capacities, which need to be *cultivated*. We should not take that participle in a narrow sense, as though it concerned especially the fine arts. However, they differ in that one is (always or sometimes) superior in some respects, the other in others. They enjoy recognising these superiorities, but they seek

to learn from and emulate one another, following 'the path of development'. (Cf. p. 538f) Perhaps Mill would agree that 'identical in opinions'
is going somewhat too far, and might be willing to substitute, in accordance with Ch. II of *On Liberty*, 'equally ready to submit opinions to
critical scrutiny'.

3.8 If it be replied that men and women are complementary rather
than similar, Mill would, I think, say 'complementary and similar'—and
would urge (as in Ch. III pp. 493–503) that such differences as are commonly found (e.g., that women often have a 'capacity of intuitive perception' which men often lack, but are 'less capable of persisting long in
the same continuous effort') may well reflect differences of upbringing
rather than of nature. Even where there are marked differences in 'powers and capacities', the appropriate response, according to the passage we
have quoted, is to emulate as well as to admire one another. (Cf. p. 539d)

4. Women as Human Beings

4.1 Perhaps the most pervasive of the kinds of adverse treatment suffered by women has been the patronising assumption that they cannot
really do or understand, or even be really interested in, certain things because they are women. From this attitude comes discrimination in education, separation of the sexes at many Australian parties, and in general
stifling limitation of women's opportunity to participate. Two passages
in Ch. IV show Mill's insight into frustrations of this kind endured by
women. One is the sentence on p. 544f:

> There is nothing, after disease, indigence and guilt, so fatal to the pleasur-
> able enjoyment of life as the want of a worthy outlet for the active faculties.

The other echoes (perhaps it echoed Harriet Taylor) a kind of cry of relief that women utter, at least in their own hearing, when they are at last
'simply treated as human beings', without sexist exclusion, hostility or
patronizing. This passage also is just one sentence, but too long for quotation in full. It occurs on p. 527, and Mill urges that, through the aban-
donment of the idea that subjects of a general kind are men's business,

> the mere consciousness a woman would then have of being a human being
> like any other,

able to choose pursuits, widen interests and express opinions, would alone

> effect an immense expansion of the faculties of women, as well as enlargement of the range of their moral sentiments.

4.2 Mill's primary reply to Britton would be 'Do you not think of men and women as having a similarity so great as to make their differences relatively small, that is, the similarity they have in that both are human beings?' That remains a most pertinent question at a time when in both sexes exaggerated claims, angry resentments and disorderly imaginations give such prominence to the distinction between male and female human beings. Asked to say more about what it is to be a human being, Mill would talk about faculties, capacities and sensibilities and the possibility of developing them autonomously.

5. 'Eccentric Limitation'?

5.1 It remains to ask whether we should reject Britton's view that Mill's conception of human nature suffered from an 'eccentric limitation', in that he suspected (the word is modest) that 'it is the second-rate people of the two sexes that are unlike', whereas the best are alike in that they have similar qualities.

5.2 It is noteworthy that Britton provides absolutely no argument for his criticism. That in itself is grist for the feminist's mill. We are invited to recognise from our own experience that Mill is mistaken.

5.3 What does Mill mention in *Subjection* which supports the claim that 'the second-rate people of the two sexes' are unlike? Among the type-portraits he draws—and those are a large part of the work's value—are two of men and two of women. There is the husband and father, who, because of the 'almost unlimited power' he enjoys, is characterised by

> wilfulness, overbearingness, unbounded self-indulgence, and a double-dyed and idealised selfishness . . . (Ch. II, p. 469)

There is the boy who

> grow[s] up to manhood in the belief that . . . by the mere fact of being born a male he is by right the superior of all and every one of an entire half of the human race. . . .

That, from Ch. IV, p. 522f, is only part of a vivid paragraph in which 'the self-worship of the male' is described. But Mill writes also of the woman who, from lack of opportunity to develop wider interests, exerts her influence to distract her husband from disinterested purposes (p. 472) or reformist causes (pp. 534–536); and the philanthropic woman who, lacking breadth of experience and general ideas, bestows 'charity' which demoralizes (p. 532f).

5.4 The second-rate man is so, at least in many cases, because from boyhood he has been unchecked in the supposition that his being a male gives him a reason for attributing to himself superiority; the second-rate woman, because of the narrowness of vision which comes from subordination and her consequent lack of opportunity for a wider cultivation of capacities and influences. Neither has learned 'the love of liberty', (p. 544d) and without it they are distorted in these different ways.

5.5 The deficiencies in men and women often lie in their limited sympathies; and the sympathies are, of course, limited in different ways, reflecting upbringing and the desire to impress other members of one's own sex as well as, supposedly, members of the other. 'When I go out with an Australian boy', said an Italian girl, a student, to me in the early '70s, 'he never asks me about myself'. Among the wealthier students in Australian universities, there is not uncommonly the girl who has little thought for anything beyond the kaleidoscope of dress, parties and guys to impress or gratify.

5.6 I conclude, then, that Mill and our own experience both give us good reason for rejecting Britton's view that Mill suffers from an eccentric limitation in his view of men and women. It may well be that Britton profoundly valued the unlikeness of some of the women he knew to all or almost all of the men he knew. To refute Mill, however, one needs not merely to point to the rare and valuable characteristics of such women; one would have to argue that it was unrealistic to seek such qualities in men. Thirty years on, there has been enough change of roles for us to have grounds for believing that men are not by nature less able to provide care and compassion. We certainly need to give to sexuality more importance than did Mill (though there, too, complementarity does not imply complete difference of nature). We can hardly find a better guide to that love of liberty, justice and human development without which women's and men's liberation is impossible.

5.7 '. . . *is* there really any distinction between the highest masculine and the highest feminine character?' That was the question which Mill put to Carlyle two sentences before the one quoted by Britton. Wollheim, at the end of his Introduction to the Oxford edition of 1975, says that 'central to the essay . . . is the thesis that the distinction between male and female corresponds to no significant difference in psychology', and quotes Freud as saying that Mill had overlooked the fact that the distinction between men and women 'is the most significant one that exists'. Wollheim then makes the extraordinary move of maintaining that what is central to Mill's essay 'is not central to the argument of the essay': Mill could concede Freud's point and insist that

> it is only in an atmosphere of equal freedom that people can work out different plans of life that will then correspond to the differences between them.

5.8 I hope that I have shown in this paper that central to Mill's argument are the two themes of justice and development of human faculties and sensibilities, and that Mill believes that the conditioning women have received has obscured the similarity of these faculties and sensibilities in men and women. His essay would have been very different indeed had he thought it necessary to argue in Wollheim's fashion; and, if he had, he would have done justice to the theme of autonomous development of a human nature which men and women share. Mill, rather than Freud, is the emancipator.

Notes

1. Britton's reference was to Elliot's edition of the *Letters*, Vol. 1, p. 70. The whole letter is on pp. 180–184 of the *Collected Works*, Vol. XII (University of Toronto Press, 1963). See also 5.7 of this paper.

2. I refer, for both *On Liberty* and *The Subjection of Women*, to the two Oxford editions which combine them with *Representative Government*, and which have the same pagination: the World's Classics volume (1912) and the O.U.P. paperback (1975). I use the letters a to c to indicate parts of a page. Chapter numbers are given for *Subjection*. Ch. I begins at p. 427; Ch. II, p. 460; Ch. III, p. 484; Ch. IV, p. 521.

3

John Stuart Mill's Feminism

The Subjection of Women and the Improvement of Mankind

Susan Moller Okin

Okin focuses on Mill's view of human beings as fundamentally pro-
gressive, that is, capable of improvement. She interprets his egalitarian-
ism in terms of this ideal and, like Howes, places his arguments for gen-
der equality in the context of his defense of freedom. Yet unlike Howes,
Okin maintains that in The Subjection of Women Mill goes beyond his
concerns in On Liberty to argue that gender inequality is both in-
equitable and socially harmful. Okin contends that the central argu-
ment of The Subjection of Women is an argument from expediency tied
to Mill's conception of happiness: gender discrimination is unjust, but,
more generally, gender inequality thwarts the ideal of improvement
generally and women's happiness particularly.

JOHN STUART MILL DIED A HUNDRED YEARS AGO, on 8 May 1873. In view
of the recent renaissance of the feminist movement in the Western
world, it seems especially pertinent to remember and pay tribute to the
very significant influence which he had in the early struggle for women's
rights. It is well-known that, as M.P. for Westminster, Mill provoked the
first substantial debate on women's suffrage in the House of Commons,
and it is generally acknowledged that the publication of his *The Subjec-*
tion of Women in 1869 was a catalyst for the suffrage movement in Great
Britain. What is not so generally known, however, is the influence, well
demonstrated by Patricia Grimshaw in her recent book, *Women's Suf-*
frage in New Zealand,[1] which Mill's ideas and enthusiasm exerted on the

New Zealand feminists of the same period. As Ms. Grimshaw relates, Mill corresponded with the early Nelson feminist, Mary Muller, whose pamphlet *An Appeal to the Men of New Zealand* was published in the same year as his own *Subjection of Women*—commending and encouraging her by saying 'You have made an *excellent* beginning'.[2] Mill's ideas were discussed at meetings of the Women's Christian Temperance Union, backbone of the struggle for female enfranchisement; and prominent New Zealand suffragists of both sexes, including Kate Sheppard, Sir John Hall and Sir Robert Stout, were either reaffirmed in their feminist convictions, or converted to the cause, by reading Mill's convincing and decidedly unhysterical arguments. Thus it is trebly relevant, in this centennial year, in this New Zealand journal, and at this time of revived and wide-spread agitation for female equality, to understand and to examine critically the substantial contribution of this great thinker to the feminist cause.

The fact that John Stuart Mill was an ardent and active feminist is particularly interesting for two reasons, which are developed as themes of this essay. First, as anyone who has recently glanced at the 'Feminist Studies' or 'Women's Liberation' shelves of a bookstore must have noticed, very few feminist works are written by men. So far as I am able to ascertain, the only substantial piece of writing on the subject by a man, prior to the publication of Mill's *Subjection of Women*, was a little-known work by the Owenite Socialist, William Thompson, which he graced with the title *An Appeal of One Half the Human Race, Women, against the Pretensions of the Other Half, Men, to retain them in Political, and thence in Civil and Domestic Slavery.*[3] And since Mill's *Subjection of Women*, too, there have been no feminist writings by men which approach its forcefulness, comprehensiveness and lucidity. One of the questions I propose to discuss, then, is why this nineteenth century philosopher had such strong convictions about the inequity of the treatment of women and what were the influences which bore upon this aspect of his thought.

Secondly, Mill's feminism is a striking example of the application of political theory. Though far from the abstractness of Plato or Hegel, Mill was a philosopher who was concerned with the broadest and most profound issues affecting the life of man in political society. Liberty, individuality, justice and democracy were his values, and at the root of his whole philosophy was his conviction that the utilitarian goal of 'the greatest happiness of the greatest number' could not be achieved apart from the greatest possible advancement, moral and intellectual, of the human race. Thus, for Mill, unlike Bentham and James Mill, one of the principal purposes of social and political institutions was to develop human potential to the highest possible stage. One of the most intriguing things about his feminist writings, then, is that they are clearly an application of his most dearly-held principles to a specific case where he felt they were being most flagrantly ignored. His feminism was definitely not a 'sideline': rather it constitutes, for the student of Mill, a valuable opportunity to see how he applied his central ideas about human beings in a social setting. For the emancipation of women to a level of equality with men was not, for Mill, aimed solely at the increased immediate happiness of women themselves, although this was an important part of it. It was also a very important prerequisite for the improvement of mankind.

John Stuart Mill's opposition to the prejudices and beliefs which kept women in a subordinate position in all aspects of social and political life was based on convictions formed very early in his life which found expression in many of his works on political and ethical subjects. At the beginning of the work he devoted specifically to the subject, *The Subjection of Women*, he states that 'the legal subordination of one sex to the other . . . is wrong in itself, and now one of the chief hindrances to human improvement' is 'an opinion which I have held from the very earliest period when I had formed any opinion at all on social or political matters, and which . . . has been constantly growing stronger by the progress of reflection and the experience of life'.[4] Evidence for his continual concern with the position of women is offered by his various biographers and in his letters; he often judged peoples, philosophical systems and periods of history, according to their attitudes towards women and their role in society.[5] It will not suffice, then, to confine the following discussion to *The Subjection of Women* alone, since it is possible to find in some of his other published works and in his letters a fuller treatment of some ideas that are rather summarily dealt with in that work. For example, both to guard his own and Harriet Taylor Mill's personal reputations, and in order to avoid endangering the respectability of the incipient movement for women's rights, he played down or omitted some of his more radical ideas about divorce and contraception. Where this occurs, I shall make reference to his more explicit discussions of these subjects, and I shall also point out instances in which Harriet's ideas, as expressed in her writings on the subject of women, are significantly different from those which Mill himself ever espoused.[6]

Alien though Mill's radical ideas about women were to the mid-nineteenth century climate of opinion in general, it is easy to find stimuli to the development of his feminist convictions amongst several of the groups of thinkers with whom he was in contact in his formative years. The Utilitarians amongst whom he was educated were certainly not unconcerned with the issue. Bentham, for instance, although he considered the actual question of women's suffrage to be an insufficiently urgent one to be allowed to distract attention from or endanger his greater purposes, did concede the crucial points that existing differences between the sexes had certainly not been shown to be innate or inevitable ones, and that therefore there was no reason why women should not vote on the same terms as men, since clearly their interests were equally involved in the outcome.[7] Of his father, John Stuart Mill notes in his *Autobiography* that 'he looked forward . . . to a considerable increase of freedom in the relations between the sexes, though without pretending to define exactly what would be, or ought to be, the precise conditions of that freedom'.[8] On the subject of female suffrage, however, James Mill had, in his *Essay on Government*, committed a gross 'faux pas' in the eyes of the other philosophical radicals, by suggesting that women might well be excluded from voting without any bad consequences.[9] A violent controversy was produced in utilitarian circles, by this single, most unacceptable sentence, from which Mill junior tells us that he and his associates, including Bentham, 'most positively dissented'.[10] It is obvious from his use of the phrase in his subsequent writings about women, that the young Mill was particularly struck at this time by the rather exaggerated statement in Macaulay's critical attack on the *Government* essay, that the interests of women were no more identical with those of their husbands than the interests of subjects with their kings.[11] The whole controversy must surely have stimulated John Stuart Mill's concern with feminism. The Utilitarians' mouthpiece, the *Westminster Times*, had established itself as an early champion of the cause of women's rights, and as early as 1824, Mill himself had published in that periodical an article attacking the prevalent custom of regarding morality and personal characteristics in completely different lights with reference to the different sexes.

Secondly, Mill's feminism derived inspiration from the early French and English Socialists. Although there is no evidence that Mill ever read

William Thompson's *Appeal*, he does mention it in a passage in the *Autobiography* in which he talks of meeting Thompson, whom he considered 'a very estimable man', through his youthful contacts with the Owenite Socialists.[12] He said that he considered it 'the signal honour of Owenism and most other forms of Socialism that they assign [to women] equal rights, in all respects, with those of the hitherto dominant sex'.[13] We know, also, from his letters, that he was very interested in the ideas of Enfantin and the other Saint-Simonian 'missionaries' who came to London in the early 1830s,[14] and tempered though his admiration was by his subsequently justified suspicions of their fanaticism and charlatanry, he continued to recognize the debt owed to them by the feminist cause. In the *Autobiography* he wrote: 'In proclaiming the perfect equality of men and women, and an entirely new order of things in regard to their relations with one another, the St. Simonians, in common with Owen and Fourier, have entitled themselves to the grateful remembrance of future generations'.[15]

Another influence which must have tended to confirm Mill's already strongly-held feminist ideas was his connection with W. J. Fox and the Unitarian periodical, the *Monthly Repository*. As early as 1823, when Harriet Martineau contributed on the subject of equal education for women, but especially in the 1830s, when Fox was editor, this magazine published articles advocating female suffrage, a more rational attitude towards divorce, and the correction of the countless other injustices in the treatment of women by society. In his history of this periodical, Francis Mineka says: 'Altogether, the *Repository*'s record on the emancipation of women is a distinctly honorable one. For its day, it was far in advance of common opinion; no contemporary periodical so consistently advocated an enlightened policy'.[16] Mill wrote for the *Repository* in the early and mid-1830s, and his frequent correspondence with Fox over these years shows that the latter was a distinct spur to his feminist principles.[17]

Finally, we cannot ignore the direct influence on Mill's ideas about women that must have come from the women themselves whom he met in the intellectual circles in which he moved. Such talented and intelligent, educated and productive women as Harriet Martineau, Sarah Austin, Harriet Grote, and Eliza and Sarah Flower (to the former of whom he refers to 'a person of genius'), cannot fail to have made their impression on his attitude to their sex and the way it was regarded by contemporary society. Most important of all in this respect, however, was Harriet Taylor.

There has been much dispute about the extent of Harriet Taylor's influence on Mill, and the originality of her contribution to his work.[18] This stems from the extreme divergence between, on the one hand, Mill's enraptured statements about her limitless genius and his claims that a great proportion of his later work was, in fact, based on ideas that were hers, so that she played Bentham to his Dumont,[19] and, on the other hand, the decidedly unfavourable impression she made on their contemporaries, and the hardly startling quality of her own extant writings. I am much inclined to agree with H. O. Pappe, who concludes his examination of the evidence by saying that it was only Mill's grossly distorted impression of her abilities that suggests that Harriet was endowed with any qualities of genius. However, it is not necessary in the context of Mill's feminist ideas to go deeply into this controversy, for several reasons.

First, Mill has left us with a very clear statement, in his *Autobiography*,[20] about Harriet's effect on his feminist beliefs. He stresses that she was certainly not the source of his convictions about the complete equality of men and women, and of course this statement is borne out by his many letters and several publications on the subject which date from before their first meeting. He says, in fact, that it may well have been his strong views on this subject which initially attracted her to him. However, he adds that, in the course of their long relationship and eventual marriage, she had played the role of transforming what had been 'little more than an abstract principle' into a real appreciation of the practical, day-to-day effects of women's lack of rights and opportunities, and also of 'the mode in which the consequences of the inferior position of women intertwine themselves with all the evils of existing society and with all the difficulties of human improvement'.[21] Thus, although there is no doubt that Mill was a convinced feminist quite independently of the influence of Mrs. Taylor, the existence and the difficult circumstances of their relationship must have increased the fervour of his convictions and his determination to do what he could to have women's many disabilities remedied.

Secondly, it is impossible to tell which of the ideas that Mill and Harriet Taylor expressed on the subject of women originated in his mind and which in hers, with the possible exception of those they expressed to each other in two short essays on marriage and divorce, very early in the relationship.[22] From this evidence, one derives the distinct impression that her ideas were somewhat more extremist than his, though not necessarily in a consistent direction. For on the one hand, she asserts that the total responsibility for bringing a child into the world belongs to the woman, and that therefore in the case of a separation or divorce the woman should bring up any children of the marriage; but on the other hand, she argues that even married women have just as much right as men to a career and to earning their own subsistence, an opinion which Mill never expressed in his writings on the subject. After these first two pieces they wrote for each other, it appears that their ideas must have become very enmeshed on this subject, which was so important to them both. Many of the ideas and arguments which appear in *The Subjection of Women*, which was actually written after Harriet's death, appeared first in their pamphlet *The Enfranchisement of Women*, but this is certainly not evidence enough for us to be able to say that they were originally her ideas, since although the pamphlet was published under her name, it was referred to at least once by Mill as though he had written it himself. Most probably they worked on it together, or at least were constantly in touch about the ideas it contained. As Mill himself said, they came from 'the fund of thought which had been made common to us both, by our innumerable conversations and discussions on a topic which filled so large a place in our minds'.[23]

Thus, to feminist convictions which J. S. Mill claimed to have held from very early in his life were added the influences of a number of the groups of thinkers with whom he mixed or at least had considerable contact: the Utilitarians, the early Co-operative Socialists and Saint-Simonians, and the Unitarian radicals. He had come into contact with a number of women whose qualities strongly contradicted contemporary stereotypes of what women were and should be like, and he had had a lengthy and intimate relationship with a woman who had directly suffered the effects of discrimination against her sex, particularly in the spheres of the marriage laws and of the denial of educational opportunities. It appears, then, to be after all not surprising that he should decide to apply his most basic principles to arguing for the cause of female emancipation.

In a passage which parallels that in *On Liberty*, in which Mill eschews any appeal to 'abstract right, as a thing independent of utility',[24] in *The Subjection of Women*, too, Mill felt obliged to answer those who might accuse him of advocating 'a social revolution in the name of an abstract right'.[25] In other works, however, in spite of this protestation, he does come very near to sounding like a natural rights theorist, rather than a simple utilitarian, for instance when talking in *The Subjection of Women* of the injustice of denying to women 'the *equal moral right* of all human beings to choose their occupation (short of injury to others) according to their own preferences'.[26] Despite a few un-utilitarian 'lapses' such as this, however, the basic arguments of the work on women, as of *On Liberty*, are made in the name of utility—that is, in the name of John Stuart Mill's version of utility. The appeal of *The Subjection of Women*, too, is to 'utility in the largest sense, grounded on the permanent interests of man as a progressive being'.[27]

John Stuart Mill had vehemently rejected the narrow, Benthamite conception of human nature, explicitly in the essay on Bentham,[28] but also implicitly in all his other works. 'Human nature', he says in *On Liberty*, 'is not a machine to be built after a model . . . but a tree, which requires to grow and develop itself on all sides according to the tendency of the inward forces which make it a living thing'.[29] Whether Mill's totally unmechanistic conception of human nature prevents him from being called a real utilitarian is a much debated issue. Some have argued that the emphasis he places on the *development* of the human faculties takes him so far away from 'the greatest happiness of the greatest number' that he cannot be considered a utilitarian in the Benthamite sense. He certainly did not believe that 'pushpin is as good as poetry', but I do not consider that he ever gave up the 'greatest happiness' principle. The basic reason for this is that he was convinced that the moral and intellectual advancement of mankind would result in greater happiness for everybody. Believing as he did that the higher pleasures of the intellect yielded far greater happiness than the lower pleasures of the senses,[30] and that consequently, 'next to selfishness, the principal cause which makes life unsatisfactory is want of mental cultivation',[31] he could only conclude that a principal pathway to the greatest happiness was to open up to everybody the greater joys of poetry and the other higher pleasures. He also believed that continuing intellectual advancement would lead to greater discoveries and greater knowledge that could be applied in such a way as to increase the general utility. The moral development of humanity would likewise lead to ever greater happiness, because to a moral being the feeling of virtue was not just a means, but actually a part of his or her own happiness;[32] and also because the decline of selfishness would mean that people would be united in aiming at the greatest happiness of all, rather than just pursuing their own individual pleasures. Thus, Mill's utilitarianism was certainly different from Bentham's in that one could not find the answer to the question 'Is the greatest happiness presently being experienced?' simply by asking everyone how happy they are feeling. As Mill made clear, particularly in the 'Socrates and the pig' passage, he did not consider that people were at all capable of knowing how happy they were, in comparison with how great and profound their happiness could be, if their full intellectual and moral potential were developed.

There is, undoubtedly, a strong current of intellectual élitism running through Mill's thought. While he had criticized Bentham for basing his concept of human nature on his own narrow and unimaginative person, Mill proceeded to commit exactly the same fallacy, except that the content is different. He assumed that the model for humanity is the intellectual and ascetic aesthete that he himself personified. However, once this bias is acknowledged, it cannot be maintained that he *rejected* the greatest happiness principle in favour of a 'greatest human development' principle; the point was that he was quite convinced that only the cultivated could achieve the greatest happiness available to mankind.

The purpose of this somewhat lengthy digression from the specific subject of women was to explore the importance in J. S. Mill's version of utilitarianism of his concept of man as a progressive, a morally and intellectually improvable being. My conclusion is that he believed that such improvement was a prerequisite for the eventual achievement of the greatest human happiness. In *The Subjection of Women* and in those parts of his other works in which he argues the need for female emancipation, the theme of human advancement is a frequently recurring one. It is probably most succinctly summarized in a passage of the *Principles of Political Economy*, where he wrote: "The ideas and institutions by which the accident of sex is made the groundwork of an inequality of legal rights, and a forced dissimilarity of social functions, must ere long be recognized as the greatest hindrance to moral, social, and even intellectual improvement."[33] Whereas there are two other principles that figure very prominently in *The Subjection of Women* and his other feminist arguments—liberty, or the opportunity for self-determination, and justice, in the sense of equality of consideration or impartiality—both of these other concerns are explicitly related to that of the moral and intellectual advancement of mankind, as well as to the happiness of women themselves.

As is clear from his *On Liberty*, Mill was deeply concerned about the value of individual freedom, regarding it as such an important means to happiness and self-development that it could be justifiably sacrificed only to the extent that is absolutely necessary for the maintenance of security and social co-operation. 'After the primary necessities of food and raiment', he asserted, 'freedom is the first and strongest want of human nature',[34] and he recalled the joys of emerging from the tutelage of childhood into the responsibilities of adulthood, as indicative of the feeling of added 'aliveness' that self-determination could give. Thus freedom was such an essential part of human well-being that Mill concluded 'that the only purpose for which power can be rightfully exercised over any member of a civilized community, against his will, is to prevent harm to others'.[35]

There was no question that this strongly held value could find copious scope for application to the issue of the contemporary social and legal position of women, and it is not surprising that liberty and self-determination are recurrent themes of Mill's arguments against the gross inequality of the marriage laws and the severe discrimination suffered by women in the spheres of educational and occupational opportunity. Indeed, he states that the most direct benefit he envisages will arise from the emancipation of women is the added happiness of women themselves, resulting from the difference between 'a life of subjection to the will of others, and a life of rational freedom'.[36] Whereas a woman at the time he wrote had practically no opportunity of any occupation (outside of unskilled labour and a few of the service industries), except that of wife, in a marital relationship in which she was legally bound to obey her husband and had no rights to own property, it was obvious to Mill that an inestimable increase in happiness would result from giving women a real choice of how to spend their lives. Convinced as he was that "if there is anything vitally important to the happiness of human beings, it is that they should relish their habitual pursut",[37] it was essential that all the careers open to men should be made equally available to women, so that the choice of whether to marry or not would be a meaningful one, and not the only means of escape from the despised dependency of 'old maidhood'. It was also essential that those who chose to marry should be granted an equal share in the rights and responsibilities of that relationship, and although he did not express his most radical ideas on the subject of marriage in *The Subjection of Women*, Mill believed that it should be a free contract in the sense of being dissoluble at the wish of the contracting parties, provided that any children that had resulted from the marriage were well provided for. His dissent from the contemporary view of the biding nature of the marriage contract is summed up in his statement that 'surely it is wrong, wrong in every way . . . that there should exist any motives to marriage except the happiness which two persons who love one another feel in associating their existence'.[38] Any denial of liberty which was not for the sake of protecting some third party from harm was anathema to him.

It was not only, however, for the sake of the added happiness of women themselves, that Mill advocated giving them complete freedom of choice about how they would use their lives but also for the good, and particularly the progress, of society as a whole. For as he had said in *On Liberty*, 'the only unfailing and permanent source of improvement is liberty since by it there are as many possible permanent centers of improvement as there are individuals'.[39] The extension of education and the opening up of careers to women, freeing them from the bondage of conformity and narrow domesticity, would have the beneficial effect of 'doubling the mass of mental faculties available for the higher service of humanity'.[40]

In addition to this vast increase in available talent, Mill was certain that freeing women to become educated and to work at whatever career they desired would have most valuable effects on men. Both the stimulus of female competition, and the companionship of equally educated partners, would result in the greater intellectual development of men. He was most impressed by the fact that since men were becoming less bound up in outdoor pursuits and what were regarded as exclusively masculine activities, their domestic lives were becoming more important, and the influence of their wives, with whom they were tending to spend more time, was therefore continually increasing. Taking the rather pessimistic point of view that any society or individual which is not improving is deteriorating, he stresses the insidious effects that the constant companionship of an uneducated and frivolous wife could have on a man, even though he might have previously had serious intellectual interests. He asks how it could be considered anything but detrimental to a man's development to be confined for a large proportion of his life with a partner whose mind has been so studiously concentrated on trivia, who is utterly ignorant about matters which should be of the highest concern, and who is bound because of the narrowness of her education to consider the immediate and material interests of her own family of greater importance than any public-spirited or intellectual aspirations that her husband might wish to pursue. 'With such an influence in every house', Mill asks, 'is it any wonder that people in general are kept down in that mediocrity of respectability which is becoming a marked characteristic of modern times?'[41] Thus women in their present state of subjection and lack of opportunity were in Mill's view acting as a continual force against progress; liberating them would reverse this force.

Second only to freedom, in the arguments set out in *The Subjection of Women*, is the principle of justice. Just treatment, no less than liberty, is regarded both as essential for the happiness of women themselves and as a necessary condition for the advancement of humanity. Mill's most comprehensive discussion of justice, at which it is necessary to look in order for us to be able to understand its importance in his feminism, is found in the last chapter of *Utilitarianism*. Here, having stressed the central idea of impartiality, or treating like cases alike, he proceeds to show that the reason that different societies have had such divergent conceptions of what constitutes just treatment, is that they have regarded different qualities as relevant grounds for departing from impartiality. Whereas it is, then, crucial to the idea of justice that 'all persons are deemed to have a *right* to equality of treatment, except when some recognized social expediency requires the reverse',[42] different conceptions of what constitutes social expediency have resulted in societies' regarding slavery, caste systems, and many other unequal arrangements, now considered completely unjust, as thoroughly justified by the requirements of their circumstances. This meant that when social inequalities ceased to be considered expedient, they became regarded as not only inexpedient, but also as unjust. However, people tend to be 'forgetful that they themselves perhaps tolerate other inequalities under an equally mistaken notion of expediency.'[43] And a paradigmatic case of this was the subjection of women. Believing fervently that the society of equals was society in its most desirable form, and that all instances of command and obedience were but temporary evils, to be tolerated no longer than necessary, Mill looked forward to the day when discrimination on grounds of colour, race and sex would follow that based on nobility of birth into disrepute and oblivion.

In order to rest his case for female equality on what he regarded as the universally-accepted value of just treatment, Mill felt that he was obliged to demonstrate two things. First he set out to show, against the strong force of contemporary opinion, that the reasons which had always been

considered ample grounds for treating women differently from men—
that is, that they are naturally inferior, less rational, and so on—were not
based on good evidence and were probably all false. Secondly, even when
he had demonstrated this as far as anyone could at that time, Mill considered it important, as a utilitarian who did not want to be accused of
making a social revolution in the name of an abstract right, to show that
doing away with the unequal treatment of women would be expedient
in the sense of contributing significantly to the welfare of society.

In arguing the first of these two claims, Mill had to contend not only
with popular prejudice, but also with the violent reaction which many
influential intellectuals of the mid-nineteenth century were expressing
against the excessive importance which French eighteenth-century educational theorists, such as Helvétius and d'Holbach, had attributed to
environmental factors in the formation of the human character and intelligence. For Mill, following to some extent in the footsteps of the latter, claimed that certainly most, and probably all, of the existing and allegedly innate differences of character and intellect between men and
women were caused by the very different attitudes of society towards
members of the two sexes from their earliest infancy, and the vastly different types and qualities of education they were given. In his fragment
on the subject of marriage, written about 1832, he had vehemently denied any natural inequality between the two sexes apart from that of
physical strength (and even this, he said, admitted of doubt).[44] He was,
however, so opposed to dogmatism on any issue that he later modified
his position to the assertion that none of the alleged differences between
the mental and moral capacities of the sexes had been proved to be the
inevitable consequences of innate factors, though some of them might
possibly be.[45] His only dogmatic assertion was that nothing was yet certainly known on the subject: 'If it be said that the doctrine of the equality of the sexes rests only on theory, it must be remembered that the contrary doctrine has only theory to rest upon.'[46] For as long as what was
called 'women's nature' was such a very artificial product, resulting from
'forced repression in some directions, unnatural stimulation in others',[47]
like a tree that has been reared with one half in a vapour bath and the
other half in the snow, it was impossible to assess that natural differences
between this distorted creature and her male counterpart. What was
'natural' to the two sexes could only be found out by allowing both to
develop and use their faculties freely. For, as Harriet Taylor had written

in her *Enfranchisement of Women* pamphlet, the 'proper sphere for all human beings is the largest and highest which they are able to attain to'[48] and the narrow channeling of the activities of the entire female sex was a most glaring example of the non-application of this principle.

Mill considered that anyone who took the trouble to consider the very different way in which nineteenth-century boys and girls were educated, and their different assigned tasks in adult life, could readily explain a great many of the intellectual incapacities and special moral qualities attributed to women. Those who summarily assessed the female sex as 'naturally' practical and intuitive, capable in small, day-to-day affairs but lacking in any capacity for rational thought, had only to look at the way girls were trained to cope with domestic trivia, while boys were educated in the classics and the sciences. A woman's mistakes were therefore often like those of a self-educated man, who might grasp the common-sense factors of a situation, some of which might elude the theorist, but who was likely to suffer from a lack of knowledge of general principles and a lack of ability to grasp the abstract, conceptual aspect of the problem.[49]

Mill was no more prepared to accept any innate distinctions drawn in favour of the female character, than to accept allegedly innate inferiorities, and counted as equally absurd as the claim that women are mentally inferior to men, the claim that they are by nature morally superior.[50] Women, like Negro slaves, he said, have had scarcely any opportunity to commit crimes, and so it is not remarkable nor particularly laudable that they have not often been criminals, and all such qualities as unselfishness and moral restraint can be explained in terms of their particular circumstances of dependence on and accountability to others. He concluded: 'I do not know a more signal instance of the blindness with which the world, including the herd of studious men, ignore and pass over all the influences of social circumstances, than their silly depreciation of the intellectual, and silly panegyrics on the moral, nature of women.'[51]

Any attempt to refute the prevailing notion that women were innately and irremediably inferior in ability to men, Mill felt, was difficult because of the very unadvanced state of psychology. The contemporary preoccupation with the biological sciences and the deplorable lack of attention paid to the influence of environment on the formation of the human character had led, he thought, to far too great a reversal of the Helvétian claim '*l'éducation peut tout*,' to the point where organic characteristics were now supposed capable of explaining everything.[52] Mill's chief adversary, in his battle to win recognition for the importance of environmental factors in the character-formation of women, was Auguste Comte, with whom he carried on a substantial correspondence on the subject during 1843[53]—a correspondence which, however unsatisfactorily it ended with regard to this issue, formed an important part of Mill's thinking about this aspect of his case for the emancipation of women.

Comte was a clear example, among political and social theorists of the time, of the confident conviction that the physical sciences were not just potentially capable of solving all human problems, once their findings were 'applied' by the social sciences, but that they had found practically all the important answers already. Thus he was sure that, although biology was still unable to answer every important question, it was already 'able to establish the hierarchy of the sexes, by demonstrating both anatomically and physiologically that, in almost the entire animal kingdom, and especially in our species, the female sex is formed for a state of essential childhood, which renders it necessarily inferior to the corresponding male organism'.[54] With a pre-Darwinian confidence in the uniqueness of the human species, he asserted that 'the organic condition must certainly prevail, since it is the organism and not the environment that makes us men rather than monkeys or dogs, and which even determines our special type of humanity, to a degree much more circumscribed than has often been believed'.[55] Thus, far from its being simply a question of social expediency that women should be subordinate to men, to attempt any other arrangement of society was biologically absurd. The causes of all mental characteristics were to be found in the physical organism, the brain, and women, with their physically weaker constitution, must therefore be intellectually inferior to men, though Comte granted generously that they were compensated to some extent by being endowed by nature with greater delicacy of feeling and sympathy. They were to be pampered, worshipped, even prayed to, in the society Comte envisaged for the future, but to expect them to be capable of any sort of decision-making or political participation that required reasonable or objective thought, was to go against nature in a way that could only be disastrous both for women and for society as a whole.

Mill, who initially acknowledged the gaps in his knowledge of biology which he was valiantly attempting to remedy,[56] adopted a tone that seems extremely humble and conciliatory, especially in contrast to

Comte's arrogant confidence in his own convictions,[57] but was simply not prepared to accept that biology could have achieved any conclusive findings on the subject. While admitting the possibility that there might one day be proved to be certain physiological differences between the brains of the sexes (that, for example, as had been suggested, women's brains might be smaller but finer in quality, so that they could work faster but would be sooner exhausted—though he was certainly far from being confined of any such hypothesis), he stressed in answering Comte that there was, as yet, no definite knowledge of the precise relationship that held between the physical characteristics of the brain and the intellectual powers of its owner. To rely, then, on such an oversimplification as the contention that men, being bigger than women, have bigger brains and therefore greater mental powers, was to lay oneself open to the charge that big men are more intelligent than little ones, and that elephants and whales are more intelligent than either.[58]

Mill was convinced that the sort of reasoning that Comte was engaging in, on the issue of the different capacities of the sexes, was likely to produce no sound conclusions, as long as the study of the environmental influences on character development, or ethology, remained so neglected. In *The Subjection of Women*, he spoke urgently of the need for the advancement of this science, saying that 'of all the difficulties which impede the progress of thought, and the formation of well-grounded opinions on life and social arrangements, the greatest is now the unspeakable ignorance of mankind in respect to the influences which form human character'.[59] He was not, however, under any illusions as to the ease of carrying out such a study. The difficulties of isolating causal factors in a study in which experimental, laboratory conditions are impossible should be obvious, he thought, to anyone who has thought seriously about the complexity of the subject of education, or who has read Helvétius' or Rousseau's works on the subject. Despite the difficulties, however, he was convinced that this area of science, so crucial for the advancement of society, must not continue to be so neglected, and in the *Logic*, in a chapter headed 'Of Ethology, or the Science of the Formation of Character',[60] he set out some preliminary ideas for such a science, though he went no further in carrying it into operation. He was sure, though, that until that science was well advanced, no differences between the intellectual and moral characteristics of the two sexes could be reasonably held to be caused by innate, physiological factors. 'No one', he wrote bluntly in *The Subjection of Women,* 'is thus far entitled to any positive opinion on the subject.'[61]

Therefore, with knowledge in its limited state, it could certainly not be demonstrated that women were incapable of the same levels of intellectual achievement as men, and such a belief could certainly not be regarded as just grounds for keeping them subordinate in society and denying them all opportunity to show what they could in fact achieve. Further, Mill argued, in many fields women had already achieved a considerable measure of success, despite the weight of circumstance, lack of education, and force of prejudice which worked against them. Though this claim was to rest the case for women on very humble grounds, 'when we consider how sedulously they are all trained away from, instead of being trained towards, any of the occupations or objects reserved for men',[62] he cited the achievements of women such as Mme. De Staël and George Sand in the field of literature, and applied the argument most forcefully in the case of politics, in which women had proved themselves so competent at the top executive level. Here the reader was not confined to speculation about what women might be capable of if suitably educated: what some women had achieved in the political sphere was most persuasive in itself. At the top political level, Mill pointed out, which is practically the only sphere of public affairs to which they have ever been admitted, the great qualities of a proportionately larger number of queens than kings has demonstrated that 'Exactly where and in proportion as women's capacities for government have been tried, in that proportion have they been found adequate'.[63] Citing such examples as Elizabeth, Margaret of Austria, Deborah and Joan of Arc,[64] he argued that these and other examples of women who had been expert governors or leaders made it quite ridiculous to regard women as a sex as unfit to participate on all other levels of political life. For their potential in the field, he said, has already been demonstrated to be at least equal to that of men.

Speaking generally of all the spheres of human endeavour, Mill concluded that there were very few fields in which, however little opportunity they had had to prove themselves, some women at least had not reached a very high level of accomplishment. The fact that they had not, so far, achieved first-class works of genius and originality could, he thought, be explained by their lack of the thorough education which is necessary in order to reach original conclusions once all the first principles in a field are established, by the fact that women were traditionally expected to be always available to the beck and call of men and children, and therefore seldom had sustained periods in which to concentrate, and by the circumstances of their coming, like the Romans after the Greeks, second to men chronologically in all fields of study and art. Thus, he regarded what women had achieved as conclusive proof of what they were capable of, but refused to treat what they had not so far achieved as conclusive proof of anything at all.

However, Mill did not consider that he had finished arguing the case for female equality by demonstrating to his contemporaries that their grounds for discriminating against women were scientifically undemonstrable, and in many cases had been refuted by the facts of history. For, as he had pointed out in the last chapter of *Utilitarianism*, people in general had shown themselves consistently unwilling to admit to the unjust nature of any social discrimination, until they had concluded that it was inexpedient also. Thus he felt obliged to argue not only that the unjust treatment of women was inequitable, but that it was socially harmful as well, and the treating women as equals would be beneficial for the happiness and advancement of all. Justice, then, like liberty, is linked in Mill's feminist ideas with the constant theme of the improvement of mankind.

Mill believed that inequality was undesirable because of its direct moral effects on the parties involved. While this might at first seem not to be a utilitarian point of view, when we recall that in Mill's view the feeling of inner morality or virtue was itself an important part of individual happiness, it becomes compatible at least with his esoteric version of the principle of utility. He believed that 'society in equality is its normal state', and moreover that 'the only school of genuine moral sentiment is society between equals';[65] thus, in Mill's view, the very fact of the everyday assumption by men of their superiority over women was constantly detracting from the value of their own lives as well as women's. There could be nothing approaching the highest potential of human companionship between two beings one of whom was convinced of his greater capacities and value, and of the justice of his taking precedence over the other. What hopes, Mill asked, could there be for the moral advancement of society, when the domestic atmosphere in which all its members received their earliest moral education was based, in theory even if not always in practice, on such an unjust distribution of rights and powers? If marriage were to be recognised by law and in society as a co-operative partnership between equals, the family would at last have a chance of becoming, for the children, 'the real school of the virtues of freedom . . . , a school of living together in love, without power on one side or obedience on the other.'[66] Only then could their upbringing prepare children for what he regarded as the 'true virtue of human beings', that is, 'fitness to live together as equals'.[67]

The unjust treatment of women had, Mill thought, another detrimental effect on society; they attempted to gain influence in subversive ways and to use it for selfish purposes, as happened in other cases in which legitimate access to power was denied. Under existing conditions, he argued, women were forced to resort to cunning and underhanded tactics in order to have their wishes fulfilled in family matters in which they and their husbands disagreed, instead of such issues being discussed openly and rationally between them. As far as their political influence was concerned, he was sure that the indirect influence they exerted, through their pressure on their enfranchised husbands, was bound to be unconcerned with the welfare of anyone but their own immediate families. If they were themselves enfranchised, and thereby given their own legitimate means of influencing the political process, they would become far more likely, at least in the course of time, to use these means responsibly and in a more humanitarian spirit. Convinced as he had become by de Tocqueville's impressions of the educative effects of political participation, he was convinced that women who exercised their political right would 'receive that stimulus to their faculties, and that widening and liberalizing influence over their feelings and sympathies, which the suffrage seldom fails to produce on those who are admitted to it'.[68] Thus, by admitting women to the franchise, society would benefit doubly—by minimizing the selfish and narrow influences which many of them already exerted, via their husbands, and by increasing the selflessness and responsibility of the total electorate. Not only the quality of ethical life in the family, but also the standard of politics, would be raised, Mill argued, by the granting of just and equal treatment to women.

It is generally recognized that, despite the fact that Mill had omitted from *The Subjection of Women* his most radical views about sexual relations and divorce, it nevertheless earned him more antagonism than anything else he wrote.[69] Several of his friends, including his biographer, Bain, dissented strongly from the views expressed in it, and periodicals such as the *Saturday Review* and *Fraiser's Magazine* published hostile reviews of it.[70] Among Mill's most serious critics on this subject of female emancipation were the Stephen brothers—both Leslie, the more liberal, who was generally sympathetic to his utilitarian principles, and James Fitzjames, who disagreed violently with so much of what Mill believed about human equality. Leslie Stephen took great exception to Mill's references to the 'accident of sex', being definitely on Comte's side of the argument about innate sexual differences. 'It is not', he wrote, 'apparently, a case of two otherwise equal beings upon which different qualities have been superimposed, but of a radical distinction, totally inconsistent with any presumption of equality.'[71]

James Fitzjames Stephen attacked Mill in a far more vigorous manner. It is highly significant that, being totally opposed to Mill's central conviction that society was progressing towards a state of equality among individuals that was its 'normal' and its most desirable state, Stephen used Mill's arguments for the equal treatment of the sexes as a kind of test case, by means of which to attack this central principle.[72] In his *Liberty, Equality, Fraternity,* Stephen referred to *The Subjection of Women* as 'a work from which I dissent from the first sentence to the last',[73] and his objection, too, is the very basic one that sex, like age, is an undeniable inequality which exists by nature, and which must be recognized by society in its institutions, customs and laws. He considered that the inequality of the sexes is one of those facts which is so obvious that it is very difficult to prove specifically: 'The physical differences between the two sexes affect every part of the human body, from the hair of the head to the soles of the feet, from the size and density of the bones to the texture of the brain and the character of the nervous system. . . . All the talk in the world will never shake the proposition that men are stronger than women in every shape. They have greater muscular and nervous force, greater intellectual force, greater vigour of character. . . . These are the facts, and the question is whether law and public opinion ought to recognize this difference.'[74] Such were the words of a highly educated man, writing just one hundred years ago in 1873.

In spite of the fact that most of the political and legal rights for which Mill specifically argued have since been won, throughout most of the world, and most of the educational and career opportunities are no longer denied in principle, though still very often in fact, John Stuart Mill and Harriet Taylor's feminist principles and arguments continue to sound relevant to a remarkable degree. The main reasons for this are probably that they understood the immense complexity of the issue, they appreciated how much deep-rooted and strongly-felt prejudice was involved in this subject which affected the lives of everybody, both men and women, in a very intense way, and they realized that the emancipation they advocated would require change on a revolutionary scale, though not necessarily at a revolutionary speed, before it could be fully accomplished in practice. Far from thinking that a well-argued case would have immediate results, Mill acknowledged at the very beginning of *The Subjection of Women* that 'The difficulty [of the case] is that which exists in all cases in which there is a mass of feeling to be contended against. So long as an opinion is strongly rooted in the feelings, it gains rather than loses in stability by having a preponderating weight of argument against it.'[75] He also appreciated, as did Harriet Taylor, the great difficulties that stood in the way of persuading women themselves to fight for equality, because of the extent to which almost every one of them was dependent, both for her livelihood and her social standing, on a man; the intimacy of this master/slave relationship and the love that existed in many instances of it, made extensive 'Uncle Tomism' a certainty.[76] It is really hard for us, accustomed to the relative legitimacy of protest, to appreciate as Mill and Taylor did the personal sacrifices which the early feminists must have made.

It is a tribute to the far-sightedness of Mill's and Taylor's thought that there are only two aspects of his feminism and one of hers that would probably be found objectionable by most present day Women's Liberationists. The first of these, which was a product of the nineteenth-century environment and which they both undoubtedly shared, was their attitude towards sexuality. Although they regarded the mores of their time as unbearably restricting, in the sense that they saw people's self-regarding behaviour as a matter of private morality in which the law had no justifiable right to intervene,[77] it is clear form a number of passages that the purpose of their desire for people's sexual lives to be regarded as their own business was not the increase of sexual freedom and pleasure, but rather that what they saw as an unhealthy preoccupation with sexuality might then diminish.[78] Far from wanting women to feel that they had a right to derive pleasure from their sexuality, as men felt that they could, they thought that the emancipation of women, already the less sensually-preoccupied sex, would accelerate the movement of men away from a trait which they regarded as befitting humanity only in its semi-barbarous state. One of the 'improvements of mankind' which they hoped would result from female equality, then, was sexual asceticism.

Secondly, Mill though not Harriet Taylor, continued to assert that, if a woman chose to marry, she chose marriage in place of a career of her own, and that if she had children, it was her proper role to look after them. Although in those days of primitive contraceptive techniques, it would have been far harder for him that it is for us to conceive of the sharing of child-rearing and domestic chores, it is interesting that in spite of his adherence to the principle that one could not say what men and women are innately like until they were educated in the same way, Mill assumed that it was the woman's function to manage the household, and the man's to earn their livelihood.

In his early essay on marriage and divorce, this position is put much more dogmatically than later, and in terms which he could not consistently use in *The Subjection of Women*. This, then, is one area in which it seems highly likely that his views were at least modified in the certainty with which they were stated (though not substantially changed) by Harriet Taylor's more radical views. For in 1832, having just asserted that 'there is no natural inequality between the sexes', he proceeded to say that, in a home where there are no servants, it is 'good and will *naturally* take place . . . that the mistress of a family shall herself do the work of servants', and that, where there do not exist the means of hiring teachers for the children, 'the mother is the *natural* teacher'. He concluded, with little attention seemingly being paid to their own preferences, that 'the great occupation of women should be to *beautify* life . . . and to diffuse beauty, elegance and grace everywhere', since women are '*naturally*' endowed with greater elegance and taste.[79]

By the time he wrote *The Subjection of Women*, Mill could no longer say that women's domestic role was natural, in so many words, since in that work he asserted that 'natural' is such a subjective term that 'everything which is usual appears natural', and asks 'was there ever any domination which did not appear natural to those who possessed it?'[80] In spite of the alteration in terminology, however, he still adhered to the traditional division of labour within marriage. 'Like a man when he chooses a profession', he wrote, 'so, when a woman marries, it may in general be understood that she makes choice of the management of a

household, and the bringing up of a family, as the first call upon her exertions, during as many years of her life as may be required for the purpose; and that she renounces, not all other objects and occupations, but
all which are not consistent with the requirements of this'.[81] Thus, in
spite of the fact that he had drawn attention to women's continual preoccupation with domestic detail, in order to help explain that they had
never achieved any works of genius because they were always amateurs
in terms of time and concentration, Mill was not prepared to concede
that the tiresome details of domesticity should be shared by both sexes.
Although certainly a very forward-looking feminist, Mill was not prepared to follow his own theory to the point of seeing the injustice and
inequality of opportunity involved in the practice of a man's being free
to choose to have a full career and a family, whereas a woman was free
to choose only one or the other. We might well cite this as an instance of
that phenomenon to which he himself draws our attention in *Utilitarianism*, in the discussion of justice—that is, that people who have come
to recognize previously practised inequalities as unjust and tyrannical,
are 'forgetful that they themselves perhaps tolerate other inequalities
under an equally mistaken notion of expediency. . . .'[82] Mill, at any rate,
was so far from being a dogmatist that he would certainly not have
claimed to have said the last word on the subject of women's position in
society.

Harriet Taylor, however, would find herself more in agreement with
modern feminist feelings about a woman's right to have both children
and a career. Although she did not go into the specifics of how this might
be arranged when there were no servants, she asserted in *The Enfranchisement of Women* that it was not only necessary for women to have the
capacity and training to be *able* to earn their own subsistence (which was
Mill's formulation in *The Subjection of Women*),[83] but that women's position in the family would improve substantially 'if women both earned,
and had the right to possess, a part of the income of the family'.[84] And
from several other passages of this work, from which Mill did *not* draw
in composing *The Subjection of Women*, it becomes clear that Harriet was
more of a radical feminist with regard to the role of the married woman.
She spoke out more strongly than Mill ever did in favour of the married
woman's need to have a life and a career of her own, so as not to be 'a
mere appendage to a man', attached to him 'for the purpose of bringing
up *his* children, and making *his* home pleasant to him'.[85] These were

probably aspects of her thought which Mill, whom we know from letters to have been extremely dependent on her as far as domestic arrangements were concerned, did not feel at all comfortable with.

However, on all the other important feminist principles, they were agreed, and were collectively far in advance of their time. In her recent introduction to John Stuart Mill's and Harriet Taylor's collected *Essays on Sex Equality*, sociologist and feminist Alice Rossi says: 'In 1970 the movement is much broader [than the suffrage movement] and its goals more diffuse, for the women's liberation movement seeks nothing short of full equality of the sexes. In this sense contemporary activists are closer to the perspective of John Mill and Harriet Taylor than of the majority of turn-of-century American suffragists.'[86] This fact, though of course a striking tribute to them, is not surprising, considering their intelligence, their visionary capacities, their great concern with liberty and justice, and their strongly held belief that abolishing the unequal treatment of women would contribute inestimably to the happiness of both men and women and the moral and intellectual improvement of mankind.

Notes

1. Auckland University Press, 1972. I am indebted to Ms. Grimshaw for most of the information in this paragraph.

2. Grimshaw, p. 15.

3. London, 1825.

4. J. S. Mill, *The Subjection of Women*, London, 1912, p. 427.

5. See, for example, Michael St. John Packe, *The Life of John Stuart Mill*, London, 1954, pp. 90, 294–5, F. A. Hayek, *John Stuart Mill and Harriet Taylor: Their Correspondence and Subsequent Marriage*, London & Chicago, 1951, pp. 208, 248, and *The Subjection of Women*, p. 451.

6. The two essays on the subject of marriage and divorce which J. S. Mill and Harriet Taylor wrote for each other some time in 1832, are reprinted in Hayek, and also in Alice Rossi's edition of their *Essays on Sex Equality*, where the pamphlet *The Enfranchisement of Women*, which was probably although not certainly written by Harriet Taylor, is also to be found.

7. Jeremy Bentham, *Plan of Parliamentary Reform in the Form of a Catechism* in *Works*, ed. Bowring, 1843, III, 463–4, and *Constitutional Code*, in ibid., IX, 107–9.

8. J. S. Mill, *Autobiography*, London, 1873, p. 107.

9. James Mill, 'Government', written for the 1820 Supplement to the *Encyclopedia Britannica*, and reprinted as a pamphlet, 1821, p. 21.

10. Mill, *Autobiography*, p. 104.

11. Packe, p. 90.

12. Mill, *Autobiography*, pp. 124–5.

13. J. S. Mill, *Principles of Political Economy*, in *Collected Works*, Toronto, 1963, II, 209.

14. R. K. P. Pankhurst, *The Saint-Simonians, Mill and Carlyle: A Preface to Modern Thought*, London, 1957, pp. 3–4, 108–9.

15. Mill, *Autobiography*, pp. 167–8.

16. Francis Mineka, *The Dissidence of Dissent: The Monthly Repository, 1806–1838*, Chapel Hill, 1944, p. 296.

17. J. S. Mill, *The Earlier Letters, (1812–1848)*, in *Collected Works*, XII.

18. Until the 1960s, twentieth-century biographers of Mill, such as Ruth Borchard, Hayek, and Packe, had tended to accept Mill's estimate of the great extent of Harriet Taylor's intellectual influence on him, especially Packe, p. 317, who talks as if she all but wrote all of Mill's major works except the *Logic*. In recent years, however, there has been considerable reaction against his view, from Jack Stillinger, who edited the earlier draft of Mill's *Autobiography*, H. O. Pappe, in a short work entitled *John Stuart Mill and the Harriet Taylor Myth*, Melbourne, 1960, and John M. Robson, in his study of Mill's thought, *The Improvement of Mankind*, Toronto, 1968. None of these writers disputes that Harriet Taylor was a very important part of Mill's life, and that she provided him with the emotional well-being without which he may well not have been nearly so productive: what they are disagreeing about with the earlier critics, and with Mill himself, is that the principal ideas of his works were hers, not his.

19. Letter from J.S.M. to H.T., in Hayek, p. 185; for other examples of Mill's hyperbolic references to Harriet Taylor, see, for example, his introduction to *The Enfranchisement of Women*, his *Autobiography*, passim, and the inscription which he placed on her tombstone, in Hayek, p. 34.

20. Mill, *Autobiography*, p. 244, note.

21. Loc. cit.

22. Reprinted in Hayek, ch. iii, and in Rossi.

23. Mill, *Autobiography*, p. 266. However, I have assumed (p. 125) that those more radical views expressed in the *Enfranchisement of Women*, which Mill did not repeat in the *Subjection*, were hers alone.

24. *On Liberty*, p. 16.

25. *The Subjection of Women*, p. 521.

26. Ibid., p. 487.

27. *On Liberty*, p. 16.

28. Essay on *Bentham*, p. 97.

29. *On Liberty*, p. 73.
30. The famous argument about the quality of pleasures is found at the beginning of Chapter 2 of the essay *Utilitarianism*, pp. 258–62. Taken simply as it is presented there, without the unspoken premise that Mill took his own highly intellectual nature as his model of human nature no less than Bentham used his, the argument is quite unsatisfactory. Mill certainly fails to convince us that Socrates really knew what it was like to be a happy pig, any more than Mill himself did.
31. *Utilitarianism*, p. 265.
32. Ibid., pp. 289–90.
33. *Principles of Political Economy*, p. 765.
34. *The Subjection of Women*, p. 542.
35. *On Liberty*, p. 15.
36. *The Subjection of Women*, p. 542.
37. Ibid., p. 547.
38. Quoted in Hayek, p. 63.
39. *On Liberty*, p. 87.
40. *The Subjection of Women*, p. 525.
41. Ibid., p. 536, and see also p. 540.
42. *Utilitarianism*, p. 320.
43. Loc. cit.
44. In Hayek, op. cit., p. 64.
45. In a letter written in 1869 and quoted by Pappe, p. 27, Mill actually says: 'it is not certain that the differences spoken of are not partly at least natural ones'.
46. *The Subjection of Women*, p 450.
47. Ibid., pp. 451–2.
48. Harriet Taylor, *The Enfranchisement of Women*, p. 100, in Rossi.
49. *The Subjection of Women*, p. 495.
50. Ibid., pp. 518–9.
51. Ibid., p. 519.
52. Mill did, however, concede that Helvétius' claim for the powers of education was exaggerated.
53. Mill, *Earlier Letters*, in *Collected Works*, XIII, 590–611, and Comte, *Lettres d'Auguste Conte à John Stuart Mill* (1841–6), Paris, 1877, pp. 175–212.
54. Comte, p. 175.
55. Ibid., p. 199.
56. He reports having read several volumes of the works of the biologist, Gall, during the correspondence.
57. Comte assumes the superior attitude that the only explanation for the divergent opinion of the two great thinkers on such a fundamental subject is that

Mill is going through a passing phase—as had Comte himself when struck by 'the strange work of Miss Mary Wooltonscraft' [*sic*]—from which he will soon, no doubt, recover. Comte, p. 184.

58. And anyway, Mill reports, for the benefit of those who are impressed by such statistics, that he knew of a man who had weighed many human brains, the heaviest of which was that of a woman. *The Subjection of Women*, p. 503.

59. *The Subjection of Women*, p. 452.

60. J. S. Mill, *Logic*, London, 1875, pp. 451–63.

61. *The Subjection of Women*, p. 453.

62. Ibid., p. 489.

63. Ibid., p. 493; and see also *Representative Government*, p. 293.

64. Ibid., pp. 490 and 492.

65. Ibid., p. 477.

66. Ibid., p. 479.

67. Loc. cit.

68. 'Speech of John Stuart Mill, M.P., on the Admission of Women to the Electoral Franchise', spoken in the House of Commons, May 20th, 1867, and published as a pamphlet, 1867, p. 12; see also *Representative Government*, pp. 292–3.

69. See, e.g., Packe, p. 495, and J. A. and O. Banks, *Feminism and Family Planning in Victorian England*, Liverpool, 1964, p. 25.

70. Banks, pp. 51–52 and p. 118.

71. Leslie Stephen, *The English Utilitarians*, London, 1900, III, *John Stuart Mill*, pp. 283–4. I cannot, as a feminist affronted by such bigotry, resist the temptation of pointing out that Leslie Stephen's daughter, Virginia Woolf, was undeniably a greater genius than he was.

72. James Fitzjames Stephen, *Liberty, Equality, Fraternity*, London, 1874, pp. 219–59, passim.

73. Ibid., pp. 219–20.

74. Ibid., pp. 227–9.

75. *The Subjection of Women*, p. 427, and see also pp. 439, 433–5, and 520.

76. See, for example, *the Enfranchisement of Women*, in Rossi, pp. 118–9.

77. Although Mill stressed that people should be held responsible for the care of any children resulting from their sexual relations, he said: 'to have held any human being responsible to other people and to the world for the fact itself, apart from this consequence, will one day be thought one of the superstitions and barbarisms of the infancy of the human race.' Quoted by Packe, p. 319.

78. See, e.g., Mill's implied approval of his father's thought on this issue in the *Autobiography*, p. 107, and Harriet Taylor's early essay on marriage and divorce, in Rossi, pp. 84–85.

79. Reprinted in Rossi, pp. 73–77 (italics added).

80. *The Subjection of Women*, pp. 440, 441.

81. Ibid., p. 484, and see also *Principles of Political Economy*, pp. 395–6, for another statement of the same position.

82. *Utilitarianism*, p. 320.

83. *The Subjection of Women*, p. 483, where Mill says 'the power of earning is essential to the dignity of a woman, if she has not independent property'. The conditional clause implies that he is concerned with the financial aspect of dignity, rather than with personal self-esteem or professional status.

84. *The Enfranchisement of Women*, in Rossi, p. 105, text and note.

85. Ibid., p. 107.

86. Rossi, Introduction, p. 62.

4

Mill and the Subjection of Women

Julia Annas

Annas argues that there are two incompatible lines of argument in The Subjection of Women. In her view, Mill oscillated between what she calls the "reformist approach" to arguing for gender equality and the "radical approach." The reformist approach targets primarily inequality in the law and unequal opportunities, while the radical approach targets the systematic thwarting of women's natures achieved by broader social attitudes towards the relationship between the sexes. Annas maintains that Mill's argument in The Subjection of Women is a "confused mixture" of these two approaches, which rely respectively on utilitarian arguments and arguments from justice. Ultimately, however, she believes that Mill's approach is reformist rather than radical.

WHEN MILL'S *THE SUBJECTION OF WOMEN* WAS PUBLISHED in 1869 it was ahead of its time in boldly championing feminism.[1] It failed to inaugurate a respectable intellectual debate. Feminist writers have tended to refer to it with respect but without any serious attempt to come to grips with Mill's actual arguments. Kate Millett's chapter in *Sexual Politics* is the only sustained discussion of Mill in the feminist literature that I am aware of, but it is not from a philosophical viewpoint, and deals with Mill only in the service of an extended comparison with Ruskin.

It is, however, simply false to say that Mill's essay is mostly concerned with legal technicalities which have since been changed, and so of no great interest today. *The Subjection of Women* is concerned with women's legal disabilities only in so far as they reflect profound social and economic inequalities between the sexes. While today there are few ways in which women are under legal disabilities compared with men (though it would be a mistake to think there are none) women are still subject to economic and social discrimination in a variety of ways, and it is extraordinary to think that Mill's essay no longer contains anything interesting or controversial just because there have been a few changes in the law. To take only one example: today a battered wife is no longer under legal compulsion to return to her husband, as she was in Mill's day, but until very recently the pressure for her to do so was overwhelming; the informal ways in which society enforces conformity to the institution of the family have never been stronger. Although we are more receptive to the ideal, we are nowhere near achieving in practice the kind of equality between the sexes that Mill looks forward to. It will be a good day when *The Subjection of Women* is outdated, but it is not yet.

Ryan has another objection: 'Mill's coolness towards sexual issues makes *The Subjection of Women* an awkward work to place in twentieth-century arguments about sexual equality'. It is true that Mill's actual references to sex are all very Victorian in the worst sense, but it does not follow that this undermines his argument, unless it can be shown that his main contentions are based on his false view of women's sexuality. Since Mill does not put forward purported facts about female sexuality as the main support for any of his conclusions, argument is needed, which Ryan does not provide, to show that what Mill says about women should be revised substantially in the light of our greatly altered beliefs about women's sexuality. Mill has often been dismissed on the ground that, being pre-Freudian, he failed to understand the basic importance of sex in determining personality.[2] However, Mill's non-Freudian approach may nowadays be thought a positive advantage, given the extremely contentious character of Freud's views on women and the history of dispute in the psychoanalytic movement on this topic.

The predominant view seems to be that *The Subjection of Women* is obviously right but of little importance. I believe, on the contrary, that it is of great importance, but, far from being obviously truistic, contains very deep confusions; this paper is an attempt to disentangle some of them. I should say at the outset, however, that the reason why I think this is worthwhile is that Mill's confusions are not shallow ones; they come rather from a desire to have things too many ways at once, to do justice to all the complexities of a topic which even now is far from being adequately clarified. If this were not so, it would indeed be perverse to search for faults in what Millett justly calls his 'splendidly controlled humanist outrage'.

I shall begin by distinguishing two ways in which one might protest at exiting sexual inequalities.

1. The reformist approach. One can claim that it is unfair for women to be excluded from opportunities that are open to men, because women are in fact capable of doing what men do, and do in fact resent being excluded. This is a straightforwardly factual claim; the available openings are not in fact commensurate with women's desires and needs, and what is therefore required is reform of the existing social system. The most obvious justification for this is utilitarian: if desires are no longer frustrated, this will lead to greater happiness for women, and if unused abilities are put to work, everyone will benefit; in both cases the benefits are such as to be so regarded already by both men and women. This argument is quite compatible with there being many important empirically established differences of nature between the sexes; all that it excludes is that these differences should justify inferior opportunities for women in the respects in which their contribution can be recognized.

2. The radical approach. One can also claim that the subjection of women is unfair, but not from observation of actual frustrated desires and unfulfilled capacities. Rather it may be admitted, and even stressed, that most women lack ambition and serious concentration, but argued that this very fact shows that their natural impulses have been suppressed by a system that brings them up to think submissiveness and dependence virtues, and that what is required is that they (and men) be liberated from this system. This is not a straightforwardly factual claim, for the appeal is to women's nature, but this nature is not something that can be ascertained from women's present behaviour and achievements. This approach is not exactly *a priori*, for it may well appeal to known facts about human nature; but these will be extremely general and theory-laden, as opposed to the sort of facts that can be read off from people's observed behaviour. The radical approach will have little use for reform of the existing system; to a radical, this would be merely futile, enabling a few women to get ahead by adopting male values, but doing nothing for the mass of women whose natures have been systematically thwarted. What is required is a radical change in the whole framework of society's attitudes to the relations between the sexes; and the justification of this radical change will be one of justice and of women's rights, not a utilitarian one. As I am using 'utilitarian' in this connection, a utilitarian justification is one that appeals to the satisfactions of desires that people actually have, not those they would have in some ideal condition.[3] Changes that merely produce the maximum satisfaction of desires in the system as it is will be rejected by the radical, because integral to the system are the institutions and attitudes that according to the radical systematically deform women's natures. In contrast to the reformist, the radical does seem committed to holding that there are no large and interesting differences of nature between men and women, none, at any rate, that could justify any institutionalization of sexual differences.

Mill's argument throughout *The Subjection of Women* is a confused mixture of these two approaches. He lurches from a less to a more radical position and back again, and this creates strain at several points. In what follows I shall try to show that although Mill is clear about what he is opposing he fails to consider that there are different possibilities on the positive side, and that different arguments carry different commitments and can be incompatible.

In the argument of Chapter 1 of the essay, Mill seems to presuppose the radical approach. He objects, for example, that the existence of patriarchy is not something that can count in its favour, because it has no theoretical basis. It is not the case that patriarchy is the result of fair experiment, trials and refutations. Experience shows us only that we *can* survive under patriarchy, not that we could not do a good deal better otherwise. (p. 129)[4] So 'experience, in the sense in which it is vulgarly opposed to theory cannot be pretended to have pronounced any verdict'. Further, 'the adoption of this system of inequality never was the result of deliberation, or forethought, or any social ideas, or any notion whatever of what conduced to the benefit of humanity or the good order of society'. It arose simply because women have always been weaker, being at a biological disadvantage. It is just 'the primitive state of slavery lasting on'. The opponent presumably wants to argue that biology is destiny; Mill's counter to this is to deny it is relevant at all. What matter more are considerations of what is just and right, and these cannot be read off from ordinary experience.

Mill also overrides the objection that women do not object to the present system. While insisting that some do, as is shown by franchise agitation, etc., he admits that most do not; yet insists that 'there are abundant tokens how many *would* cherish [similar aspirations] were they not so strenuously taught to repress them as contrary to the proprieties of their sex' (p. 140). He adds that the fact that each woman complains individually about her husband shows that women would collectively complain about the position of men if their education were not aimed at getting them to think of themselves as dependents with subservience to men as their natural goal. This may well be true, but it is not a datum of experience, and Mill does not think that it is; he is getting us to discount the views of most women as presently expressed. He even gets us to disallow most of what women have written as inauthentic. The desires and interests which women now have are thus not given utilitarian weighting; they are explained away, as not reflecting women's real nature.

That this is the radical and not the reformist approach is made even clearer by Mill's eloquent rejection of the opponent's claim that men and women are naturally fitted for their present functions and positions: 'What is now called the nature of women is an eminently artificial thing—the result of forced repression in some directions, unnatural stimulation in others. It may be asserted without scruple, that no other class of dependents have had their character so entirely distorted from its natural proportions by their relation with their masters . . .' (p. 148). Mill insists that nobody is in a position to know anything about women's nature, because so far we have not seen anything that we could call natural; all we have seen is manifestations of the altogether understandable desire to conform to stereotype. He uses the occasion to criticize men who think, from a negligible basis, that they completely understand women. Consistently with this, Mill, in Chapter 1, uses no argument directly from what women want or can do. His main argument works by analogy: the dissatisfaction that most women feel with marriage shows that they would object to the position of men in general if it were not for the submissiveness inculcated by their education, just as complaints about misuse of tyrannical power by one class against another in the past have always led in the end to demands that the power itself should be abolished. Given Mill's strong assertions about the impossibility of demarcating female nature, this kind of argument from analogy is the most he can consistently offer.[5]

Mill argues (p. 185) that if even a few women are fit to hold office then legally excluding women 'cannot be justified by any opinion which can be held respecting the capacities of women in general'. He adds, with a connection of thought which is for him uncharacteristically loose and vague, 'But, though this last consideration is not essential, it is far from being irrelevant. An unprejudiced view of it gives additional strength to the argument against the disabilities of women, and reinforces them by high considerations of practical utility.' The progress of Mill's thought here seems to be: to exclude women from jobs, etc., on the ground that they are unfit for them is irrational, because we cannot know whether they are unfit or not (never having tried). But it is *also* actually rebutted by the existence of some women who *are* fit—and if some women are fit, it must surely increase utility to include them among the employables. Mill obviously thinks that he has merely brought in a supplementary argument which will strengthen the first, and so he would have if he had stuck to the above formulation of his point; but Mill in the course of making his appeal to utility makes exactly his opponents' dubious move of arguing from a few examples to the capacity of women in general in a specific respect—e.g., from a few women rulers to women's bent for the practical. Yet he had himself earlier (p. 149) pointed out the fallacy of arguing from the behaviour of a few to the behaviour of all members of a class like women or members of other nations. Worse: if, as Mill has argued at length in Chapter 1, we have no real knowledge of women's natures, then we cannot argue from some cases that women are fit to hold jobs, etc., any more than we can argue from some other cases that women are *not* fit. Indeed, this is dangerous ground for a feminist; as Mill seemed aware earlier on, there have always been many more women who have failed to rise above their education than have succeeded—that was why he was so anxious to argue that in this matter we cannot argue from experience. Yet here he seems not to see that the argument cuts both ways, and cuts more sharply against him than for him.

It seems, then, that in his anxiety to add a utilitarian argument to the argument from rights, Mill is trying to occupy ground already undercut by his own earlier arguments. This emerge strongly in the rest of the arguments of Chapter 3. Throughout them we find Mill in untypically embarrassed and tortuous positions. He demands that we 'make entire abstraction of' all considerations suggesting that differences between the sexes are the product of the suppression by education of women's natures, admitting uncomfortably that this leaves only 'a very humble ground' for women, and apparently unaware that earlier he had argued that such abstraction, far from leading to an unprejudiced view, is illegitimate.

Mill makes much of the fact that women have been excellent rulers when they have had a chance to rule. His case perhaps depends on his selection of examples (the Empresses of Russia and China have been worse, if anything, than their male counterpart); but more disturbing is the fact that he concludes that this fits what we do know of 'the peculiar tendencies and aptitudes characteristic of women' (p. 189). Women in general have a bent towards the practical. They are capable of intuitive perception of situations, 'rapid and correct insight into present fact' (p. 190). This is a talent which, while it does not fit one for scientific thought or abstract reasoning on general principles, is of great use in practical matters, where what is required is sensitivity to the realities of the present situation. Women's intuition is thus a valuable corrective to man's tendency to abstract reasoning. It prevents the latter becoming uselessly over-speculative, and it ensures that sound reasoning is put into practice in a competent way.

Here is the oldest cliché in the book: women are intuitive while men reason. If any cliché has done the most harm to the acceptance by men of women as intellectual equals, it is this, and it is distressing to see Mill come out with it. It is even more distressing to find him patronizingly recommending to any man working in a speculative subject the great value of an intuitive woman to keep him down to earth (p. 102). It is true that Mill prefaces these remarks with an awkward and apologetic passage (pp. 189–190) in which he says that they apply only to women in their actual state, not as they could be. None the less, it is his own choice to defend women's supposed intuition on utilitarian grounds; and a very backhanded defence it is. If it were sound, it would actually undermine many radical proposals. There would be no good ground, for example, for giving the sexes the same type of education; it would be appropriate to train boys to go in, at least predominantly, for subjects requiring analytical reasoning and development of theory, and to train women rather for subjects requiring no sustained reasoning but rather 'human contact' and easily appreciable practical applications. We do not need to be reminded that our educational system is still run largely on these assumptions, and that girls are still notoriously inhibited from going in for subjects on the science and mathematics side, particularly in mixed schools, for fear of being thought too 'masculine'.[6] As for the utility of women's famous intuition,

Mill unwittingly exposes the catch when he points out its utility for a *man* engaged in speculative thought. Why should a woman be pleased by the fact that she is a usefully earthy check on some man's theories? Instead of claiming the usefulness of this function (which is surely very limited anyway) would it not be more rational for her to claim the right to produce theories too, if she can, just as speculative as a man's, and to have them taken seriously? As long as one admits that women are intuitive and men suited to reasoning, one's best efforts at valuing women's contribution will be patronizing and damaging, encouraging women to think that the most highly regarded intellectual achievements are not for them.

No less unhappy is Mill's treatment of the objection that women have greater 'nervous susceptibility' than men and so are unfit for proper employment (p. 194). Firstly he tries to explain this supposed fact away: much of it is the result of having excess energy unused or wasted on trivia, and much is artificially cultivated as the result of an unhealthy upbringing. But he then adds that some women *do* have nervous temperaments, and tries to present this in as favourable a light as possible. He points out that it is not confined to women, that it often accompanies genius, that if allied to self-control it produces a very strong character. In short, what is wrong with being nervous and excitable? But Mill, in spite of the changed direction of his defence, is too honest to claim that excitability is really a virtue. He admits that women would do as well as men 'if their education and cultivation were adapted to correcting instead of aggravating the infirmities incidental to their temperament'. So it seems that nervous susceptibility, in spite of Mill's awkward praise of it, is a defect after all. As if realizing how damaging this admission is, Mill launches on to another type of defence: even if women's minds are more 'mobile' than those of men, and thus less capable of sustained intellectual effort, this does not mean that they are any the less to be valued: 'This difference is one which can only affect the kind of excellence, not the excellence itself.' Mill's confused and tangled attempts to show the useful qualities of women's special way of thinking thus ends up with the dangerous cliché so beloved of inegalitarians: women are not *inferior* to men, just *different*.

It is no accident that efforts to get the position of women improved by praising their special, womanly qualities usually end up in a position very similar to that of the opposition, with merely a difference of emphasis. This is because, as Mill so clearly saw in Chapter 1, the special qualities that are ascribed to women, and for which they are praised, are created within a male-dominated society, and it is very unlikely that the roles that give them content can within that society achieve a genuinely high value. Their qualities are the qualities of the inferior, and praising them will not make their owners equal—indeed, it may well have the opposite effect by encouraging women to fall back lazily on their 'female intuitions' rather than learn to argue on equal terms with men. Mill sees very clearly what is wrong and harmful with the Victorian praise of women for having more moral virtue than men. It is surprising that he does not see what is wrong with his own very similar attempts to praise women as less abstractly rational than men and more sensitive to the human dimension.

Mill's discomforts increase when he comes to deal with the alleged fact that men have bigger brains than women. Firstly he dismisses it quite decisively: the alleged fact is dubious; anyway the principle appealed to is ridiculous, for according to it whales would be much more intelligent than men; further, the relationship between size of brain and quality of mind is, to say the least, not the subject of general agreement. But then, amazingly, he backtracks and admits that probably men do have bigger brains than women, but slower cerebral circulation; this would explain why men's thoughts are slower and steadier, while women's are more rapid and ephemeral! This is the only place in *The Subjection of Women* where the argument is quite pathetic, and one is mainly surprised that Mill feels that he needs to argue at all on this level. That he does can only be put down to his anxiety to add as many arguments as possible based upon women's actual (and supposedly actual) qualities, in spite of having pointed out clearly all the pitfalls of this approach in Chapter 1.

As if unhappy about this argument, Mill repeats his sound earlier point that we can know practically nothing about natural differences, because of the meagerness of the research done so far and the inevitability of cultural prejudices. At once he disregards his own good advice and starts speculating on the possible causes of what is represented as the greatest difference between the sexes, namely that there have been no great women philosophers, artists, etc. He defends this uneasily: 'I am not about to attempt what I have pronounced impossible; but doubt does not forbid conjecture'. But Mill's tone is not subsequently very tentative; and in any case he has already shown amply the futility of all such conjectures, if women's natures have been systematically deformed by their upbringing in male-dominated society. He now, however, takes seriously the question, 'Why have there been no great women artists, etc.?' as a question to be answered by appealing to actually existing features of women's character.

He begins by saying that it is not surprising that there have been no women geniuses, since it has not been very long since women could even enter the stakes for intellectual excellence. This looks at first like a good argument, but if one looks at the facts more closely a good deal of its force seems to evaporate. It cannot explain why women have been so much more prominent in fields like literature than in fields like the visual arts, when they have been open to them for roughly the same length of time.[7] Mill speaks as though women have made slow but increasing progress on all fronts, uniformly achieving competence so far but nothing great. One begins to suspect that he is dominated by a linear picture of progress.

Even without any belief in Progress, however, one can agree that women have not so far (even now, to any extent) 'produced any of those great and luminous new ideas which form an era in thought, nor those fundamentally new conceptions in art, which open a vista of possible effects not before thought of, and found a new school' (p. 204). Mill's explanation is strange and forced. He argues that in the past, when 'great and fruitful new truths could be arrived at by mere force of genius' women were socially prevented from artistic expression, and nowadays, when the latter is no longer the case, few women have the erudition required to say something new. In other words, women were not allowed to join in when originality was easy to come by and now when it is hard to come by they start with an educational handicap. Mill seems to be thinking of culture as cumulative, each generation having more homework to get through before they can add anything new. What is puzzling is why he thinks he needs this bizarre and implausible picture. For he has already made clear at some length why it is unlikely that a woman could come out with a profoundly original idea; women are not brought up to be self-reliant and are much more likely (like Harriet Taylor) to express their best insights through the work of some man.

Equally bizarre is Mill's explanation of why women's literature has been so derivative from that of men. He compares it with that of the Romans, who found a whole literature, the Greek, already in existence when they began to write. But surely *all* writers, men and women, stand to earlier literary achievements as the Romans stood to the Greeks. The comparison also renders wholly inappropriate Mill's claim that in time women will come to write their own original literature. But in any case he has already provided us with the real answer, or at least part of it, back in Chapter 1: 'The greater part of what women write about women is mere sycophancy to men' (p. 153). The dependence displayed by women who falsify their own experience to fulfill male expectations is quite unlike the literary dependence of the Romans on the Greeks.

Mill's awkwardness in arguing on his chosen humble ground shows up most clearly when he points out that women fail to achieve works of genius partly because they lack ambition to immortalize their names— 'whether the cause be natural or artificial'—this in spite of the fact that he has already shown at length that it is unreasonable to think that women are naturally passive and spiritless, just as it is in the case of serfs or black slaves; the limitations and narrow focus of their standard ambitions are quite adequately explained by their upbringing and the expectations of the roles they fill.

Mill's attempts in Chapter 3 to argue for reform on utilitarian grounds, basing himself on women's nature as they are, amount to total failure. I have dwelt on these arguments at length because they are so unexpectedly bizarre and weak; Mill's awkwardness betrays his confusion as again and again he puts forward grounds which are undermined by his own earlier arguments.

Mill seems unaware of this, as he seems likewise to be unaware that Chapter 3 is not co-tenable with some of the arguments of Chapter 4 either.

In Chapter 4 he argues that great benefits will accrue from the liberation of women, including among these the vast improvement of women's influence over men. He describes how as things are a woman is nearly always a moral drag on her husband; her narrow conception of their interests often forces him to sacrifice principle to money and status. 'Whoever has a wife and children has given hostages to Mrs. Grundy' (p. 229). Mill's eulogy of marriage as between equals gives great emphasis to the unsatisfactory nature of marriage as it is, largely on the ground that artificially fostered differences of tastes and inclinations make the marriage something that lowers the husband intellectually and morally. We are told similarly that liberated women will help others in a useful and rational way, rather than putting their energy into harmful and patronizing charity, as at present; again there is much stress on the improvements from others' points of view if women are liberated from their present rigid and thwarted characters. Now even if this long cata-logue of women's shortcomings is true, it should make one wonder afresh what the status of the arguments in Chapter 3 can possibly be. If women's influence as it stands is baneful, why should we hasten to em-ploy women in public and private jobs? What can be the utility of press-ing into service all these narrow and repressed natures? And can women's vaunted intuition and nervous susceptibility be worth very much after all, if their effects are those described in Chapter 4? Mill can-not have it both ways. If women even as they are deserve employment in the same way as men, then there is no reason to think that a fundamen-tal change of the relations between the sexes will bring great benefits. On the other hand, if a great change here *will* bring vast benefits, is it not suspicious to try to increase utility by making use of women in their present corrupted state?

Apart from the conflicts I have tried to draw out between Chapter 3 and Chapters 1 and 4, there are less localized signs throughout the essay that Mill is having trouble in combining his different arguments. One is his struggle with 'nature'. We are told over and over again that we can-not read off women's nature from their present state. On the other hand, we are assured that women are schooled into suppressing their desires for freedom and self-expression 'in their natural and most healthy di-rection' (p. 238).[8] So we are to be stopped from arguing that it is natu-ral for women to be passive but we must argue that it is natural for them to want to be free and self-determining in the way that men are. It is not clear, in fact, that there is a real incoherence here. What is needed is a distinction between facts about human nature that can be supported by some very general theory, and supposed facts that are merely superficial inferences from what happens to be observed. But none of this is made clear in *The Subjection of Women* itself; the reader is left with the im-pression that nature has been expelled from the argument as an enemy only to be brought in again by the back door.

A more troubling problem is that it is constantly unclear, throughout the essay, just what changes Mill thinks *are* appropriate. Since he is so in-sistent that women are not constrained by natural inferiority, and re-peats several times that what is desirable is that the sexes compete on an equal basis, one would assume that he thinks that women and men will tend to fill the same roles; his remarks at the theoretical level would all tend to imply the radical approach. Yet what he actually says on the subject is timid and reformist at best. He assumes that most women will in fact want only to be wives and mothers, 'the one vocation in which there is nobody to compete with them' (p. 183)—which is not even true, if we mean child-rearing and not just the physical process of birth. He thinks it undesirable for the wife to earn as well as the husband, for having a job will make a woman neglect the home and family. He argues that to have self-respect a woman must be *able* to earn her own living, but that in fact few women will, and he seems to envisage jobs being held only by the unmarried, or by middle-aged women whose children have grown up. This is clearly most unsatisfactory. How can women's education be a serious affair if it is known that most will not use it? In any case, how can it be argued that women really do want to be free and equal with men, and have political and educational parity, if it is taken to be a fact that the reformed state of affairs will make no difference to the majority of women? Mill's position here seems to be simply confused, because he is trying to argue both from the way women actually are, and from their right to become entirely different.

So far I have pointed to some confusions that arise from the fact that Mill attempts to combine the radical approach with the reformist approach. I shall finally try to show that the radical argument as it appears in Chapter 4 creates a further problem for Mill if he wants to apply utilitarian considerations.

In Chapter 4 Mill sets himself to answer the question 'which will be asked the most importunately by those opponents whose conviction is somewhat shaken on the main point. What good are we to expect from the changes proposed in our customs and institutions? Would mankind be at all better off if women were free?' (p. 216). This looks like a utilitarian argument, and Mill in fact goes on to list advantages to be gained from the liberation of women. However, though it is clearly an appeal to consequences, the argument cannot be utilitarian in the present restricted sense of taking into account only people's actual desires and needs; for what Mill cites as benefits would often only satisfy people *already* liberated from former attitudes. He first, for example, mentions the benefit of having the most basic human relationship run justly instead of unjustly; but if most people in a society are not liberated, they will presumably not see the present system of relations between the sexes as unjust, nor see anything wrong with the attitudes engendered by it. This comes out clearly from Mill's eloquent passage on the selfish and self-worshipping attitudes encouraged in men under patriarchy (pp. 218–220). The obvious retort to this is that, if it is true, then most men would not think of change as a *benefit*. Why should men want to change a system so favourable to themselves? Mill assumes that they will do so when they see the injustice of it; but that is the whole problem, for he has emphasized the way they are brought up to accept it as perfectly natural and just.

Similar remarks apply to what Mill says about the increase in happiness in marriage when it becomes a union of equals. Mill assumes that men will appreciate the greater profitability of a rational union between equals rather than a marriage where the husband has all the authority and all the wife does is obey. 'What . . . does the man obtain by it, except an upper servant, a nurse or a mistress?' (p. 233). But what if men have been so brought up that that is precisely what they do want out of a marriage? Should these desires not count? As we are aware from Rawls,[9] Mill will have trouble finding a utilitarian ground for discounting desires that can only be satisfied in an unjust system because they are engendered within it. Mill clearly thinks that these desires should *not* count, any more than women's expressed desires to remain happily dominated by men should count; they show nothing except how warped the nature of both men and women can get. But his justification for doing this cannot be a utilitarian one.

This means that Mill faces more of a problem than he is aware of when he represents the effects of liberation as uncontroversially benefits. In any society hitherto, Mill's or ours, the number of people, men and women, who are dissatisfied with the present state of relations between the sexes is very small. Not only do most men derive satisfaction from their dominant position, and would resent its removal; most women accept their position and do not see it as unjust.[10] So for the effects of liberation such as Mill details to be generally agreed to be benefits, there would have to be large-scale changes in people's desires, and for this to come about there would have to be fundamental changes in the way both sees think about sex differences and sex roles. Nowadays we know that this entails changes right from the beginning of education; if girls and boys learn from books where sexual stereotypes are presented, they will naturally tend to perpetuate those stereotypes. Our whole approach to education has to be changed if people are not to continue to learn the attitudes which lead to discrimination even where legal disabilities disappear.

In this respect there is some truth in the accusation that Mill's thinking about sexual differences is shallow. He is not aware of the massive changes required in people's desires and outlooks before sexual equality becomes a reality and its effects something that people see as beneficial. Consequently, he does not pay enough attention to the extensive interference in people's lives necessary to ensure that the liberation of women becomes a real change and not just the same attitudes under another name. He rejects reverse discrimination, and says nothing about re-educating people's desires by reforming school-books, etc. If he had been aware of this, he might as an individualist, have been disturbed. We know from *On Liberty* how he rejects, as unjustified, state interference in people's lives even where this would be agreed to lead to moral improvement He regards Prohibition as completely unjustifiable, though all would agree that it is better and morally preferable to be without drunkenness and its results. Presumably he would feel quite unhappy about state-aided programmes to help women, quotas for employing women, revision of books, etc. There is a real problem here, since the only effective means of removing injustice appears to involve injustice itself. Mill never faces this problem because he does not see the extent to which people have to be forcibly led to make sexual equality work. In this sense Mill *is* too much of a rationalist about sex and sexual roles; what is wrong is not that he lacked Freud's supposed truths but that he assumes that when people clearly perceive the injustice of sexual inequality they will come to desire its removal, and find greater satisfaction in liberation from it. But unfortunately this is not true.

In *The Subjection of Women*, then, Mill is sure what he is against, but he is not sure whether he is committed to a radical or a reformist approach, and in trying to have it both ways blurs what he is saying.[11] He has seen neither the problems inherent in pressing the argument from the benefits of liberation, given his individualistic beliefs, nor the difficulties lurking in his attempt to combine both his main lines of thought.

It is intriguing here to notice the way in which *The Subjection of Women* contrasts with an earlier essay on the same theme, *The Enfranchisement of Women*. There are three points at which, by adopting a more radical position than *The Subjection of Women*, and ignoring or rejecting the reformist approach, it achieves a more consistent and stronger argument.

Firstly, *The Enfranchisement of Women* argues firmly that 'The proper sphere for all human beings is the largest and highest which they are able to attain to. What this is, cannot be ascertained, without complete liberty of choice' (p. 100). It is therefore a complete waste of time to argue about women's peculiar aptitude or capacities. What women are like, and are able to do, will be decided by what they actually do when they are free to have a choice, and in no other way. Thus we find avoided, and on clear grounds, Mill's various disastrous attempts to argue, in Chapter 3 of *The Subjection of Women*, the usefulness of women's 'special gifts', intuitions, etc. Like Mill, the author of the earlier essay says that it cannot be true that women are incapable of political life on the basis of there having been capable women rulers, but because no attempt is made to argue from a few examples to a supposed fitness for practical matters on the part of all women, there is no incompatibility with the main line of argument.

Secondly, *The Enfranchisement of Women* argues that women should earn a living (p. 105). Where Mill was confused and cool towards this, the earlier essay argues that it would be a good thing even if the effect on wages were all that the most alarmist suggest. Even if man and wife together earned only what he earns now, 'how infinitely preferable is it that part of the income should be of the woman's earning, . . . rather than that she should be compelled to stand aside in order that men may be the sole earners, and the sole dispensers of what is earned'. Women discover self-respect if they earn, and equality of standing with the man; and this is much more important, from the viewpoint of sound relationships between the sexes, than mere economic improvement in the family position. How much more realistic this is than Mill's timid declaration that a woman should draw self-respect from an ability to earn which she in fact makes no use of when married. His position here is sentimental; the earlier essay is more aware of the realities of power.

It is also clear that if women are really to have equality, their education must be seriously intended to fit them for serious jobs. Here the author foresees conflict with what are called 'the moderate reformers of the education of women', which would appear to include the author of *The Subjection of Women*. Women should be taught 'solid instruction', not 'superficial instruction on solid subjects'. They must be educated in a way that makes them independent beings; it is merely fudging the issue to bring them up to be fit companions for men who will none the less do all the earning and thus retain all the economic power. Mill's confused and sentimental position is here demolished with a few effective words: 'they do not say that men should be educated to be the companions of women'.

Lastly, *The Enfranchisement of Women* is both frank and clear about the claim that liberation will lead to greater happiness for women (pp. 117 ff.). Women are not in general aware of frustration, and tend not to feel their position intolerable, but this does not matter: Asian women do not mind being in purdah, and find the thought of going about freely shocking, but this does not mean that they should not be liberated from seclusion, or that they would not appreciate freedom once they had it; and the same holds for European women who cannot appreciate why it is important for them to be financially independent. 'The vast population of Asia do not desire or value, probably would not accept, political liberty, nor the savages of the forest, civilization; which does not prove that either of those things is undesirable for them, or that they will not, at some future time, enjoy it' (p. 117). This is a bold but consistent position: people's present desires are discounted in favour of the desires that would be had if their natural selves were not repressed. Here we find the radical approach put forward boldly, with no attempt at compromise with the reformist approach; and the application to women is made straightforwardly. 'How does the objector know that women do not desire equality and freedom? He never knew a woman who did not, or would not, desire it for herself individually. It would be very simple to suppose, that if they do desire it they will say so. Their position is like that of the tenants or labourers who vote against their own political interests to please their landlords or employers; with the unique addition that submission is inculcated on them from childhood, as the peculiar grace and attraction of their character' (p. 118).

The earlier essay is thus more coherent as argument than the later; it quite avoids the struggles that occupy Mill over natural differences, and it avoids his tendency to lapse back into a more timid position than his radical premises would suggest.

I have so far spoken non-committally about 'the author of *The Enfranchisement of Women*' because there is some uncertainty about whom to call the author. It was published under Mill's name, but in an introduction to it Mill says that it is Harriet's work, in a stronger and more definite way than in his customary avowals of general intellectual indebtedness.[12] Taking it to be Harriet's work would certainly offer a neat solution to the problem of the discrepancies I have noted. However, I do not wish here to make a contribution to the debate about the extent of Harriet's contributions to Mill's work, which is too complicated a topic to raise here. What is important is simply that *The Subjection of Women* puts forward a position more complicated (as well as more lengthily expressed) than that of *The Enfranchisement of Women*, and in the process, I maintain, introduces deep confusions. It is certainly true that the position put forward in the earlier essay needs much more argument to back up its basic premises before it can be regarded as defensible; but at least it is clear and provides a basis for a coherent practical programmer. In *The Subjection of Women*, I believe, we can see Mill doing something strikingly similar to what he does in *Utilitarianism*. Anxious to do justice to all sides of a question he sees to be complex and important, and unwilling to commit himself definitively to one simple line of thought, he qualifies an originally bold and straightforward theory to the point of inconsistency.[13]

Notes

1. It became at once unpopular and neglected; it was the only book of Mill's ever to lose his publisher money (A. Ryan, *J. S. Mill*, p. 125). In 1867, when he was an MP, Mill tried to amend the Reform Bill in such a way as to secure the franchise for women, but only 73 MPs voted with him.

2. Freud translated Mill's essay, and discussed his dislike of it in the famous letter to his fiancée in which he says, 'If . . . I imagined my gentle sweet girl as a competitor it would only end by my telling her . . . that I am fond of her and that I implore her to withdraw from the struggle into the calm uncompetitive activity of my home'.

3. Of course I am not claiming that Mill clearly or consistently thinks of 'utilitarian' arguments as those that confine themselves to desires and needs that people actually have, without reference to any idealizing of the situation. (If he did, there could hardly be room for controversy as to whether he espoused 'act-' or 'rule-' utilitarianism.) My distinction is intended to hold apart two lines of thought which Mill seems to employ in the essay, and they would remain distinct even if both of them were brought under the heading of some very broad conception of utilitarianism.

4. All references to *The Subjection of Women* and *The Enfranchisement of Women* come from the useful collection *Essays on Sex Equality* by John Stuart Mill and Harriet Taylor Mill, edited by A. Rossi (University of Chicago Press, 1970).

5. We should note in passing that this argument depends heavily on our being able to predict a very large-scale change in society from the occurrence of similar changes in the past, and also on the assumption that progress in the required direction will not be blocked by large-scale movements in society based entirely on irrational or destructive forces. Mill could not foresee the inroads made on women's rights by fascism, for example.

6. In 1972, for example, the percentage of girls studying mathematics and science subjects at A-level was higher in single-sex schools than in mixed schools, tiny in both (18.7 per cent as against 13.4 per cent).

7. For some preliminary clarifications on this, see the excellent article by L. Nochlin, 'Why are there no great women artists?' in *Women in Sexist Society*, Gornick and Moran (eds.), also (abbreviated) in *Art and Sexual Politics*, Hess and Baker (eds.).

8. Cf. the quotation on p. 182; and what is said about equality on p. 173: 'society in equality is its normal state'. This is hardly something we can learn from experience, when history presents us with nothing but hierarchies.

9. Mostly in part 1 of *A Theory of Justice*.

10. One small but striking example (quoted from the *Daily Telegraph* of 16 December 1963 by J. Mitchell, *Women's Estate* p. 126): 'All four hundred employees at the Typhoo Tea Works, Birmingham, went on unofficial strike yesterday because a forewoman reprimanded a workman. A shop-steward said, "The forewoman should have referred any question of discipline to the man's foreman . . ." '. 470 people, in fact, struck over this issue; 300 of them were women.

11. Commentators generally see one or the other strand, but not the fact that Mill combines both. McCloskey curtly sums up the essay by saying (op. cit., p. 136), 'Obviously the utilitarian arguments [from the abuses of power, etc.] have greater force and relevance here than elsewhere'. Ryan, on the other hand, sums up just as curtly (op. cit., pp. 157–158), 'the argument is essentially the argument from individuality', and notes that arguing 'for the higher and better happiness which stems from self-respect and personal autonomy' is 'not a very obviously utilitarian appeal'.

12. '. . . the following Essay is hers in a peculiar sense, my share in it being little more than that of an editor and amanuensis. Its authorship having been known at the time and publicly attributed to her' (p. 91). Rossi (pp. 41–43) discusses other evidence for Harriet's authorship, which she accepts.

13. I am grateful for helpful comments and discussion to A. O. J. Cockshut, J. Dybikowski and G. Segal.

5

John Stuart Mill, Radical Feminist[1]

Keith Burgess-Jackson

Criticizing Annas, Burgess-Jackson argues that Mill's views on the legal and social status of women align him with contemporary radical feminism. Burgess-Jackson maintains that the primary target of Mill's critical arguments in The Subjection of Women *is the systemic inegalitarian social framework, notably institutions ranging from education to family. Like contemporary radical feminists, Burgess-Jackson contends, Mill challenged the received liberal distinction between the public and private realms, insisting that ending women's oppression requires a radical shift in social attitudes, values, and beliefs. Central to his case for Mill as radical feminist is an analysis of Mill's views on the pervasiveness and corruptibility of power.*

[A] much more important consideration still [than the ability of a man to support a large family], is the perpetuation of the previous degradation & slavery of women, no alteration in which can be hoped for while their whole lives are devoted to the function of producing & rearing children.[2]

The natural desire of consideration from our fellow creatures is as strong in a woman as in a man; but society has so ordered things that public consideration is, in all ordinary cases, only attainable by her through the consideration of her husband or of her male relations, while her private consideration is forfeited by making herself individually prominent, or appearing in any other character than that of an appendage to men.[3]

JOHN STUART MILL IS widely if not universally regarded as a liberal feminist. This is puzzling, all the more so because some of those who regard Mill as a liberal feminist—Julia Annas, Susan Moller Okin, and Leslie Goldstein, to name just three—are, among other things, prominent Mill scholars. It would seem that one ought to defer to their judgment, coming as it does after years of careful study. But that would be intellectually irresponsible, for much of what Mill wrote is accessible to the curious reader. Independent judgment is possible, feasible, and in the end necessary. What puzzles is that Mill's views on the social and legal status of women are more closely aligned with those of contemporary *radical* feminists than with those of contemporary liberal feminists.

It may seem trivial to argue about the type of feminist Mill was—he was surely a feminist of some sort[4]—but the matter is not trivial, and the disagreement not therefore a quibble. Not only is it unfair to Mill to mischaracterize him (which I believe has occurred and is occurring), but part of the project of contemporary radical feminism is to reclaim its past, and Mill, whatever his shortcomings as a feminist theorist, strategist, and practitioner, is an important part of that past. My aim in this essay is to inaugurate the radical-feminist reclamation project.

The essay has four parts. In the first I distinguish liberal and radical feminism, showing in what respects these ideologies are alike and in what respects they differ. I am careful to define terms in such a way that even those with whom I disagree—that is, even those who classify Mill as a liberal feminist—can accept them; otherwise I run the risk of persuasive definition. In part two I make what I consider a prima facie case for classifying Mill as a radical feminist, appealing primarily, although not exclusively, to his 1869 essay *The Subjection of Women*[5] in which Mill's mature thought on sexual equality is set forth. If successful, this argument shifts the burden of persuasion to those who maintain that Mill was, at most, a liberal feminist.

In part three I respond to two of Mill's critics, Annas and Okin, both of whom are feminists who have taken Mill to task for being at best a half-hearted liberal feminist. I also respond to a third and different sort of critic, David Stove, who argues that Mill's feminism, whether characterized as liberal or radical, is hopelessly, even laughably (Stove's word) confused. I argue that it is Stove, not Mill, who is confused. In part four, I speculate about the source(s) of what to my mind is a pervasive misdiagnosis of Mill as a liberal feminist. Anyone who challenges a received view, as I do in this essay, has this minimal explanatory burden. I believe that there are several factors at work, each of which rests on either fallacious reasoning or a misunderstanding of what Mill wrote.

Before entering the fray, however, I wish to comment on source material. It is not unusual for those who are involved in politics, as Mill was,[6] to espouse one set of views for public consumption and another privately. This is not necessarily duplicitous. Politics raises questions of strategy and tactic as well as principle. It engages the heart as well as the mind. It is messy, dirty, and full of compromise. Timing matters. The way one says something can alienate those who would otherwise concur and provide support for a cause. One might employ different premises when arguing to an audience of prospective voters or legislators than when arguing to a gathering of philosophers. One might privately have reservations about a particular topic, but not express them publicly for fear of dampening the enthusiasm of those whose assistance one needs. In short, there are nonmalicious reasons for moderating one's publicly expressed views, just as, in a particular case, there may be nonmalicious reasons for exaggerating one's views.

Anyone who has read Mill's diaries or private correspondence knows that he was acutely aware of, and made shrewd calculations concerning, the practical effect of his utterance, especially late in life when his views carried great weight with his peers and the voting public. He timed the publication of certain essays so that they would have maximum political effect.[7] The question therefore arises whether, in trying to understand or characterize Mill, one should consider all of his extant writings or only those prepared for public consumption. I believe that if everything he wrote were to be considered, Mill would come across quite convincingly as a radical feminist in the sense in which I use the term herein. It is common knowledge that Mill worked long and hard to enhance the legal and social status of women, especially during his later years, and would not have published anything that he thought would have done the cause more harm than good. For this reason one would expect Mill's private writings to be more radical than his public writings, and for the most part they are.

But I shall not rest my case on Mill's private writings, although I will not hesitate to refer to or quote from them to illustrate or support a point. I believe that the public Mill—the Mill in particular of *The Subjection of Women*, his most sustained treatment of the topic—is best characterized as a radical feminist. If that case can be made, then it can only be strengthened by consideration of his private writings. The point of the present essay is not, in other words, to bring previously unknown writings to light so that we have a more complete picture of Mill the person; it is to argue that Mill's *known* writings have been misread, misunderstood, and, regrettably, misappropriated.

1. Liberal and Radical Feminism

Theorists differ, as one might expect, in their understanding of liberal and radical feminism, but there seems to be a core of agreement about the difference, a core that I will try to extract and use. Both types of feminist maintain that women are and have been oppressed by men, that the oppression was and is unjustified and that steps ought to be taken to rectify the oppression that presently exists.[8] This is what makes them feminists. Radical feminists go further than liberal feminists in two ways: first, in their analysis of the roots of oppression (the descriptive difference); and second, in their proposals for change (the prescriptive difference). Liberal feminists, qua liberals, see oppression as an irrational encrustation on the surface of society. Men and women, they believe, have a common rational nature and are equally capable of performing the various private and public functions of social life. Laws and customs that segregate men and women into different occupations, or enforce sex roles, or both, are seen as the problem to be solved. The liberal solution is to repeal such laws and change the customs.

Historically, liberal feminism has been concerned to grant women legal rights to be educated, to vote, to enter previously male-only occupations, and to own and transfer property. It has also striven to change laws of marriage that subject wives to their husbands.[9] In the words of one scholar, this type of feminist "concentrates on the reformist, liberal pursuit of widening and consolidating the legal rights of women in the political and economic spheres."[10] Liberal feminism accepts the public sphere as it is and seeks to bring women into it on the same terms as men.

Radical feminists do not of course reject these practical objectives; rather, they see them as an essential first step toward true sexual equality and justice. While radical feminists do not agree among themselves in every descriptive or prescriptive detail,[11] any more than liberal feminists do, they do share the view that the source of women's oppression lies in various social structures, institutions, and processes, ranging from education to heterosexuality to marriage to childbirth and childrearing. According to Annas,

> The radical approach will have little use for reform of the existing system; to a radical, this would be merely futile, enabling a few women to get ahead by adopting male values, but doing nothing for the mass of women whose natures have been systematically thwarted. What is required is a radical change in the whole framework of society's attitudes to the relations between the sexes.[12]

Radical feminists, as such, question the liberal distinction between public and private, insisting that all aspects of human life, even those that occur "behind closed doors," be evaluated in terms of whether they support or undermine the existing inegalitarian social framework. The personal, it is said, is political. Radical feminists, unlike liberal feminists, do not automatically accept the attitudes, values, and beliefs that they find in society, for these phenomena may themselves be the result of oppressive social structure and processes. Inequality, in other words, may be institutionalized and therefore invisible (or hard to see). To the radical-feminist mind, every practice, institution, law, and person is tainted by sexism, which pervades society.

So conceived, the difference between liberal and radical feminism is one of both kind and degree. To the extent that liberal and radical feminists give different analyses of women's oppression, they differ in kind. One feminist theorist goes so far as to say that liberal and radical feminists have different conceptions of human nature.[13] To the extent that liberal and radical feminists advocate some but not all of the same reforms, however, they differ in degree. As I suggested above, radical feminists join liberal feminists in advocating repeal of laws that limit women's liberty or legal powers or otherwise treat them as inferior to men.

But whereas liberal feminists are content with equal opportunity under the law and equal access to the main benefits of social life, radical feminists are not. In a society permeated by sexism, distorted by power relations, and laboring under the weight of centuries of oppression, equal opportunity under the law is held to be insufficient; it fails to address or rectify the real situation of women. Radical feminists want to change attitudes as well as laws, values as well as customs, beliefs as well as behavior.[14] Radical feminists, as their self-chose name implies, want to get at the root of women's oppression, thereby killing its toxic fruit.

2. A Prima Facie Case for Mill Being a Radical Feminist

My aim in this part of the essay is to show that, given the preceding conceptions of liberal and radical feminism, which, as I have shown, track those of Mill's critics,[15] Mill should be understood as a radical feminist rather than as a liberal feminist. My strategy is to quote pertinent passages from Mill's published writings, showing (a) that what he says is consistent with the conception of radical feminism set out above and (b) that his expressed views have close affinities to what paradigmatic contemporary radical feminists[16] have to say. The case is prima facie and cumulative. I shall also refer from time to time to the secondary literature to support my main contention or to defuse a criticism.

Mill's feminism was based on—or rather, a response to—two beliefs that loomed large in his overall thought: first, the malleability of human character; and second, the corruptibility and pervasiveness of power.[17] A study of history, Mill wrote, would convince anyone who cared to investigate the matter of "the extraordinary susceptibility of human nature to external influences, and the extreme variableness of those of its manifestations which are supposed to be most universal and uniform."[18] To those who claim that women's nature can be "read off" their actual behavior or aptitudes, Mill's response was always that what one sees is as likely the effect of socialization as of nature. Mill was emphatically agnostic about women's nature, insisting repeatedly that nobody, including him, "knows, or can know, the nature of the two sexes, as long as they have only been seen in their present relation to one another."[19] Mill did not claim to know, as critics often suggest, that men and women have a common nature, rational or otherwise.

What we do know, Mill said, is that different social conditions produce different human characters.[20] This could be seen clearly in the case of women:

> All women are brought up from the very earliest years in the belief that their ideal of character is the very opposite to that of men; not self-will, and government by self-control, but submission, and yielding to the control of others. All the moralities tell them that it is the duty of women, and

all the current sentimentalities that it is in their nature, to live for others; to make complete abnegation of themselves, and to have no life but in their affections. And by their affections are meant the only ones they are allowed to have—those to the men with whom they are connected, or to the children who constitute an additional and indefeasible tie between them and a man.[21]

Mill, like many of today's most prominent radical feminists, sees sexist socialization as the root of women's oppression by men.[22] Women have been conditioned to devote themselves to men, to identify with male interests, and, perhaps most insidiously, to see themselves as incomplete and unfulfilled unless they are affiliated with a particular man. These are not the sentiments of a liberal feminist whose sole or main concern is repealing inegalitarian laws, although Mill was certainly interested in doing that. They are the sentiments of a radical, one who wishes to change society at the root by first understanding and then altering the processes that make us what we are.[23]

Mill's belief in human malleability ties in with the second of his beliefs, which is that power is a distorting and corrupting influence in human affairs. Mill devoted several paragraphs of the first chapter of *SW* to identifying what he called the "regulating principle of the world's affairs"—namely, "the law of the strongest," or what he elsewhere refers to as "the system of right founded on might."[24] To Mill's mind, this odious principle had long since faded from view, except—and this he saw as a grave anomaly—with respect to the relations between the sexes. There, he pointed out, the principle not only survived but flourished; and as long as law and other institutions conferred rights on men that were denied to women, men would wield power over women in such a way as to solidify their advantages.

The effect of this use of power on women was, not surprisingly, devastating. First and most obviously, women were denied the opportunity to support themselves economically. This dependence inevitably led to other forms of dependence, ranging from emotional to spiritual to physical. The cumulative effect of the various female dependencies was to make women virtual slaves to their husbands—and to men generally. "Men," Mill wrote, "do not want solely the obedience of women, they want their sentiments. All men, except the most brutish, desire to have, in the woman most nearly connected with them, not a forced slave but a willing one, not a slave merely, but a favourite." Indeed, given "the natural attraction between opposite sexes," "the wife's entire dependence on the husband," and the fact that a woman's sole opportunity for social mobility was through a husband, "it would be a miracle if the object of being attractive to men had not become the polar star of feminine education and formation of character."[25] To Mill, power corrupts. It corrupts men and degrades (de-grades, lowers the status of) women.[26]

The parallels between Mill and contemporary radical feminism are striking. In her book *The Politics of Reality*, in which, among other things, she analyzes the nature of oppression, radical feminist Marilyn Frye asserts that women are oppressed functionally rather than geographically or in some other way. The function of women at all times and places, Frye says, is "the service of men and men's interests as men define them, which includes the bearing and rearing of children."[27] Frye elaborates:

> Whether in lower, middle or upper-class home or work situations, women's service work always includes personal service (the work of maids, butlers, cooks, personal secretaries), sexual service (including provision for his genital sexual needs and bearing his children, but also including "being nice," "being attractive for him," etc.), and ego service (encouragement, support, praise, attention).[28]

Mill, to his credit, anticipated this line of thought, even if he did not develop it to the extent Frye and others have.

Like Mill, contemporary radical feminists focus on the power imbalances that exist between men and women—and the effects of those imbalances on the formation of character and on interpersonal relations such as those involved in marriage. As Richard Krouse recently argued, Mill recognized that "as realms of power and authority, [marriage and the family] are intrinsically *political* institutions."[29] Mill did not draw a sharp line between the public and the private, as liberals are wont to do. The Millian focus on power is exemplified by the radical-feminist preoccupation with women's reproductive capacities, the thought being that unless and until women gain control of (secure power over) their reproductive lives, they will be dependent on men in the ways described above—and hence unequal in the most fundamental sense.[30] Mill's views on this are set out in one of the introductory quotations.

That Mill went beyond liberal feminism in his analysis of and proposals to eradicate the oppression of women by men can be seen in the fact that he viewed equal educational opportunities, a longstanding liberal preoccupation, as merely the "first and indispensable step"[31] toward women's liberation. His aim was to secure for women the sort of education that would undermine dependence "either on her father or her husband for subsistence: a position which in nine cases out of ten, makes her either the plaything or the slave of the man who needs her, and in the tenth case, only his humble friend."[32] Mill realized that an uneducated, unskilled woman had inferior prospects in the occupational world, and this made her vulnerable to power-hungry males who were eager to press her into their service. As long as a woman had the skills and aptitude for gainful employment, Mill believed, she would not be at the mercy of men. She would have leverage and the self-respect that derives from it.

At this point I rest my prima facie case for Mill being a radical feminist. Not only did Mill *not* subscribe to the view that men and women have a common nature (he was officially agnostic on the question); he very much questioned existing institutions such as the family, the educational system, and the church.[33] He wanted more than reform and superficial changes in the law, although he advocated at least that. Mill viewed human beings as malleable organisms who could be and had been corrupted by the desire for power. Women in particular had suffered from the corruption and, accordingly, had the most to gain from its destruction, although society as a whole would also benefit. Alice Rossi summarizes Mill's feminism as follows: "Mill attempted to probe beneath the surface of social forms to find the latent function served by that form, not, however, to pinpoint its 'social utility' but to identify the root cause which must be changed to effect the release of women from their subjection."[34] This search for the roots or underlying causes of women's oppression, together with a willingness to change what he finds there, identifies Mill as a radical feminist.

3. A Reply to Mill's Critics

I now address a number of criticisms that have been lodged against Mill the feminist. One group of critics, represented by Annas and Okin, maintains that Mill did not go far enough in his feminism—that he was at best a half-hearted liberal and cannot therefore be counted among

radical-feminist numbers. These criticisms are made from *within* feminism by individuals who are sympathetic to its objectives. The second
group of critics, represented by Stove, maintains that Mill's feminism is
self-contradictory (and hence untenable). This criticism is made from
without feminism by individuals who are unsympathetic, or positively
antagonistic, to its objectives. I hope to show, in my responses to both
types of criticism, that Mill's feminism is not only consistent but consistently radical. His critics either misunderstand what he said or ignore
the parts of what he said that weaken or undermine their claims. In the
final section of the essay I speculate about why Mill, who was a careful
and articulate writer, continues to be thought, spoken, and written of as
a liberal feminist.

In an essay published in 1977, Annas took Mill to task for trying "to
have things too many ways at once."[35] This, she says, generates "deep
confusions," not to mention "strain,"[36] embarrassment, and "pathetic"
argumentation.[37] The two ways Mill tries to "have it" correspond to
what I have identified as liberal and radical feminism. On the one hand,
Annas says, Mill appeals to the desires women actually have as the basis
for change. Repealing inegalitarian laws (Mill argues) liberates women
to perform the various functions of social life, thus ending their frustration, increasing the pool of qualified job candidates, and promoting
overall happiness. The underlying assumptions are that men and
women have a common rational nature and that, given equal opportunities, men and women are equally competent to perform most, if not
all, of life's diverse functions.

At the same time (and here Annas finds a contradiction), Mill appeals
to idealized or counterfactual desires—those that women would have if
they had not been systematically oppressed by men. That women in general have little or no desire to enter certain occupations is irrelevant, in
this view; the question is whether the lack of desire has been inculcated
under oppressive conditions. If it has, then the desire has little or no
normative weight. Annas's criticism is that "Mill's argument throughout
The Subjection of Women is a confused mixture of these two approaches."[38] She says that he would have been on more solid ground had
he stayed with the "radical approach" throughout.[39]

With all due respect to Annas, she has misread Mill. She is right, of
course, that the first chapter of *SW* is a sustained defense of the radical
approach, but she errs in thinking that Mill backslid in subsequent

chapters, especially chapter three. For instance, Annas criticizes Mill for perpetuating the "cliché" that "women are intuitive while men reason."[40] What Annas fails to see is that Mill is responding to an argument rather than making one. The argument to which he is responding is that, because women are by nature intuitive and practical rather than analytical and theoretical, they are unfit for public affairs.

Mill's response is complex, interesting, and not in the least inconsistent with radical feminism. First he challenges the premise concerning women's nature. Even if it is true, he says, that "women as they are known in experience"[41] are intuitive and practical, it does not follow that they are so by nature. For all we know, what we see is the result of oppressive socialization. But (and here enters the complexity) even if one concedes the truth of the premise, it still doesn't follow that women are unfit for public affairs. That depends on the utility or disutility of intuitiveness and practicality in that realm. Mill stands the argument on its head by claiming that, far from disqualifying women, these (admittedly learned) attributes *qualify* them for the performance of public functions by making them attentive to the details and subtleties of situations. Men, with their (over)emphasis on the abstract and general, are distinctly unqualified for these offices. Mill isn't perpetuating a cliché so much as hoisting those who use it with their own petards.

Mill makes this pre-emptive move at least three other times in SW, once in response to the claim that women have a greater "quickness of apprehension" than men, again in response to the claim that women have a greater "nervous susceptibility" than men, and finally in response to the allegation that women's minds are more "mobile" than those of men. A liberal feminist would accept the implication, as Annas apparently does, that each of these qualities is inferior, thus requiring that the premise be rejected. But Mill stubbornly refuses to do so, and in this respect he reveals his radical feminism.

Radical feminists do not reject traditional feminine attributes out of hand, for that would be to "buy into" the patriarchal value scheme in which whatever is feminine is devalued. Men, traditionally, have not valued such qualities as intuitiveness, practicality, nervous susceptibility, and mental mobility, all of which (not coincidentally) have been assigned to women. Rather than perpetuate the negativity of these characteristics, radical feminists seek to revalue them and that is precisely what Mill does. Nervous susceptibility, for example, is a good-making characteristic of executives (although not, he says, of judges). So if anything, the fact that women have this characteristic *qualifies* them for executive positions— just the opposite of what had been maintained! Mill, in short, is cutting off the argument that because women have characteristic X, X is inferior. Whether X is an advantage or a disadvantage to those who possess it, Mill says, depends on its relation to the task at hand.

Annas is therefore off the mark in accusing Mill of backsliding. It is she who, as evidenced by her remarks, buys into the prevailing value scheme, thinking that women must have precisely those attributes that have traditionally been associated with or valued by men. Perhaps men should take on the attributes traditionally assigned to women! Annas writes: "Mill's confused and tangled attempts to show the useful qualities of women's special way of thinking thus ends up with the dangerous cliché so beloved of inegalitarians: women are not *inferior* to men, just *different.*"[42]

Mill is not at all confused. He is making a conditional argument: *Even if* women are different, as non- or antifeminists maintain, they are not necessarily inferior. The work of developmental psychologists such as Carol Gilligan shows that in the realm of moral reasoning and decision-making, for example, women speak with a "different voice" than do men;[43] but it is not assumed on that account that women are inferior. Indeed, the recent thrust of work by radical feminists has been to exalt women's distinctive "care" perspective on moral and social issues.[44] It may be that women are not only different than but superior to men, a claim anticipated and defended by Mill more than a century ago.[45]

I want to address one other of Annas's criticisms, for it seems to me to reflect a deeper misunderstanding of the type of argumentation in which Mill engages—and the motive with which he does so. Annas criticizes Mill for "deal[ing] with" the argument that because men, on average, have larger brains than women, women are unfit for various public functions.[46] "This," she writes, "is the only place in *The Subjection of Women* where the argument is quite pathetic, and one is mainly surprised that Mill feels that he needs to argue at all on this level."[47]

Annas has wrenched Mill out of context. One must keep in mind that Mill had both theoretical and practical motives in writing and publishing *SW*. Indeed, he waited some eight years to publish the essay, wishing for it to have maximal practical effect.[48] Elsewhere in *SW*, Mill laments the time and energy he must expend in responding to bad arguments, for example the argument that "queens are better than kings, because under kings women govern but under queens, men."[49] Mill: "It may seem a waste of reasoning to argue against a bad joke; but such things do affect people's minds; and I have heard men quote this saying, with an air as if they thought there was something in it."[50]

It may be that Mill had heard the brain argument repeatedly in connection with the debate over sexual equality and saw that it was having an effect on people. If his goal was to respond to the arguments that those with whom he disagreed found persuasive, then practically speaking he was compelled to address it. No *philosopher* would have adduced such an argument, of course, but then Mill wasn't addressing himself solely to philosophers. For that reason it is unfair of Annas and others to criticize Mill on this score. He took the arguments as he found them and said what needed to be said against them.[51]

Okin's criticisms have a different thrust. In the chapter of *Women in Western Political Thought* entitled "John Stuart Mill, Liberal Feminist," Okin criticizes Mill for failing to accept the full implications of his feminism—or rather, for failing to draw the appropriate radical-feminist conclusions from his analysis of female oppression. But as in the case of Annas, Okin misunderstands Mill. Example: Okin claims that Mill "never suggested that the contractual basis of marriage be abolished."[52] But why does this count against Mill's being a radical feminist? Just as radical feminists such as Adrienne Rich distinguish the *institution* of motherhood from the *experience* of motherhood,[53] condemning only the former, one can and should distinguish the institution of marriage (marriage as it has existed and does exist under patriarchy) from the experience of marriage (marriage as it might exist or in some few cases does exist).

The *institution* of marriage is arguably unjust, although surely it is less so now than when Mill wrote; but Mill was dead set against precisely those unjust features of the institution, referring to it, and to the family around it, as a "school of despotism."[54] He went so far as to say that in some respects the lot of women in marriage was worse than—not just on a par with—that of slaves. A strong claim! What Mill advocated, and in his own life practiced (so far as we know), was perfect egalitarianism within marriage.[55] His ideal is set forth in chapter four of *SW*:

> What marriage may be in the case of two persons of cultivated faculties, identical in opinions and purposes, between whom there exists that best kind of equality, similarity of powers and capacities with reciprocal superiority in them—so that each can enjoy the luxury of looking up to the

other, and can have alternately the pleasure of leading and of being led in the path of development—I will not attempt to describe. To those who can conceive it, there is no need; to those who cannot, it would appear the dream of an enthusiast. But I maintain, with the profoundest conviction, that this, and this only, is the ideal of marriage.[56]

Mill had no illusions that this marital ideal had been, or would soon be, implemented. In correspondence he observed that "marriage has not had a fair trial. It has yet to be seen what marriage will do, with equality of rights on both sides; with that full freedom of choice which as yet is very incomplete anywhere, and in most countries does not exist at all on the woman's side."[57]

Now, had Mill advocated or insisted on marriage for all, independently of inclination or circumstance, he could rightly have been accused of lacking proper radical credentials; but he didn't. In fact, he went out of his way to point out that, ideally, "marriage, on whatever footing it might be placed, would be wholly a matter of choice, not, as for a woman it now is, something approaching to a matter of necessity."[58] In 1870, just three years before his death, Mill told a correspondent that "the purpose of that book [*SW*] was to maintain the claim of women, *whether in marriage or out of it*, to perfect equality in all rights with the male sex."[59] This shows that Mill both contemplated and accepted the prospect of unmarried women. If a woman married, it would be because she wanted to, not because she needed to.

For Mill, equality of opportunity in education and employment were inextricably linked to egalitarianism in marriage. Unless women had ambition, skill, and a real opportunity for gainful employment, they would never be equal partners in marriage; nor would any decision on their part to marry be completely free. In 1832, some twenty-nine years before drafting *SW*, Mill wrote:

[W]omen will never be what they should be, nor their social position what it should be, until women, as universally as men, have the power of gaining their own livelihood: until, therefore, every girl's parents have either provided her with independent means of subsistence or given her an education qualifying her to provide those means for herself.[60]

Thus were liberty, equality, and power linked. Liberty to work or to remain unmarried made a decision to marry a free one, which had the ef-

fect of equalizing power in the marital relationship. Mill can and perhaps should be criticized for being an idealist, and certainly he was an
elitist,[61] but no radical feminist can challenge the *content* of his marital
ideal. Egalitarian marriage as a legally sanctioned relationship is no
more objectionable than any other legal partnership entered into for
mutual benefit. It increases a person's options; it does not foreclose
any.[62] Mill, as I have said, was trying to get at the root of women's oppression, and "perfect equality,"[63] in and out of marriage, was his means
to achieve it.[64] But Mill saw marriage as far more than an instrumental
arrangement, although it was at least that. He saw it "as a locus of mutual sympathy and understanding between autonomous adults"[65] and as
embodying "friendship of the highest order."[66] In Rich's terms, Mill defended the experience and not the institution of marriage.

Another powerful but ultimately misguided criticism of Mill lodged
by Okin has to do with his views concerning the administration of the
marital household. Mill, she says, "argues in favor of the traditional division of labor within the family."[67] It is true that Mill addresses this
topic and that he makes comments that do and should disturb contemporary radical feminists, but his comments must be kept in perspective.
In discussing the law of property in marriage (which, by the way, Mill
sought to reform radically),[68] he says that "when the support of the family depends, not on property, but on earnings, the common arrangement, by which the man earns the income and the wife superintends the
domestic expenditure, seems to me in general the most suitable division
of labour between the two persons."[69]

Elsewhere Mill writes that when a woman marries, "it may in general
be understood that she makes choice of the management of a household, and the bringing up of a family, as the first call upon her exertions,
during as many years of her life as may be required for the purpose; and
that she renounces, not all other objects and occupations, but all which
are not consistent with the requirements of this."[70] To Okin, these and
other passages constitute a "defense of traditional sex roles within the
family [that] amounts to a denial of freedom of opportunity and individual expression of talents to that majority of women whom he assumes would always choose to marry."[71]

The first thing to observe is that Mill neither advocated nor expected
that all women of marrying age would marry. As we have seen, he
wanted women to be independent of men so that a decision to marry, *if*

made, would be truly free, and so that the relationship within marriage would be one of equality and friendship. Second, Mill did not advocate that the law enforce the division of labor he expected to find. That would have been distinctly illiberal and would have taken him out of the liberal-feminist camp as well as the radical-feminist camp. The division of household labor was to be entirely up to the men and women involved. In 1867 he wrote: "Neither do I think that the adaptation of the [household] work of each person to his or her special endowments or position is a thing to be reappointed by society."[72] Third, Mill, like the political economist Adam Smith, was a firm believer in the economic benefits of dividing labor among individuals, whether in the household or in the workplace. A division of labor was more efficient, and thus best for both those in the household and those in society. This explains, although it does not justify, his remarks.

Fourth, and importantly, Mill did not advocate that married couples have children, let alone suggest that they have a duty to do so.[73] But if they did so choose, it may be prudent for them (Mill says) to divide the household labor, and since he believed, rightly or wrongly, that women had a comparative advantage in the realm of nurturing skill, it was only prudent that they—women—nurture the children, leaving the husband to earn the income for the family. This proposition stinks in radical-feminist nostrils, but it must be remembered that the suggestion was no part of Mill's feminist argument. Had a particular couple arranged to do things differently, with, say, the woman earning the income and the man nurturing the children, Mill would not, at least as I read him, have objected.[74] He would probably have celebrated the diversity. He loved and encouraged experiments in living. His remarks on household responsibilities should be interpreted in that light; we should read them as gratuitous (and misguided) practical advice to married couples rather than as essential components of his feminist vision or argument.[75]

Okin concludes by saying that "Mill's feminism is severely constrained. He in effect condoned the continuation of considerable differences in power and in opportunity, for men and married women. Thus, though he argued that women must be admitted to citizenship, there is no way that the realities of the lives he envisaged for them could allow them to be equal citizens."[76] I believe that Okin and other critics of Mill fail to make a basic distinction: between Mill's feminist argument for "perfect equality"[77] on the one hand (an argument based on principle) and Mill's *prediction* about what most women will do on the other.[78]

In terms of his ideal marital arrangement, as we have seen, Mill in no sense "condoned the continuation of considerable differences in power and in opportunity." He was adamant in his conviction that women be free to marry or not marry, bear or not bear children, work or not work outside the home, perform or not perform public functions. Though I cannot demonstrate this, I suspect that Mill would have been delighted with familial experiments that allowed women to have both families and public responsibilities to the same extent as and in the same way that men have always had.[79] The conjunction of the qualifying phrase "in effect" to the already weak "condoned" indicates the tentativeness of Okin's conclusion. I submit that it is not only tentative but inaccurate and, for that reason, unfair to Mill, whose radical-feminist credentials remain solid (if not impeccable).

In a recently published essay on Mill's feminism, Stove accuses Mill of flagrant inconsistency. Mill, he says, embraces the following "self-contradictory" conjunction: "I know that subjection of women to men is unnatural" and "The nature of women is quite unknown, or else there is no such thing."[80] Leaving aside the dubious claim that these propositions are inconsistent,[81] it is simply not the case that Mill accepts the first of the conjuncts; nor is he committed to it by anything he does say. To be sure, the bulk of the first chapter of *SW* is devoted to responding to those who maintain that the subjection of women to men is natural, from which these individuals infer that (a) the subjection cannot be changed and (b) nobody has an obligation to attempt to change it. Mill's response is that nobody *knows* what is natural for men or women.[82] It does not follow from "Nobody knows whether the subjection of women is natural" that "I know that the subjection of women is unnatural," as Stove apparently thinks. His criticism therefore misses its mark.

Stove accuses Mill of a second and related inconsistency: claiming to know that women are the intellectual equals of men while denying that anyone has this knowledge. But not only does Mill nowhere assert what Stove calls the "equality theory"—namely, that "the intellectual capacity of women is equal to that of men"[83]—he is not committed to it. Mill explicitly says that for practical purposes the question of women's nature is moot. "Happily," he writes, "no such knowledge is necessary for any practical purpose connected with the position of women in relation to society and life. For, according to all the principles involved in modern society, the question rests with women themselves—to be decided by their own experience, and by the use of their own faculties."[84] In other words, what women *can* do will be determined in the crucible of experience; but they must be at liberty to act before any reliable results come in. It will take time. If anything, Stove has given an argument in favor of women's liberation, not, as he thinks, against it.[85] He is confused.

4. Why Has Mill Been (Mis)diagnosed as a Liberal Feminist?

Suppose I am right that Mill was, in the sense specified, a radical feminist. Why have so many scholars persisted in classifying him otherwise, most often as a liberal feminist? It is not because there is an equivocation on terms, for I have argued that on the definitions of the critics who do the classifying—Annas, Rossi, and Okin—Mill is a radical feminist. One explanation is that in social and political theory generally, Mill is a liberal—indeed, the paradigmatic liberal.[86] As I have said, liberal feminism is liberalism (the social and political theory) applied to issues of sexual equality. But it doesn't follow from this that Mill was a liberal feminist. I have tried to show that Mill made an exception in the case of women. Mill was clear in stating that sexual inequality is sui generis in at least one respect: it is the last vestige of the idea that individual rights, status, and opportunity may legitimately rest on the accident of birth.[87] For this reason he may have deemed a more radical approach necessary.

Another explanation of the prevailing misdiagnosis is that, in comparison with Mill's wife and partner, Harriet Taylor, Mill was less radical, at least in the early essays. A number of Mill scholars have made this observation.[88] Taylor, for example, advocated the repeal of all laws concerning marriage,[89] while Mill, as we have seen, sought only to equalize the rights and responsibilities of marital partners. But if, as I have suggested, radicalism is a matter of degree, one cannot infer *non*radicalism from the fact that one is *less* radical than someone else. Both Taylor and Mill, in fact, were quite radical in their analysis of and prescriptions for ending women's oppression.

A third explanation is that many or most feminists of Mill's day, including those who sought to reform laws in the United States, were liberal feminists. This fact may have led scholars unthinkingly to lump Mill with them, seeing him as part of a social movement rather than as an independent thinker. We moderns tend to view feminism in stages. The first stage (so the story goes) had as its objective the repeal of sexist laws such as those that forbade married women to own property and enter certain occupations. The second stage, the first having been nearly completed, was designed to root out the remaining causes of women's oppression at the hands of men.[90] But this historical approach ignores the possibility that certain individuals were ahead of their time. I have argued in this essay, in large part by allowing Mill to speak for himself, that Mill is such an individual.[91] He belongs in, even if he hasn't always been seen as a member of, the radical-feminist camp. Those who deny Mill's radicalism in matters of sexual equality would do themselves well to reread what he wrote and rethink what he said.[92]

Notes

Copyright 1995 by *Social Theory and Practice*, Vol. 21, No. 3 (Fall 1995)

1. My title is a deliberate and subversive play on Susan Moller Okin's "John Stuart Mill, Liberal Feminist," the title of chapter 9 of her book *Women in Western Political Thought* (Princeton: Princeton University Press, 1992; orig. publ. 1979).

2. John Stuart Mill to Professor (Henry?) Green, 8 April 1852, in *Collected Works of John Stuart Mill* [hereafter "*CW*"], 33 vols., gen. ed. John M. Robson (Toronto: University of Toronto Press, 1963–91), vol. 14: *The Later Letters of John Stuart Mill, 1849–1873* [hereafter "*Later Letters*"], ed. Francis E. Mineka and Dwight N. Lindley (Toronto and Buffalo: University of Toronto Press, 1972), p. 88. Mill also wrote that "any great improvement in human life is not to be looked for so long as the animal instinct of sex occupies the absurdly disproportionate place it does therein; . . . to correct this evil two things are required, both of them desirable for other reasons, *viz.*, firstly that women should cease to be set apart for this function, and should be admitted to all other duties and occupations on a par with men. . . ." Mill, diary entry of 26 March 1854, in *CW*, vol. 27: *Journals and Debating Speeches*, ed. John M. Robson (Toronto and Buffalo: University of Toronto Press, 1988), p. 664 (italics in original).

3. John Stuart Mill, *The Subjection of Women*, ed. Susan Moller Okin (Indianapolis: Hackett Publishing Company, 1988; orig. publ. 1968), p. 82.

4. Goldstein, who criticizes Mill for not drawing out and accepting the radical implications of his principles, nonetheless says that "Mill deserves his reputation as

a sincerely committed feminist." Leslie Goldstein, "Mill, Marx, and Women's Liberation," *Journal of the History of Philosophy* 18 (1980), p. 319.

5. *The Subjection of Women* (hereafter "*SW*") was written in 1861 but withheld from publication until 1869, when Mill thought it would have the greatest practical effect. See Alice S. Rossi, "Sentiment and Intellect: The Story of John Stuart Mill and Harriet Taylor Mill," in John Stuart Mill and Harriet Taylor Mill, *Essays on Sex Equality*, ed. Alice S. Rossi (Chicago and London: The University of Chicago Press, 1970), p. 4.

6. For a recitation of Mill's main political activities on behalf of women, including those undertaken as a Member of Parliament, see Zillah R. Eisenstein, *The Radical Future of Liberal Feminism* (Boston: Northeastern University Press, 1993; orig. publ. 1981), p. 128.

7. See, e.g., Nadia Urbinati, "John Stuart Mill on Androgyny and Ideal Marriage," *Political Theory* 19 (1991), p. 640.

8. See, e.g., Rosemarie Tong, *Feminist Thought: A Comprehensive Introduction* (Boulder and San Francisco: Westview Press, 1989), p. 1. Tong claims that every feminist theory makes these claims.

9. See, e.g., Wendell Robert Carr, "Introduction," in John Stuart Mill, *The Subjection of Women* (Cambridge, Mass., and London: The M.I.T. Press, 1970), p. vii; Goldstein, "Mill, Marx, and Women's Liberation," p. 321.

10. Rossi, "Sentiment and Intellect," p. 7.

11. Tong points out, rightly that "Radical feminism is still evolving in several directions at once, and so any attempt to define it is bound to stress some of its aspects more than others." Tong, *Feminist Thought*, p. 71. What binds radical feminists, Tong says, is their "insistence that women's oppression is the most fundamental form of oppression." Ibid.; see also Alison M. Jaggar, *Feminist Politics and Human Nature* (Totowa, N.J.: Rowman & Littlefield, 1988; orig. publ. 1983), p. 12. Later in this essay I suggest that Mill shared this view of the primacy of women's oppression. The introductory quotations are meant to support that claim.

12. Julia Annas, "Mill and the Subjection of Women," *Philosophy* 52 (1977), p. 181.

13. I refer to Jaggar, who writes: "I find it most useful to identify fundamental differences by reference to four distinctive conceptions of human nature. These conceptions . . . are correlated with distinctive analyses of women's oppression and distinctive visions of women's liberation." Jaggar, *Feminist Politics and Human Nature*, p. 10.

14. For a discussion, see Marion Tapper, "Can a Feminist Be a Liberal?," *Australasian Journal of Philosophy*, suppl. to vol. 64 (1986): 37–47.

15. I have shown this by using the critics' own understandings of the terms. Specifically, I have used the understandings of Annas and Rossi. Later I show

that on Okin's conception of radical feminism, Mill is a radical feminist—not, as she claims, a liberal feminist.

16. By "paradigmatic contemporary radical feminist" I mean individuals who are radical feminists if anyone is. I include in this category Marilyn Frye, Catharine MacKinnon, Adrienne Rich, Shulamith Firestone, Mary O'Brien, Andrea Dworkin, Ann Oakley, Kate Millett, Marilyn French, Charlotte Bunch, and Sarah Lucia Hoagland. There are of course many others. I refer to the work of some of these radical feminists in what follows.

17. See Carr, "Introduction," p. xvi; Goldstein, "Mill, Marx, and Women's Liberation," p. 324.

18. *SW* has appeared in many editions. I cite it by chapter and paragraph. The quotation just given appears in chapter 1, paragraph 19; hence, hereafter, "1/19." Although it is neither my intention nor my burden to defend Mill's descriptive claims about women, it is interesting to note that recent research supports his claims of human malleability. See, e.g., Hilary M. Lips, "Gender-Role Socialization: Lessons in Femininity," in *Women: A Feminist Perspective*, 4th ed., ed. Jo Freeman (Mountain View, Cal.: Mayfield Publishing Company, 1989), pp. 197–216; and Margaret L. Andersen, *Thinking About Women: Sociological Perspectives on Sex and Gender*, 3rd ed. (New York: Macmillan Publishing Company, 1993), pp. 21–51 ("The Social Construction of Gender").

19. *SW*, 1/18.

20. For a critique of Mill's distinction between the natural and the social, see Alan Soble, "The Epistemology of the Natural and the Social in Mill's *The Subjection of Women*," *The Mill Newsletter* 16 (Summer 1981): 3–9.

21. *SW*, 1/11.

22. See Keith Burgess-Jackson, "On the Coerciveness of Sexist Socialization," *Public Affairs Quarterly* 9 (1995): 15–27.

23. Gail Tulloch: "Mill perceived that feminine character was the outcome of an artificial system of cultivation via education, and that cultural conditioning produces sexual temperament appropriate to a culturally customary sexual role. Mill was thus describing what Kate Millett [in *Sexual Politics* (New York: Equinox Books, 1971)] has termed 'sexual politics' in depicting the relative status of men and women as a deliberate, perpetuated construction, though he did not use the term." Gail Tulloch, "Mill's Epistemology in Practice in His Liberal Feminism," *Educational Philosophy and Theory* 21 (1989), p. 37.

24. *SW*, 1/6.

25. Ibid., 1/11. Here is the basis of a critique of the fashion and cosmetic industries. See, e.g., Naomi Wolf, *The Beauty Myth: How Images of Beauty Are Used Against Women* (New York: Anchor Books, 1991).

26. Physical power is only one type, but it was the basis of other types. To Mill, it is "the fundamental purpose of civilization to redress as much as possible all

such natural inequalities." Mill to Richard Russell, 2 April 1867, in *CW*, vol. 16: *Later Letters*, p. 1261.

27. Marilyn Frye, *The Politics of Reality: Essays in Feminist Theory* (Trumansburg, N.Y.: The Crossing Press, 1983), p. 9.

28. Ibid.; see also Tong, *Feminist Thought*, p. 72: '[R]adical feminists have explicitly articulated the ways in which men have constructed female sexuality to serve not women's but men's needs, wants, and interests."

29. Richard W. Krouse, "Patriarchal Liberalism and Beyond: From John Stuart Mill to Harriet Taylor," in *The Family in Political Thought*, ed. Jean Bethke Elshtain (Amherst: The University of Massachusetts Press, 1982), p. 160 (italics in original). Krouse's argument, however, is that Mill's commitment to certain "institutions and practices"—for example, a traditional, sex-based division of labor within the marital household—defeated his commitment to radical change. Compare Jennifer Ring, "Mill's *The Subjection of Women*: The Methodological Limits of Liberal Feminism," *The Review of Politics* 47 (1985): 27–44. Ring says that Mill "comes close to arguing that 'the personal is political'" when he establishes parallels between a political ruler's relation to his subjects and husband's rule over his wife" (p. 37).

30. For a discussion of the practical and theoretical importance of reproduction in radical-feminist thought, see Tong, *Feminist Thought*, chap. 3; see also Catharine A. MacKinnon, *Toward a Feminist Theory of the State* (Cambridge, Mass.: Harvard University Press, 1989), chap. 10.

31. Mill used these words in his 1832 essay on marriage, published when he was twenty-six. See Mill, *Essays on Sex Equality*, p. 74.

32. Ibid.

33. Mill carried no brief for the family as he knew it. In private correspondence he wrote: "[T]he root of my difference with you is that you appear to accept the present constitution of the family & the whole of the priestly morality founded on & connected with it—which morality in my opinion thorough [*sic*] deserves the epithets of 'intolerant, slavish & selfish.'" Mill to George Jacob Holyoake, 7 December 1848, in *CW*, vol. 13: *The Earlier Letters of John Stuart Mill, 1812–1848*, ed. Francis E. Mineka (Toronto: University of Toronto Press, 1863), p. 741.

34. Rossi, "Sentiment and Intellect," p. 59.

35. Annas, "Mill and the Subjection of Women," p. 180.

36. Ibid., p. 181.

37. Ibid., p. 186.

38. Ibid., p. 181.

39. The same criticism was made three years later by Goldstein. See Goldstein, "Mill, Marx, and Women's Liberation," pp 325–28.

40. Annas, "Mill and the Subjection of Women," p. 184.

41. *SW*, 3/8.

42. Annas, "Mill and the Subjection of Women," p. 186 (italics in original).

43. See Carol Gilligan, *In a Different Voice: Psychological Theory and Women's Development* (Cambridge, Mass.: Harvard University Press, 1982).

44. See, e.g., Nel Noddings, *Caring: A Feminine Approach to Ethics and Moral Education* (Berkeley: University of California Press, 1984); Joyce Trebilcot, ed., *Mothering: Essays in Feminist Theory* (Totowa, N.J.: Rowman & Allanheld, 1984). I do not for a moment suggest that *all* radical feminists share this view. For a dissenting voice, see Sarah Lucia Hoagland *Lesbian Ethics: Toward New Value* (Palo Alto, Cal.: Institute for Lesbian Studies, 1988). There is currently a lively debate about the feminist significance, if any, of Gilligan's work.

45. For an argument that Mill's thought "resonates with some principles of a feminist ethic of care," see Wendy Donner, "John Stuart Mill's Liberal Feminism," *Philosophical Studies* 69 (1993): 155–66 (quotation from p 157). Donner's title is curious. Nowhere in her essay does she define "liberal feminism" or argue that Mill is a liberal feminist. She simply assumes that he is and tries to show that his thought has the resources to respond to communitarian critics of liberalism. I have not defined "radical feminism" in a way that necessitates a commitment to communitarianism, for I think there are noncommunitarian as well as communitarian radical feminists.

46. Mill states and criticizes the argument in *SW*, 3/13.

47. Annas, "Mill and the Subjection of Women," p. 186.

48. One of Mill's practical goals was to motivate women to enter the political arena and "break down the old barriers" in every walk of life—or, as he put it, "to stir up the zeal of women themselves." Mill to Alexander Bain, 14 July 1869, in *CW*, vol. 17: *Later Letters*, p. 1623.

49. *SW*, 3/5.

50. Ibid., 3/6.

51. Mill told a correspondent that *SW* "was written principally with a view to the state of society and opinion in England." Mill to Charles Eliot Norton, 23 June 1869, in *CW*, vol. 17: *Later Letters*, p. 1618. This suggests that Mill had a particular audience in mind, one that presumably found certain arguments but not others appealing. If Mill was to persuade that audience, as he sought, he had first of all to weaken the arguments they found appealing. For other evidence that Mill tailored his arguments to his audience, see Mill to Alexander Bain, 14 July 1869, in ibid., pp. 1623–24.

52. Okin, *Women in Western Political Thought*, p. 207.

53. See Adrienne Rich, *Of Woman Born: Motherhood as Experience and Institution* (New York: W. W. Norton, 1976). For a discussion of Rich's views, see Tong, *Feminist Thought*, pp. 87–89.

54. *SW*, 2/12.

55. In March 1851, one month before marrying his long-time companion Harriet Taylor, Mill composed a "Statement on Marriage" in which, among other things, he renounced all legal rights that devolved to him, qua male, by marriage. See John Stuart Mill, "Statement on Marriage," in *CW*, vol. 21: *Essays on Equality, Law, and Education*, ed. John M. Robson and Stefan Collini (Toronto: University of Toronto Press, 1984), p. 99 (Mill's statement was first published in 1910).

56. *SW*, 4/18.

57. Mill to Lord Amberley, 2 February 1870, in *CW*, vol. 17: *Later Letters*, p. 1693; see also Mill to John Nichol, 18 August 1869, in ibid., p. 1634.

58. Mill, *Essays on Sex Equality*, p. l 77.

59. Mill to Henry Keylock Rusden, 22 July 1870, in *CW*, vol. 17: *Later Letters*, p. 1751 (emphasis added).

60. Mill, *Essays on Sex Equality*, p. 77.

61. For a discussion of Mill's elitism, see Eisenstein, *The Radical Future of Liberal Feminism*, chap. 6.

62. For an argument to the effect that institutions such as marriage, suitably structured, can empower individuals rather than restrict them, see H.L.A. Hart, *Punishment and Responsibility: Essays in the Philosophy of Law* (Oxford: Clarendon Press, 1968), pp. 44–46.

63. *SW*, 1/1.

64. I am not suggesting that all radical feminists see marriage as a benign institution. There is a vigorous and ongoing debate on the topic, as there is on heterosexuality. But I suspect that those radical feminists who object to marriage do so because of its sordid past. Much or all of what is objectionable about marriage disappears, it seems to me, when the relationship is equalized, when divorce is easily available to both parties, and when same-sex marriages are allowed. I have no idea what Mill would have said about same-sex marriages, but I suspect that, given his general liberal outlook, he would have tolerated if not approved them.

65. Mary Lyndon Shanley, "Marital Slavery and Friendship: John Stuart Mill's *The Subjection of Women*," *Political Theory* 9 (1981), p. 230.

66. Ibid., p. 239. John Howes says that "Mill is describing a strenuous and profoundly satisfying kind of marriage." John Howes, "Mill on Women and Human Development," *Australasian Journal of Philosophy*, suppl. to vol. 64 (1986), p. 71.

67. Okin, *Women in Western Political Thought*, p. 226; see also Krouse, "Patriarchal Liberalism and Beyond," p. 164; Eisenstein, *The Radical Future of Liberal Feminism*, pp. 132–39.

68. See *SW*, 2/15. Mill advocated what is known as separate property—with the proviso that the parties to the marriage may agree to combine assets. What

Mill opposed was the rule according to which the woman's property devolved to the man upon marriage. That, he thought, was distinctly inegalitarian, and therefore unacceptable.

69. Ibid., 2/16.

70. Ibid.

71. Okin, *Women in Western Political Thought*, p. 229.

72. Mill to John Allen, 27 May 1867, in *CW*, vol. 16; *Later Letters*, pp. 1273–74.

73. Mill was a life-long defender of the use of contraceptives. As a youth he was arrested and jailed overnight for disseminating birth-control literature in London. See Okin, "Editor's Introduction," p. xvii. Mill did not believe that individuals, male or female, have a moral or legal duty to procreate. Therefore, while it is true that "Mill was totally silent on the possibility that a woman might marry and have no children" (Goldstein, "Mill, Marx, and Women's Liberation," p. 328, n. 62), it is also true that he made no argument that women should (let alone must) have children. And anyway, I do not understand radical feminism as being opposed, in principle, to women having or raising children. Radical-feminist qualms concern the effects of childrearing on women's opportunities vis-à-vis those of men, and on the fact that, in society as it is presently constituted, having children makes a woman vulnerable in a number of ways. For a sensitive and articulate elaboration of these points, see Susan Moller Okin, *Justice, Gender, and the Family* (New York: Basic Books, 1989).

74. I infer this from Mill's discussion of household responsibilities in *SW* 2/8, where he emphasizes the importance of allowing the marital partners to decide for themselves how they shall conduct their affairs. Shanley appears to concur in this. See Shanley, "Marital Slavery and Friendship," p. 242: "Had Mill discovered that managing the household to the exclusion of most other activity created an impediment to the friendship of married women and men, *The Subjection of Women* suggests that he would have altered his view of practicable domestic arrangements, but not his commitment to the desirability of male-female friendship in marriage."

75. Goldstein writes that "The *restraints* which Mill believed should be imposed of individual liberty between the sexes—is an exception to his argument for equality of individual liberty between the sexes—an exception so enormous that it threatens to swallow up the entire argument." Goldstein, "Mill, Marx and Women's Liberation," p. 328 (emphasis added); see also Susan Heckman, "John Stuart Mill's *The Subjection of Women*: The Foundations of Liberal Feminism," *History of European Ideas* 15 (1992): 681–86, pp. 684–85. Later Goldstein suggests that Mill advocated "*channeling* the vast majority of women into 'household management.'" Goldstein, "Mill, Marx, and Women's Liberation," p. 334 (emphasis added). I have argued that Mill advocated neither restraints nor

channeling. Predicting that S will do X under certain conditions is not necessarily to advocate that S do X under those conditions or indeed under any conditions.

76. Okin, *Women in Western Political Thought*, p. 237

77. *SW*, 1/1.

78. That Mill was engaged in prediction comes through in a letter to John Allen, in which Mill writes: "Perhaps I do not differ so much from you as you suppose, as to what is *likely to be* permanently the main occupation of a very great majority of women. But I do not think that he majority should give laws to the individual action of the minority." Mill to John Allen, 27 May 1867, in *CW*, vol. 16: *Later Letters*, p. 1274 (emphasis added). The principle/prediction distinction, or something very like it, is drawn by Urbinati, who, speaking as a radical feminist, writes: "Our dissatisfaction with Mill's feminism is . . . a dissatisfaction with particular opinions that he expressed on specific problems rather than with his principles per se." Urbinati, "John Stuart Mill on Androgyny and Ideal Marriage," p. 639. Urbinati is one of the few Mill scholars who shares my view that he is a radical feminist, although she doesn't put it that way. Another is David Dyzenhaus; see his "John Stuart Mill and the Harm of Pornography," *Ethics* 102 (1992):534–51.

79. I refer again to *SW* 2/8.

80. David Stove, "The Subjection of John Stuart Mill," *Philosophy* 68 (1993), p. 12.

81. I say "dubious" because one could claim that the nature of women is irrelevant to whether their subjection to men is "unnatural." Why must one know the nature of women in order to judge that their subjection to anyone, including men, is unnatural? Logically speaking, knowledge of the nature of a relation between X and Y is different from knowledge of the nature of X and Y.

82. *SW*, 1/18.

83. Stove, "The Subjection of John Stuart Mill," p. 5.

84. *SW*, 1/23.

85. Stove makes a number of distasteful ad hominem attacks on Mill. For example, he accuses Mill of having a "weak sexual impulse," as if that fact (conceding for purposes of argument that it is a fact) has a bearing on the adequacy of Mill's arguments. Later Stove questions Mill's motives in writing *SW*, suggesting that the work was the product of frustration at being snubbed by others of his social class. See Stove, "The Subjection of John Stuart Mill," pp. 12–13.

86. See John Stuart Mill, *On Liberty*, ed. Gertrude Himmelfarb (Harmondsworth: Penguin Books, 1974; orig. publ. 1859). For a contemporary vindication of "the traditional liberalism derived from Mill's *On Liberty*," see Joel Feinberg, *The Moral Limits of the Criminal Law*, 4 vols. (New York: Oxford University Press, 1984–88) (quotation from vol. 1, *Harm to Others*, p. 15).

87. *SW*, 1/15. Actually, Mill maintained that there was one other area—royalty—in which this was the case.

88. See, e.g., Rossi, "Sentiment and Intellect," p. 22; Okin, *Women in Western Political Thought*, p. 207; Annas, "Mill and the Subjection of Women," pp. 192–94.

89. See Okin, *Women in Western Political Thought*, p. 207.

90. Tong, for example, encourages this line of thought. See Tong, *Feminist Thought*, pp. 13–31; see also Goldstein, "Mill, Marx, and Women's Liberation," p. 325. Not coincidentally, Tong classifies Mill as a liberal feminist—indeed, as a paradigmatic liberal feminist (p. 13).

91. Freud is reputed to have said of Mill that he was "the man of the century most capable of freeing himself from the domination of the usual prejudices." Ernst Jones, *The Life and Work of Sigmund Freud*, 3 vols. (New York: Basic Books, 1953–57), vol. 1, p. 116 (quoted in Krouse, "Patriarchal Liberalism and Beyond," p. 172).

92. This essay was inspired by classroom discussions in an undergraduate feminism course I taught at UTA in Fall 1993. One of the many books we read in that course was Mill's *The Subjection of Women*, which I consider a philosophical masterpiece as well as a classic of English prose literature. This book, regrettably, has been ignored by the philosophical establishment. Even those who have not ignored it have judged it inferior to other of Mill's works, such as *On Liberty* and *Utilitarianism*. *The Subjection of Women* is at least as significant, philosophically, and at least as relevant, socially and politically, as these other works.

I thank Dabney Townsend for making the feminism course—or rather, my teaching of it—possible; the UTA Women's Studies Program for sponsoring and advertising the course; and the students who eventually enrolled for making the course challenging, rewarding, and enjoyable. Tom Tuchscherer and Marcia Cirillo asked incisive questions which forced me to think long and hard about what Mill meant and about the implications of what he said. I thank my UTA colleague Susan Hekman for encouragement and for critical commentary on an early draft of the essay (although I am sure she disagrees with some or all of my conclusions). I thank an anonymous reviewer for *Social Theory and Practice* for helpful suggestions on the penultimate draft. And finally, I thank David Cortner not for help with counterfactuals, but for what I shall call counterfactual help—help he would have provided, and happily so, had I asked.

6

The Corrupting Influence of Power

Maria H. Morales

Like Burgess-Jackson, Morales maintains that key to Mill's liberating project in The Subjection of Women *is an analysis of wrongful power and its corrupting influence on everyone. Mill aimed to replace the "ethic" of command/obedience with a principle of "perfect equality" regulative of social relations between women and men. This principle is substantive and relational rather than formal and individualist. To understand what kind of good "perfect equality" is for Mill, Morales examines Mill's analysis of social and domestic tyranny. This analysis underscores that, for Mill, the principal harms of inequality are tied to inequality of power.*

So kings find it odd they should have a million subjects
Yet share in the thoughts of none.

W. H. Auden, *The Sea and The Mirror*

HUMAN BEINGS CAN FORGE LIFE-AFFIRMING BONDS only with those to whose singularity they are able to respond appropriately. Genuine love and friendship cannot be based on convenience, deceit, envy, possessiveness, or even idealization. Neither can these bonds thrive under conditions of control. The *wrongful* exercise of power[1] undermines the foundation on which are built lasting and real bonds between human beings: trust, sympathy, intimacy, openness, and freedom. Power is exercised wrongfully over someone when it involves complete, or nearly complete, authority over that person and, hence, that person's lack of autonomy. In this sense, if I am in your power, then not only can you influence my desires or, by persuasion or force, induce me to do something that I would not do otherwise. Your *superior standing* with respect to me, which is typically backed by institutions or social practices, also enables you to control me by restricting my freedom and to harm me directly (for example, in my person) or indirectly (for example, by neglecting my needs, interests, or well-being). An "ethic" of command and obedience sustains relations between human beings founded on this power differential in political, social, and personal life.

In *The Subjection of Women*, John Stuart Mill argues against the ethic of command and obedience in human relations. His principle of "perfect equality" is an inclusive and substantive moral ideal of human relations, "admitting no power or privilege on the one side, nor disability on the other."[2] *The Subjection of Women* has been read as a textbook of "liberal feminism," construed as the theoretical framework that focuses on reforming the formal structure of the so-called public realm as the necessary and sufficient means for securing gender equality. The principle of perfect equality is *formal* in that it applies to the structure of liberties, opportunities, and rights that constitute the institutional framework for human life. On this standard construal, such formal egalitarian values as equality of opportunity and equality before the law are built into the ideal of *liberty* to which liberals traditionally have given priority in their discussions of justice.[3] Yet, this way of construing the value of perfect equality is anything but standard.

It is not hard to understand why commentators overwhelmingly have classified Mill as a liberal feminist of this stamp. This categorization matches the traditional portrayal of Mill as a mildly reformist utilitarian and a committed classical liberal. Alas, this portrayal has prejudiced readings of *The Subjection of Women*. Most commentators believe that Mill was principally concerned with removing formal barriers to women's emancipation. For example, Alan Ryan claims that Mill was "almost entirely concerned with the legal disabilities of women in Victorian England."[4] Similarly, Zillah R. Eisenstein contends that Mill and Harriet Taylor were concerned with replacing "aristocratic rule with the equality of opportunity doctrine," which requires granting women political rights and equality before the law.[5] Richard Krouse admits that Mill was aware that "the destruction of patriarchal domination in the family" is necessary to secure substantive equality for women. However, he suggests that Mill proceeded "as if this latter task can in turn be accomplished by purely legal means."[6] In short, the consensus is that Mill was concerned with formal equality. His principle of "perfect equality" depends exclusively on removing obstacles to equality of opportunity between the sexes and on guaranteeing their legal equality. Most commentators conclude that, like "most liberals,"[7] Mill could not formulate a substantive vision of egalitarian human relations.

In contrast to this received view, I shall argue that perfect equality embodies a substantive relational ideal. This ideal is a key element of the rich conception of human well-being at the heart of Mill's moral and political thought. I shall focus on his insightful analysis in *The Subjection of Women* of the corrupting effects of power on *everyone*. In particular, Mill offers a compelling account of how power can corrupt those who wield it and exercise it over others. His discussion of the dire effects of tyranny on the tyrant, reminiscent of Plato in the *Republic*, helps us to understand what kind of good is at stake in debates over the value of equality.

1. Virtue as the Advantage of Perfect Equality

Commentators have tended to assess negatively Mill's arguments for the "advantages" of perfect equality. Allegedly, these arguments at best can point to the utility of gender egalitarian arrangements, where "utility" is understood as a criterion for cost-benefit analysis. Some commentators even have criticized as virtually unfeminist Mill's arguments for the beneficial consequences of gender equality not only on women, but also on men and on society generally. Most recently, Gail Tulloch suggests that these arguments are too broad and, consequently, not gender egalitarian arguments.[8] Julia Annas also complains that in *The Subjection of Women* "there is much stress on the improvements from others' points of view if women are liberated from their present rigid and thwarted characters."[9] She recognizes that Mill's condemnation of the effects of gender inequality on men's characters is "eloquent." However, in her view Mill failed to show why men should deem perfect equality beneficial, and he failed to appreciate the magnitude of the changes necessary to persuade the unconvinced, whether women or men, that perfect equality is an important good.

One *might* wonder why it is not sufficient to show that perfect equality is beneficial to women. After all, women indisputably and most directly suffer the effects of systematic gender inequality. Why need Mill, or anyone else, worry about persuading the perpetrators of this suffering that their privilege and practices are harmful to themselves? At least three responses suggest themselves. First, nothing else will motivate men to give up their privileged position. Self-interested reasons always can motivate people to action. Second, genuine changes will not be possible unless men are willing to contribute to bringing them about. This point is about the practicability of fundamental changes: everyone must facilitate their realization. Finally, the more inclusive an argument for perfect equality, the greater its force. Showing that gender equality benefits everyone establishes something important about what kind of good is at stake.

These three responses are not mutually exclusive. We should understand Mill's position as involving all of these responses, but in the following order. It is important to persuade men of the advantages of perfect equality primarily because it is an essential part of the human good. A *strength* of Mill's defense of perfect equality is that it exhibits the advantages of perfect equality *for everyone*. Mill knew that women would be the key beneficiaries of perfect equality, and he did not expect that its benefits would be patently obvious to men. Neither did he underestimate the degree of moral reform required for the complete overhaul of the command and obedience ethic in human relations. He knew that replacing this ethic with perfect equality would require dramatic changes in political, social, and personal life. Most importantly, it would require profound changes in everyone's sentiments and habits.

Mill also suggested that the lasting success of this project would depend at least in part on men's willingness to join with women in the struggle for perfect equality.[10] This suggestion is connected with his belief that genuine social reform must be premised on the reformation of the moral world. For new to replace old values, people must come *to value* the new ones. The generality of men and of women must be persuaded of the value of certain goods and ways of life for basic changes in the direction of social life to be possible and ultimately successful. Some *women* might have vested interests in perpetuating certain social arrangements, because they think that these arrangements truly benefit them. Until they are otherwise convinced, genuine change will not be possible. Thus, an inclusive and general argument of the sort that Mill offered is actually far stronger than arguments with a narrower scope.

Finally, although Mill did not believe that only self-interested reasons can motivate people, he recognized that sometimes these sorts of reasons can tip the balance in favor of good actions. Where other appeals fail, appeals to self-interest might succeed in persuading people that there is no good justification for the wrongful exercise of power over others. Mill did not object in principle to relying on self-interested arguments, even though, from his perspective, they do not count as *moral* arguments. He did hope that people who act in certain ways for self-interested reasons would gradually come to act in those ways for moral reasons, notably reasons of justice. In fact, he believed that *experiencing* the value of certain goods and ways of life that include them ultimately would convince people of their value. And appeals to people's own well-being might lead them to try different experiments of living.

Yet Mill's argument is not a straightforwardly self-interested argument, by which I mean an argument that focuses on interest understood as interest *in* the self, whatever it might be and whatever its consequences. The generality of men believe that it is in their interest to hold on to their power. Part of Mill's strategy is to try to convince them that their belief is false or, what amounts to the same thing, that it is not in their *real* interest to hold on to their power, that is, in their interest as moral and rational beings.[11] Mill argued that by holding on to their power over women, men miss out on goods that are valuable for anyone who has them and that they themselves value. The enjoyment of shared goods is impossible under conditions of inequality. Thus, a closer look at Mill's argument reveals that it focuses on self-interest broadly understood, as interest *of* the self. The interests of human beings conceived of as progressive are tied to their sympathetic and benevolent dispositions and through these, to the well-being of others.

Mill appreciated the heavy argumentative burden on those who contend that *the powerful* would benefit from egalitarian relations. To meet this burden, he mounted a forceful case against the corrupting effects of power. Mill's arguments for the "advantages" of perfect equality are anything but thin arguments of expediency. They are substantive arguments to the effect that the command and obedience ethic is wrong because it *morally corrupts* people and, in so doing, undermines the possibility of genuine happiness. More specifically, Mill argued that the command and obedience ethic undermines human beings' desire to form meaningful and life-affirming bonds with others. Perfect equality is the true human virtue, and, ultimately, for Mill, only a virtuous life is a good human life.

2. The Harms of Inequality

According to Mill, human beings' "true virtue"

> is fitness to live together as equals; claiming nothing for themselves but what they as freely concede to everyone else; regarding command of any kind as an exceptional necessity, and in all cases a temporary one; and preferring, whenever possible, the society of those with whom leading and following can be alternate and reciprocal.[12]

The principle of perfect equality prescribes shared power and privilege, as well as reciprocity and mutuality in relations between women and men. In what follows, I shall focus on the rationale for the prescription to treat others as equals in this substantive sense. Why should we prefer egalitarian associations to hierarchical ones premised on a differential of power and privilege? Why should we eradicate injustices due to imbalances of authority and esteem? Why is perfect equality the mark of the best kind of human relations? And in what sense is perfect equality a *virtue*?

I shall answer these questions by examining the other side of the coin first, namely the claim that inequality is a vice. Mill maintained that the command and obedience ethic requires fixed hierarchies in human relations, which place each person either "above" or "below" others. Where this ethic is the rule of life, human beings view themselves and others in terms of the superior/inferior or better/worse categories. This ethic is the egoistic and competitive ethic that Mill condemned in *Utilitarianism* for rendering people "cold and unsympathizing," for inducing them to regard their fellows as "struggling rivals" in the race of life, and, as a result, for undermining their well-being.[13] Complementing these criticisms, we find in *The Subjection of Women* Mill's argument that the command and obedience ethic in personal relations fosters vicious character traits and, thus, sabotages the quest for a flourishing life. The command and obedience ethic encourages people to prefer "command of any kind" to the position of a subject.[14]

The harm of inequality is most obvious on those who, like women, suffer its effects directly and immediately. In the first place, inequality harms women by warping their characters. Mill contended that women's masters have turned "the whole force of education" to subject them.[15] Men encourage in women an ideal of character entirely different from their own: "not self-will, and government by self-control, but submission, and yielding to the control of others." Worse, men represent this ideal of character to women as an "essential part of sexual attractiveness."[16] The ideal of femininity extols submissiveness and passivity as an "essential" and alluring aspect of women's sexuality. Mill turned this Freudian conception of femininity[17] on its head by arguing that it is neither "natural" nor desirable. It is a powerful artificial construct designed by men for their own benefit and to keep women dependent on them. The ideal of femininity is undesirable because it actually harms women.

How does the ideal of femininity harm women? First, Mill argued, it morally corrupts women by promoting as "feminine" virtues the *vices* of self-denial, dependence, and submissiveness. These character traits are vices because they thwart the active development and exercise of the higher faculties—intellect, judgment, choice, imagination, and feelings. Full self-development, which is a critical aspect of morality, requires the active cultivation of these faculties. For Mill, the ideal of femity is *immoral* because it is premised on devaluing women's full self-development. It encourages the over-development of their emotional faculties, consistently with a certain view of their "nature" as essentially emotional. It overemphasizes their biological constitution, consistently with a certain view of their "nature" as essentially sensual. Adding insult to injury, men complain about the overly emotional nature of women. Mill retorted that

> men, with that inability to recognize their own work which distinguishes the unanalytic mind, indolently believe that the tree grows of itself in the way that they have made it grow, and that it would die if one half of it were not kept in a vapour bath and the other in the snow.[18]

Mill rejected the contention that femininity is a natural and desirable ideal of character for women. From his perspective, men conjured up a nightmare and called it the work of nature to give it "objective" standing and circumvent responsibility. In fact, they blamed on "women's nature" the misery-inducing results of their own work.

In addition to corrupting women's characters, inequality has a profoundly disheartening effect on women. Second-class citizenship, limited
personhood, and a life exclusively devoted to pleasing others and tending
to their needs seriously weakens women's sense of themselves and of
their personal worth. Mill contended that inequality denies women even
the "mere consciousness" of being treated as human beings.[19] It deprives
women of their dignity by sustaining the notion that their value is merely
instrumental.[20] Only the "feeling of a wasted life" is left for most of them
at the twilight of their days. To the other positive evils of subjection, Mill
noted, must be added this "weariness, disappointment, and profound
dissatisfaction with life": society's payment for women's fulfillment of
their roles as wives and mothers. Mill discussed this effect of inequality
in other contexts as well. In "Coleridge," he decried the "demoralizing effect" of social and economic inequalities.[21] Inequality always affects negatively people's self-conceptions, their relations to others, and their views
on the world generally. Economic inequalities leave the powerless in ab-
ject poverty and dependent on the wills of the powerful in another way.[22]
Like Marx, Mill condemned the wage relationship for condoning and
perpetuating the wage earner's subjection to the capitalist.[23] In short,
Mill consistently maintained that the wrongful exercise of power is
premised on the powerless's lack of autonomy, which dispirits them and
defeats their pursuit of a good life.

Mill rejected the disingenuous argument that the subjection of certain
groups is actually for their good. Racial slavery had been "justified" on
similar grounds. Mill contended that the abolition of slavery was the vic-
tory of justice, not of sentimentalism. Behind the abhorrent despotism
and cruelty that masters exercised over slaves was "the love of gold" and
the concern for "god economy," which dictated "to wear [slaves] out
quickly and import more."[24] The institution of slavery was not the outcome of deliberation about the good of slaves, but of prejudice and the
noxious belief that "one kind of human beings are born servants to another kind."[25] The "utter and irrevocable extinction" of the institution of
slavery was the requirement of an age concerned primarily with the abolition of tyranny and the diminution of pain and suffering inflicted on
some human beings "by the mere will" of others.[26] The same applies to
the power of men over women. Mill found spurious men's attempts to
justify excluding women from the benefits that they themselves enjoyed.
One justification was that women "depart from their real path of success

and happiness" when they leave the domestic realm.[27] Allegedly, women acquiesce to their social condition because their roles guarantee their well-being. Mill retorted that structuring institutions and social practices around "the law of force" is inconsistent with holding that women's "natural" path of success and happiness is embodied in the division of roles along gender lines. Men seem to fear that women might prove to be real "competitors." They fear that women might not be excluded when competing with them, and that they themselves might lose the upperhand in "the free play of competition." Men view women as possible "struggling rivals" in the race of life and, hence, they do whatever is in their power to keep women from threatening their superiority and privileges—the "bounties and protective duties" in their favor. In so doing, men perpetuate the system under which everyone is either an inferior to be controlled or an enemy to be fought. They do not uphold this system out of concern for *women's* well-being. Plainly, men keep women subjected so that they will fulfill the duties that men wish women to discharge. Mill was indignant:

> I should like to hear somebody openly enunciating the doctrine . . . "It is necessary to society that women should marry and produce children. They will not do so unless they are compelled. Therefore it is necessary to compel them." The merits of the case would then be clearly defined.[28]

If women are by nature called "to marry and produce children," then it will not be necessary to compel them by direct force, including the force of education and public opinion, or by denial of meaningful alternatives. And women themselves would not demand equality in all areas of life. Mill concluded that men denied women full moral and political personhood because they did not want to give up their power and risk losing their domestic drudges. Sometimes the argument is that it is in society's interest to enforce gender roles. Yet by "the interest of society," Mill rebutted, men really mean their own interests.[29] He likened this interest to that of masters in slavery. Neither one is for the good of moral and rational beings, because the wrongful exercise of power corrupts ruler as well as subject, master as well as slave. This is Mill's strongest claim: inequality harms those who wield and wrongfully exercise power over others.

How does inequality harm those who are in a position of power? First, Mill argued, the wrongful exercise of power harms its presumed beneficiaries by fostering "self-worship," a vice common to the members of all privileged groups.[30] In families structured around the command and obedience ethic, boys learn that by birth they are superior to all women. Thus, they grow "to worship their own will as such a grand thing that it is actually the law for another rational being."[31] Paradoxically, men elevate women as morally superior. Mill rejected this "piece of tiresome cant" as simply another excuse for men's unwillingness to live with women as equals. Men did not *treat* women as if they were as good, let alone as if they were better. Mill suggested that, if anything, men's acknowledged moral inferiority to women amounted to their recognition of "the corrupting influence of power."[32] He even suggested that the wrongful exercise of power is less corrupting to slaves than to masters, because it is better to be restrained by "arbitrary" power than not to be restrained at all.[33] Nonetheless, Mill insisted, the picture of the noble slave is as contemptible as the myth of the benevolent despot. They both obscure the immense suffering that inequality brings in its wake.

Another harmful effect of inequality on the powerful is that it numbs their minds. Mill had made this point in "The Spirit of the Age," where he claimed that unearned luxuries and advantages generally dull the spirits of the privileged.[34] In *The Subjection of Women*, he argued that the wrongful exercise of power does not stimulate men to better themselves. Under the influence of the command and obedience ethic, most women's lives are narrow and their concerns superficial. Their interaction with men does not have the "moralizing" effect attributed to women's influence.[35] It could not have a moralizing effect *on women*. It fosters not only the vices of servitude, but also those of vanity, conceit, and pettiness. Understandably, associating with beings of limited aspirations and frivolous interests as many women have been made to be is neither personally fulfilling nor conducive to positive development and moral improvement.

This contention has led such critics as Annas to decry Mill's interest in men's well-being.[36] The problem is that his rhetoric is infelicitous: it seems to reproach *women* for their distorted characters. Yet Mill knew that women's distorted characters are the result of systematic inequality. To a large extent, women were what men had made them through bad education and subjection to their wills. Thus, *men* could not complain that their associations with women are unfulfilling and incompatible with their own moral improvement. In fact, everyone loses out: neither

men nor women can be fulfilled, positively develop, and morally improve living under conditions of inequality. Does this mean that people
necessarily deteriorate under such conditions? Mill suggested that whoever is not improving is deteriorating.[37] Is this suggestion sound? Mill
admitted that there had been some degree of improvement and pros-
perity under conditions of inequality.[38] He should have made plain that,
in his view, inequality is inconsistent with the best and most complete
kind of improvement: the *moral* improvement that the corrupting effects of power prevent.

The claim that society as presently constituted morally corrupts
everyone raises another concern. An implication of this claim is that it
is impossible in principle to find uncorrupted people. However, Mill did
not hold this Rousseauian view. His contention was that society organized on a systematically inegalitarian basis *tends to* corrupt people
morally. Put differently, it is generally, but not universally, the case that
under conditions of inequality people morally deteriorate. The same applies to Mill's views in *On Liberty* on how social despotism affects individual character. It is not in principle impossible to find Millean "individuals" in societies organized so as generally to render people passive
and compliant. However, despotic conditions severely inhibit the development of active and critical character traits. Inequality, despotism, and
paternalism are not conducive to the development of principled individuals. Inegalitarian, despotic, and paternalistic societies encourage
sectarianism, intolerance, and conformism.

I have discussed how the ideal of femininity warps women's characters, thus hindering their moral improvement. How does the ideal of
masculinity harm men? According to Mill, self-worship hinders men
from developing and exercising their higher faculties, notably their
moral sentiments. The feeling of innate superiority to others is inimical
to the cultivation of sympathetic and intimate ties with them. The position of superiority fosters in men 'the worst sort of pride, that which values itself upon accidental advantages, not of its own achievement."[39] It
renders them arrogant and egotistical. In short, the wrongful exercise of
power morally corrupts men by promoting as "masculine" virtues nothing other than the *vices* of despotism: "willfulness, overbearingness, unbounded self-indulgence, and a double-dyed and idealized selfishness."[40] These traits make up the ideal of masculinity, which is as phony
and undesirable as its feminine counterpart. The ideal of masculinity is

also premised on devaluing full self-development It encourages the over-development of men's intellectual faculties, consistently with a certain view of their "nature" as essentially rational. It starves their emotional constitution, consistently with a certain view of what counts as "manly" behavior. Thus, it perpetuates a conception of men as *less* than human, but, paradoxically, for that reason *better* than women!

To sum up, Mill denounced the command and obedience ethic primarily on the grounds that it morally corrupts everyone. The crux of the corrupting effects of power is that it prompts both men and women *to treat vices as though they were virtues.* The ideal of perfect equality is an ideal of human relations inseparable from an ideal of moral character. The virtues most appropriate to progressive beings are other-regarding. Human excellence, like a tree, is capable of self-development and good growth only if well attended to and rightly nurtured from the outside.[41] Foremost among the right conditions for full self-development and good growth is the cultivation of confirming associations with others. Genuine human flourishing is impossible apart from the blooming of other-regarding sentiments and affections. Thus, the central feature of Mill's conception of the moral life is the irreplaceable value to human beings of shared goods. The rationale for this conception is his view of how our concrete attachments to others affect the quality of our lives. This picture of a good human life as requiring qualitatively good relations with others rests on the assumption that we cannot live *well* without others.

The strongest argument in *The Subjection of Women* is that perfect equality is a central element of the human good. The corrupting effects of power undermine the possibility of human happiness by frustrating the pursuit of key elements of a good life: unfeigned bonds of cooperation, friendship, and love. Human beings cannot be fully happy without genuine relations of sympathetic unity with others. Despotism inhibits the prospect of forming and sustaining such relations. Thus, despotism renders the lives of despots and subjects emotionally barren and incomplete. According to Mill, sympathy plays an important role in self-knowledge and knowledge of others The despot cannot hope to find in others the confirmation of his own identity and worth that sympathetic associations with them would make possible. Neither can he really come to know another human being. Mill intimated that "thorough knowledge" of someone requires not only intimacy, but intimacy between equals.[42] A superior can inspire awe or fear, but not the trust and security characteristic of close and meaningful human relations.

Mill believed that inequality alienates women and men from one another. Genuine friendship between them is impossible if their lives exhibit the yawning gap that they do under the command and obedience ethic. As long as men relate to women as master to slave, lord to vassal, or ruler to subject, men will remain isolated in their solitary towers of arrogance and selfishness and women confined to cramped and unsatisfying lives of meekness and selflessness. Human beings are not self-sufficient. Power never compensates for the loss of happiness, nor security for the loss of freedom. The despot's longings for life-affirming relations with others are in vain. Superiority, the condition of being "above" another human being, distances superior from inferior, which precludes any real connection between them. Mill contended that genuine bonds of affection between human beings are impossible if there is power on one side and subjection on the other.[43] Perfect equality has *intrinsic* value: egalitarian relations of reciprocal affection and happiness enrich human beings' lives and, hence, constitute a qualitatively significant part of the human good.

In short, all other things equal, the just person is happier than the unjust. The wrongful exercise of power is one of the chief manifestations of injustice.[44] Justice is *better* than injustice because it enriches human life. In short, justice is *qualitatively* better than injustice.

A Millean justification of the claim that perfect equality is part of the human good can be provided by applying Mill's hypothetico-empiricist standard of value: the "decided preference" criterion.[45] The claim in need of justification is that, all other things equal, individuals with experience of both kinds of lives *would* prefer to live under conditions of perfect equality. Life with others as equals is a critical part of any plan of life that they would choose, even if they could be in a position of power under conditions of inequality. In choosing otherwise, they would be contenting themselves with impoverished lives, and no one "voluntarily chooses" to live an impoverished life.[46] Their lives would be impoverished because they would lack goods that are valuable for anyone who has them, notably shared goods. Of course, for Mill, experience of relevant alternatives is necessary, but not sufficient, for competent judgment concerning the value of different ways of life. Also necessary is full self-development, which shapes the capacity to appreciate and enjoy certain pleasures. Because full self-development is a condition for the possibility of genuine choice—that is, choice expressing competent preferences and reflecting a certain kind of moral character—the *social* revolution that the ideal of perfect equality would bring about requires first a *moral* revolution in people's sentiments. Mill's conception of a just society is not that of a timid reformer. Mill was aware that his ideal of human life was not yet readily embraced by most men or even women. The struggle to replace the rule of force and inequality with perfect equality was only at its dawn. And we are still far from having secured the conditions under which people's choices can be genuine. We have much to do before we realize Millean perfect equality, let alone go beyond it.

3. Conclusion

I have shown that Mill's arguments against the corrupting effects of power in *The Subjection of Women* are substantive moral arguments for the special value of perfect equality of human beings. They involve appeals to the intrinsic value of perfect equality as a constituent of the human good within concrete human relations, social practices, and institutional contexts. In Mill's view, human life is an "art" that requires not only practical mastery, but developing a sense of what is important to it by pursuing valuable ends and cultivating authentic commitments to others. Our commitments to others must be grounded on respect and reciprocity, sympathy and trust. The relational life is key to happiness. Developing strong and positive bonds with other human beings is ultimately what makes life worth living.[47]

Notes

1. John Stuart Mill, *Utilitarianism*, vol. 10, chap. 5, p. 256; emphasis mine. References to Mill are to *Collected Works of John Stuart Mill*, ed. John Robson (Toronto: University of Toronto Press; London: Routledge and Kegan Paul, 1963).

2. John Stuart Mill, *The Subjection of Women*, vol. 21, chap. 1, p. 261.

3. See John Rawls, *A Theory of Justice* (Cambridge, Mass.: Harvard University Press, 1971).

4. Alan Ryan, *The Philosophy of John Stuart Mill* (London: Macmillan, 1970), p. 125.

5. Zillah Eisenstein, *The Radical Future of Liberal Feminism* (Boston: Northeastern University Press, 1986), p. 127.

6. Richard Krouse, "Patriarchal Liberalism and Beyond: From John Stuart Mill to Harriet Taylor," in *The Family in Political Thought*, ed. Jean Bethke Elshtein (Amherst, Mass.: University of Massachusetts Press, 1982), p. 161.

7. Gail Tulloch, *Mill and Sexual Equality* (Hertfordshire, England: Harvester Wheatsheaf, 1989), p. 14.

8. *Ibid.*, pp. 30–31 and 63.

9. Julia Annas, "Mill and the Subjection of Women," *Philosophy*, 52 (1977), p. 188.

10. Mill, *The Subjection of Women*, chap. 3, p. 322.

11. *Ibid.*, chap. 1, p. 277.

12. *Ibid.*, chap. 2, p. 294.

13. Mill, *Utilitarianism*, chap. 2, p. 220, and chap. 3, p. 233.

14. Mill, *The Subjection of Women*, chap. 2, p. 294.

15. *Ibid.*, chap. 1, p. 271.

16. *Ibid.*, p. 272.

17. Sigmund Freud, "Femininity," in *Freud on Women: A Reader*, ed. Elisabeth Young-Bruehl (New York: W. W. Norton, 1990), pp. 342–362.

18. Mill, *The Subjection of Women*, chap. 1, p. 276–277.

19. *Ibid.*, chap. 4, p. 327.

20. *Ibid.*, p. 340.

21. John Stuart Mill, "Coleridge," vol. 10, p. 123.

22. Fred Berger, *Happiness, Justice, and Freedom* (Berkeley and Los Angeles: University of California Press, 1984), pp. 166–186.

23. *Ibid.*, pp. 183–186 in particular. Also, Mill, *Principles of Political Economy*, vol. 3, pp. 766–769.

24. John Stuart Mill, "The Negro Question," vol. 21, p. 88.

25. *Ibid.*, p. 92.

26. *Ibid.*, p. 94–95.

27. Mill, *The Subjection of Women*, chap. 2, p. 299.

28. *Ibid.*, p. 281.

29. *Ibid.*, p. 299.

30. *Ibid.*, p. 293, and chap. 4, pp. 324–325.

31. *Ibid.*, chap. 2, p. 293.

32. *Ibid.*, chap. 4, p. 320.

33. *Ibid.*, p. 321.

34. John Stuart Mill, "The Spirit of The Age, I," vol. 22, pp. 227–234, and "The Spirit of the Age, II," vol. 22, pp. 238–245.

35. Mill, *The Subjection of Women*, chap. 2, p. 290, and chap. 4, pp. 332–333.

36. Julia Annas, "Mill and The Subjection of Women," pp. 184–185 and 188.

37. Mill, *The Subjection of Women*, chap. 4, p. 335.

38. *Ibid.*, chap. 1, p. 276.

39. *Ibid.*, chap. 4, p. 325.

40. *Ibid.*, chap. 2, p. 289.

41. *Ibid.*, chap. 1, p. 276–277.

42. *Ibid.*, chap. 2, p. 279.

43. *Ibid.*, p. 278.

44. Mill, *Utilitarianism*, chap. 5, p. 256.

45. *Ibid.*, chap. 2, p. 211.

46. *Ibid.*, pp. 211–212.

47. I thank Elizabeth Anderson, Sally Haslanger, Laura Duhan Kaplan, Samuel Freeman, Patricia Matthews, Frederick Springer, and Aladdin Yaqub for helpful comments on this and earlier versions of this chapter. I also thank Rowman & Littlefield for permission to reprint some material from chapter 5 of my *Perfect Equality: John Stuart Mill on Well-Constituted Communities* (Lanham, Md.: Rowman & Littlefield, 1996).

7

Marital Slavery and Friendship

John Stuart Mill's
The Subjection of Women

Mary Lyndon Shanley

Like Burgess-Jackson and Morales, Lyndon Shanley believes that Mill's case against gender inequality in The Subjection of Women *centers on an analysis of the corruption of the relation between the sexes, especially in the so-called private realm. Lyndon Shanley maintains that Mill argued for a "visionary" ideal of marital friendship, which requires the overthrow of master-slave relations. Mill's target, in her view, is family life itself, and the root of gender inequality is men's fear of living with women as equals. This fear, Lyndon Shanley contends, is both self-defeating and self-destructive. In her view, however, Mill's vision is ultimately limited by his traditional views on the domestic division of labor.*

JOHN STUART MILL'S ESSAY *THE SUBJECTION OF WOMEN* was one of the nineteenth century's strongest pleas for opening to women opportunities for suffrage, education, and employment. Some contemporary feminists, however, have denigrated the work, questioning the efficacy of merely striking down legal barriers against women as the way to establish equality between the sexes. These contemporary critics argue that Mill's failure to extend his critique of inequality to the division of labor in the household,, and his confidence that most women would choose marriage as a "career," subverted his otherwise egalitarian impulses.[1]

I argue in this essay, however, that such critics have ignored an important aspect of Mill's feminism. *The Subjection of Women* was not solely about equal opportunity for women. It was also, and more fundamentally, about the corruption of male-female relationships and the hope of establishing friendship in marriage. Such friendship was desirable not only for emotional satisfaction, it was crucial if marriage were to become, as Mill desired, a "school of genuine moral sentiment."[2] The fundamental assertion of *The Subjection of Women* was not that equal opportunity would ensure the liberation of women, but that male-female equality, however achieved, was essential to marital friendship and to the progression of human society.

Mill's vision of marriage as a locus of sympathy and understanding between autonomous adults not only reforms our understanding of his feminism, but also draws attention to an often submerged or ignored aspect of liberal political thought. Liberal individualism is attacked by Marxist and neo-conservatives alike as wrongly encouraging the disintegration of affective bonds and replacing them with merely self-interested economic and contractual ties. Mill's essay, however, emphasizes the value of noninstrumental relationships in human life. His depictions of both corrupt and well-ordered marriage traces the relationship of family order to right political order. His vision of marriage as a locus of mutual sympathy and understanding between autonomous adults stands as an unrealized goal for those who believe that the liberation of women requires not only formal equality of opportunity but measures which will enable couples to live in genuine equality, mutuality, and reciprocity.

I. The Perversion of Marriage by the Master-Slave Relationship

Mill's reconstruction of marriage upon the basis of friendship was preceded by one of the most devastating critiques of male domination in marriage in the history of Western philosophy. In *The Subjection of Women* Mill repeatedly used the language of "master and slave" or "master and servant" to describe the relationship between husband and wife. In the first pages of the book, Mill called the dependence of women upon men "the primitive state of slavery lasting on" (1: 130). Later he said that despite the supposed advances of Christian civilization, "the wife is the actual bond-servant of her husband; no less so, as far as legal obligation goes, than slaves commonly so called." (2: 158) Still later he asserted that "there remain no legal slaves, except the mistress of every house." (4: 217) The theme of women's servitude was not confined to

The Subjection of Women. In his speech on the Reform Bill of 1867, Mill talked of that "obscure feeling" which members of Parliament were "ashamed to express openly" that women had no right to care about anything except "how they may be the most useful and devoted servants of some man."[3] To Auguste Comte he wrote comparing women to "domestic slaves" and noted that women's capacities were spent "seeking happiness not in their own life, but exclusively in the favor and affection of the other sex, which is only given to them on the condition of their dependence."[4]

But what did Mill mean by denouncing the "slavery" of married women? How strongly did he wish to insist upon the analogy between married women and chattel slaves? I believe that he chose the image quite deliberately. For Mill, the position of married women resembled that of slaves in several ways: the social and economic system gave women little alternative except to marry; once married, the legal personality of the woman was subsumed in that of her husband; and the abuses of human dignity permitted by custom and law within marriage were egregious.

In Mill's eyes, women were in a double bind; they were not free within marriage, and they were not truly free not to marry.[5] What could an unmarried woman do? Even if she were of the middle or upper classes, she could not attend any of the English universities, and thus she was barred from a systematic higher education.[6] If somehow she acquired a professional education, the professional associations usually barred her from practicing her trade. "No sooner do women show themselves capable of competing with men in any career, than that career, if it be lucrative or honorable, is closed to them."[7] Mill's depiction of the plight of Elinor Garrett, sister of Millicent Garrett Fawcett, the suffrage leader, is telling:

A young lady, Miss Garrett, . . . studied the medical profession. Having duly qualified herself, she . . . knocked successively at all the doors through which, by law, access is obtained into the medical profession. Having found all other doors fast shut, she fortunately discovered one which had accidentally been left ajar. The Society of Apothecaries, it seems, had forgotten to shut out those who they never thought would attempt to come in, and through this narrow entrance this young lady found her way into the profession. But so objectionable did it appear to this learned body that women should be the medical attendants even of women, that the narrow wicket through which Miss Garrett entered has been closed after her.[8]

Working-class women were even worse off. In the *Principles of Political Economy*, Mill argued that their low wages were due to the "prejudice" of society which "making almost every woman, socially speaking, an appendage of some man, enables men to take systematically the lion's share of whatever belongs to both." A second cause of low wages for women was the surplus of female labor for unskilled jobs. Law and custom ordained that a woman has "scarcely any means open to her of gaining a livelihood, except as a wife and mother."[9] Marriage was, as Mill put it, a "Hobson's choice" for women, "that or none" (1: 156).[10]

Worse than the social and economic pressure to marry, however, was women's status within marriage. Mill thoroughly understood the stipulations of the English common law which deprived a married woman of a legal personality independent of that of her husband. The doctrine of coverture or spousal unity, as it was called, was based on the Biblical notion that "a man [shall] leave his father and his mother, and shall cleave to his wife, and they shall be one flesh" (Genesis ii, 22–23). If "one flesh," then, as Blackstone put it, "by marriage, the husband and wife are one person in law." And that "person" was represented by the husband. Again Blackstone was most succinct: "The very being or legal existence of the woman is suspended during the marriage, or at least is incorporated and consolidated into that of the husband."[11] One of the most commonly felt injustices of the doctrine of spousal unity was the married woman's lack of ownership of her own earnings. As the matrimonial couple was "one person," the wife's earnings during marriage were owned and controlled by her husband.[12] During his term as a member of Parliament, Mill supported a Married Women's Property Bill, saying that its opponents were men who thought it impossible for "society to exist on a harmonious footing between two persons unless one of them has absolute power over the other," and insisting that England has moved beyond such a "savage state."[13] In *The Subjection of Women* Mill argued that the "wife's position under the common law of England [with respect to property] is worse than that of slaves in the laws of many countries: by the Roman law, for example, a slave might have his *peculium*, which to a certain extent the law guaranteed to him for his exclusive use" (2: 158–159). Similarly, Mill regarded the husband's exclusive guardianship over the married couple's children as a sign of the woman's dependence on her husband's will (2: 160). She was, in his eyes, denied any role in life except that of being "the personal body-servant of a despot" (2: 161).

The most egregious aspects of both common and statute law, however, were those which sanctioned domestic violence. During the Parliamentary debates on the Representation of the People Bill in 1867, Mill
argued that women needed suffrage to enable them to lobby for legislation which would punish domestic assault:

> I should like to have a Return laid before this House of the number of
> women who are annually beaten to death, or trampled to death by their
> male protectors; and, in an opposite column, the amount of sentence
> passed. . . . I should also like to have, in a third column, the amount of
> property, the wrongful taking of which was . . . thought worthy of the same
> punishment. We should then have an arithmetical value set by a male leg-
> islature and male tribunals on the murder of a woman.[14]

But the two legal stipulations which to Mill most demonstrated "the assimilation of the wife to the slave" were her inability to refuse her master "the last familiarity" and her inability to obtain a legal separation
from her husband unless he added desertion or extreme cruelty to his
adultery (2: 160–161). Mill was appalled by the notion that no matter
how brutal a tyrant a husband might be, and no matter how a woman
might loathe him, "he can claim from her and enforce the lowest degradation of a human being," which was to be made the instrument of "an
animal function contrary to her inclination" (2: 160). A man and wife
being one body, rape was by definition a crime which a married man
could not commit against his own wife. By law a wife could not leave her
husband on account of this offense without being guilty of desertion,
nor could she prosecute him. The most vicious form of male domination of women according to Mill was rape within marriage; it was particularly vicious because it was legal. Mill thus talked not of individual
masters and wives as aberrations, but of a legally sanctioned system of
domestic slavery which shaped the character of marriage in his day.[15]

Mill's depiction of marriage departed radically from the majority of
Victorian portrayals of home and hearth. John Ruskin's praise of the
home in *Sesame and Lilies* reflected the feelings and aspirations of many:
"This is the true nature of home—it is the place of Peace; the shelter, not
only from all injury, but from all terror, doubt, and division. . . . It is a sa-
cred place, a vestal temple, a temple of the hearth watched over by Household Gods."[16] Walter Houghton remarked that the title of Coventry Pat-
more's poem, *The Angel in the House*, captured "the essential character of

Victorian love," and reflected "the exaltation of family life and feminine character" characteristic of the mid-nineteenth century.[17] James Fitzjames Stephen, who wrote that he disagreed with *The Subjection of Women* "from the first sentence to the last," found not only Mill's ideas but his very effort to discuss the dynamics of marriage highly distasteful. "There is something—I hardly know what to call it; indecent is too strong a word, but I may say unpleasant in the direction of indecorum—in prolonged and minute discussions about the relations between men and women, and the character of women as such."[18]

The Subjection of Women challenged much more than Victorian decorum, however; it was a radical challenge to one of the most fundamental and preciously held assumptions about marriage in the modern era, which is that it was a relationship grounded on the consent of the partners to join their lives. Mill argued to the contrary that the presumed consent of women to marry was not, in any real sense, a free promise, but one socially coerced by the lack of meaningful options. Further, the laws of marriage deprived a woman of many of the normal powers of autonomous adults, from controlling her earnings, to entering contracts, to defending her bodily autonomy by resisting unwanted sexual relations. Indeed, the whole notion of a woman "consenting" to the marriage "offer" of a man implied from the outset a hierarchical relationship. Such a one-way offer did not reflect the relationship which should exist between those who were truly equal, among beings who should be able to create together by free discussion and mutual agreement an association to govern their lives together.

In addition, Mill's view of marriage as slavery suggested a significantly more complicated and skeptical view of what constituted a "free choice" in society than did either his own earlier works or those of his liberal predecessors. Hobbes, for example, regarded men as acting "freely" even when moved by fear for their lives. Locke disagreed, but he in turn talked about the individual's free choice to remain a citizen of his father's country, as if emigration were a readily available option for all. In other of his works Mill himself seemed overly sanguine about the amount of real choice enjoyed, for example, by wage laborers in entering a trade. Yet Mill's analysis of marriage demonstrated the great complexity of establishing that any presumed agreement was the result of free volition, and the fatuousness of presuming that initial consent could create perpetual obligation. By implication, the legitimacy of many other relationships, including supposedly free wage and

labor agreements and the political obligation of enfranchised and un-
enfranchised alike, was thrown into question. *The Subjection of Women*
exposed the inherent fragility of traditional conceptualizations of free
choice, autonomy, and self-determination so important to liberals,
showing that economic and social structures were bound to limit and
might coerce any person's choice of companions, employment, or citizenship.

Mill did not despair of the possibility that marriages based on true
consent would be possible. He believed that some individuals even in his
own day established such associations of reciprocity and mutual support. (He counted his own relationship with Harriet Taylor Mill as an
example of a marriage between equals.)[19] But there were systemic im-
pediments to marital equality. To create conditions conducive to a marriage of equals rather than one of master and slave, marriage law itself
would have to be altered, women would have to be provided equal educational and employment opportunity, and both men and women
would have to become capable of sustaining genuinely equal and reciprocal relationships within marriage. The last of these, in Mill's eyes,
posed the greatest challenge.

II. The Fear of Equality

Establishing legal equality in marriage and equality of opportunity
would require, said Mill, that men sacrifice those political, legal, and
economic advantages they enjoyed "simply by being born male." Mill
therefore supported such measures as women's suffrage, the Married
Women's Property Bills, the Divorce Act of 1857, the repeal of the Contagious Diseases Acts, and the opening of higher education and the professions to women. Suffrage, Mill contended, would both develop
women's faculties through participation in civic decisions and enable
married women to protect themselves from male-imposed injustices
such as lack of rights to child custody and to control of their income. Access to education and jobs would give women alternatives to marriage.
It would also provide a woman whose marriage turned out badly some
means of self-support if separated or divorced. The Divorce Act of 1857,
which established England's first civil divorce courts, would enable
women and men to escape from intolerable circumstances (although

Mill rightly protested the sexual double standard ensconced in the Act).[20] And for those few women with an income of their own a Married Women's Property Act would recognize their independent personalities and enable them to meet their husbands more nearly as equals.

However, Mill's analysis went further. He insisted that the subjection of women could not be ended by law alone, but only by law and the reformation of education, of opinion, of social inculcation, of habits, and finally of the conduct of family life itself. This was so because the root of much of men's resistance to women's emancipation was not simply their reluctance to give up their position of material advantage, but many men's fear of living with an equal. It was to retain marriage as "a law of despotism" that men shut all other occupations to women, Mill contended (1: 156). Men who "have a real antipathy to the equal freedom of women" were at bottom afraid "lest [women] should insist that marriage be on equal conditions" (1: 156). One of Mill's startling assertions in *The Subjection of Women* was that "[women's] disabilities [in law] are only clung to in order to maintain their subordination in domestic life: *because the generality of the male sex cannot yet tolerate the idea of living with an equal*" (3: 181; italics added). The public discrimination against women was a manifestation of a disorder rooted in family relationships. The progression of humankind could not take place until the dynamics of the master-slave relationship were eliminated from marriages, and until the family was instead founded on spousal equality.

Mill did not offer any single explanation or account of the origin of men's fear of female equality. Elsewhere, he attributed the general human resistance to equality to the fear of the loss of privilege, and to apprehensions concerning the effect of leveling on political order.[21] But these passages on the fear of spousal equality bring to a twentieth-century mind the psychoanalytic works about human neuroses and the male fear of women caused by the infant boy's relationship to the seemingly all-powerful mother, source of both nurturance and love and of deprivation and punishment.[22] But it is impossible to push Mill's text far in this direction. His account of the fear of equality was not psychoanalytic. He did, however, undertake to depict the consequences of marital inequality both for the individual psyche and for social justice. The rhetorical purpose of *The Subjection of Women* was not only to convince men that their treatment of women in law was unjust, but also that their treatment of women in the home was self-defeating, even self-destructive.

Women were those most obviously affected by the denial of association with men on equal footing. Women's confinement to domestic
concerns was a wrongful "forced repression" (1: 148). Mill shared Aristotle's view that participation in civic life was enriching and ennobling
activity, but Mill saw that for a woman, no public-spirited dimension
to her life was possible. There was no impetus to consider with others
the principles which were to govern their common life, no incentive to
conform to principles which defined their mutual activity for the common good, no possibility for the self-development which comes from
citizen activity.[23] The cost to women was obvious; they were dull, or
petty, or unprincipled (2: 168; 4: 238). The cost to men was less apparent but no less real; in seeking a reflection of themselves in the consciousness of these stunted women, men deceived, deluded, and limited themselves.

Mill was convinced that men were corrupted by their dominance over
women. The most corrupting element of male domination of women
was that men learned to "worship their own will as such a grand thing
that it is actually the law for another rational being" (2: 172). Such self-
worship arises at a very tender age, and blots out a boy's natural understanding of himself and his relationship to others.

A boy may be "the most frivolous and empty or the most ignorant
and stolid of mankind," but "by the mere fact of being born a male" he
is encouraged to think that "he is by right the superior of all and every
one of an entire half of the human race: including probably some whose
real superiority he had daily or hourly occasion to feel" (4: 218). By contrast, women were taught "to live for others" and "to have no life but in
their affections," and then further to confine their affections to "the men
with whom they are connected or to the children who constitute an additional indefeasible tie between them and a man" (1: 141). The result of
this upbringing was that what women would tell men was not, could not
be, wholly true; women's sensibilities were systematically warped by
their subjection. Thus the reflections were not accurate and men were
deprived of self-knowledge.[24]

The picture which merged was strikingly similar to that which Hegel
described in his passages on the relationship between master and slave
in *The Phenomenology of Mind*.[25] The lord who sees himself solely as
master, wrote Hegel, cannot obtain an independent self-consciousness.
The master thinks he is autonomous, but in fact he relies totally upon

his slaves, not only to fulfill his needs and desires, but also for his identity: "Without slaves, he is no master." The master could not acquire the fullest self-consciousness when the "other" in whom he viewed himself was in the reduced human condition of slavery: to be *merely* a master was to fall short of full self-consciousness, and to define himself in terms of the "thing" he owns. So for Mill, men who have propagated the belief that all men are superior to all women have fatally affected the dialectic involved in knowing oneself through the consciousness others have of one. The present relationship between the sexes produced in men that "self-worship" which "all privileged persons, and all privileged classes" have had. That distortion deceives men and other privileged groups as to both their character and their self-worth.[26]

No philosopher prior to Mill had developed such a sustained argument about the corrupting effects on men of their social superiority over and separation from women. Previous philosophers had argued either that the authority of men over women was natural (Aristotle, Grotius), or that while there was no natural dominance of men over women prior to the establishment of families, in any civil society such preeminence was necessary to settle the dispute over who should govern the household (Locke), or the result of women's consent in return for protection (Hobbes), or the consequence of the development of the sentiments of nurturance and love (Rousseau).[27] None had suggested that domestic arrangements might diminish a man's ability to contribute to public debates in the agora or to the rational governing of a democratic republic. Yet Mill was determined to show that the development of the species was held in check by that domestic slavery produced by the fear of equality, by spousal hierarchy, and by a lack of the reciprocity and mutuality of true friendship.

III. The Hope of Friendship

Mill's remedy for the evils generated by the fear of equality was his notion of marital friendship. The topic of the rather visionary fourth chapter of *The Subjection of Women* was friendship, "the ideal of marriage" (4: 233, 235). That ideal was, according to Mill, "a union of thoughts and inclinations" which created a "foundation of solid friendship" between husband and wife (4: 231, 233).

Mill's praise of marital friendship was almost lyrical, and struck reso-
nance with Aristotle's, Cicero's, and Montaigne's similar exaltations of
the pleasures as well as the moral enrichment of this form of human intimacy. Mill wrote:

> When each of two persons, instead of being a nothing, is a something;
> when they are attached to one another, and are not much unlike to begin
> with; the constant partaking of the same things, assisted by their sympa-
> thy, draws out the latent capacities of each for being interested in the
> things . . . by a real enriching of the two natures, each acquiring the tastes
> and capacities of the other in addition to its own [4: 233].

This expansion of human capacities did not, however, exhaust the benefits
of friendship. Most importantly, friendship developed what Montaigne
praised as the abolition of selfishness, the capacity to regard another
human being as fully as worthy as oneself. Therefore friendship of the
highest order could only exist between those equal in excellence.[28] And for
precisely this reason, philosophers from Aristotle to Hegel had consistently
argued that women could not be men's friends, for women lacked the
moral capacity for the highest forms of friendship. Indeed, it was common
to distinguish the marital bond from friendship not solely on the basis of
sexual and procreative activity, but also because women could not be part
of the school of moral virtue which was found in friendship at its best.

Mill therefore made a most significant break with the past in adopting the language of friendship in his discussion of marriage. For Mill, no
less than for any of his predecessors, "the true virtue of human beings is
the fitness to live together as equals." Such equality required that individuals "[claim] nothing for themselves but what they as freely concede
to every one else," that they regard command of any kind as "an exceptional necessity," and that they prefer whenever possible "the society of
those with whom leading and following can be alternate and reciprocal"
(4: 174–175). This picture of reciprocity of the shifting of leadership according to need, was a remarkable characterization of family life. Virtually all of Mill's liberal contemporaries accepted the notion of the natural and inevitable complementariness of male and female personalities
and roles. Mill, however, as early as 1833 had expressed his belief that
"the highest masculine and the highest feminine" characters were without any real distinction.[29] That view of the androgynous personality lent
support to Mill's brief for equality within the family.

Mill repeatedly insisted that his society had no general experience of "the marriage relationship as it would exist between equals," and that such marriages would be impossible until men rid themselves of the fear of equality and the will to domination.[30] The liberation of women, in other words, required not just legal reform but a reeducation of the passions. Women were to be regarded as equals not only to fulfill the demand for individual rights and in order that they could survive in the public world of work, but also in order that women and men could form ethical relations of the highest order. Men and women alike had to "learn to cultivate their strongest sympathy with an equal in rights and in cultivation" (4: 236). Mill struggled, not always with total success, to talk about the quality of such association. For example, in *On Liberty*, Mill explicitly rejected von Humbolt's characterization of marriage as a contractual relationship which could be ended by "the declared will of either party to dissolve it." That kind of dissolution was appropriate when the benefits of partnership could be reduced to monetary terms. But marriage involved a person's expectations for the fulfillment of a "plan of life," and created "a new series of moral obligations . . . toward that person, which may possibly be overruled, but cannot be ignored."[31] Mill was convinced that difficult though it might be to shape the law to recognize the moral imperatives of such a relationship, there were ethical communities which transcended and were not reducible to their individual components.

At this juncture, however, the critical force of Mill's essay weakened, and a tension developed between his ideal and his prescriptions for his own society. For all his insight into the dynamics of domestic domination and subordination, the only specific means Mill in fact put forward for the fostering of this society of equals was providing equal opportunity to women in areas outside the family. Indeed, in *On Liberty* he wrote that "nothing more is needed for the complete removal of [the almost despotic power of husbands over wives] than that wives should have the same rights and should receive the same protection of law in the same manner, as all other persons."[32] In the same vein, Mill seemed to suggest that nothing more was needed for women to achieve equality than that "the present duties and protective bounties in favour of men should be recalled" (1: 154). Moreover, Mill did not attack the traditional assumption about men's and women's different responsibilities in an ongoing household, although he was usually careful to say that

women "chose" their role or that it was the most "expedient" arrangement, not that it was theirs by "nature."

Mill by and large accepted the notion that once they marry, women
should be solely responsible for the care of the household and children,
men for providing the family income: "When the support of the family
depends . . . on earnings, the common arrangement, by which the man
earns the income and the wife superintends the domestic expenditure,
seems to me in general the most suitable division of labour between the
two persons" (2: 178). He did not regard it as "a desirable custom, that
the wife should contribute by her labour to the income of the family" (2:
179). Mill indicated that women alone would care for any children of
the marriage; repeatedly he called it the "care which . . . nobody else
takes," the one vocation in which there is "nobody to compete with
them," and the occupation which "cannot be fulfilled by others" (2: 178;
3: 183; 4: 241). Further, Mill seemed to shut the door on combining
household duties and a public life: "like a man when he chooses a profession, so, when a woman marries, it may be in general understood that
she makes a choice of the management of a household, and the bringing up of a family, as the first call upon her exertions . . . and that she renounces . . . all [other occupations] which are not consistent with the requirements of this" (1: 179).

Mill's acceptance of the traditional gender-based division of labor in
the family has led some recent critics to fault Mill for supposing that
legal equality of opportunity would solve the problem of women's subjection, even while leaving the sexual division of labor in the household
intact. For example, Julia Annas, after praising Mill's theoretical arguments in support of equality, complains that Mill's suggestions for actual needed changes in sex roles are "timid and reformist at best. He assumes that most women will in fact want only to be wives and
mothers."[33] Leslie Goldstein agrees that "the restraints which Mill believed should be imposed on married women constitute a major exception to his argument for equality of individual liberty between the
sexes—an exception so enormous that it threatens to swallow up the entire argument."[34] But such arguments, while correctly identifying the
limitations of antidiscrimination statutes as instruments for social
change, incorrectly identify Mill's argument for equal opportunity as the
conclusion of his discussion of male-female equality.[35] On the contrary,
Mill's final prescription to end the subjection of women was not equal

opportunity but spousal friendship; equal opportunity was a means whereby such friendship could be encouraged.

The theoretical force of Mill's condemnation of domestic hierarchy has not yet been sufficiently appreciated. Mill's commitment to equality in marriage was of a different theoretical order than his acceptance of a continued sexual division of labor. On the one hand, Mill's belief in the necessity of equality as a precondition to marital friendship was a profound theoretical tenet. It rested on the normative assumption that human relationships between equals were of a higher, more enriching order than those between unequals. Mill's belief that equality was more suitable to friendship than inequality was as unalterable as his conviction that democracy was a better system of government than despotism; the human spirit could not develop its fullest potential when living in absolute subordination to another human being or to government.[36] On the other hand, Mill's belief that friendship could be attained and sustained while women bore nearly exclusive responsibility for the home was a statement which might be modified or even abandoned if experience proved it to be wrong. In this sense it was like Mill's view that the question of whether socialism was preferable to capitalism could not be settled by verbal argument alone but must "work itself out on an experimental scale, by actual trial."[37] Mill believed that marital equality was a moral imperative; his view that such equality might exist where married men and women moved in different spheres of activity was a proposition subject to demonstration. Had Mill discovered that managing the household to the exclusion of most other activity created an impediment to the friendship of married women and men, *The Subjection of Women* suggests that he would have altered his view of practicable domestic arrangements, but not his commitment to the desirability of male-female friendship in marriage.

The most interesting shortcomings of Mill's analysis are thus not found in his belief in the efficacy of equal opportunity, but rather in his blindness to what other conditions might hinder or promote marital friendship. In his discussion of family life, for example, Mill seemed to forget his own warning that women could be imprisoned not only "by actual law" but also "by custom equivalent to law" (4: 241). Similarly, he overlooked his own cautionary observation that in any household "there will naturally be more potential voice on the side, whichever it is, that brings the means of support" (2: 170). And although he had brilliantly depicted the narrowness and petty concerns of contemporary women who were totally excluded from political participation, he implied that the mistresses of most households might content themselves simply with exercising the suffrage (were it to be granted), a view hardly consistent with his arguments in other works for maximizing the level of political discussion and participation whenever possible. More significantly, however, Mill ignored the potential barrier between husband and wife which such different adult life experiences might create, and the contribution of shared experience to building a common sensibility and strengthening the bonds of friendship.

Mill also never considered that men might take any role in the family other than providing the economic means of support. Perhaps Mill's greatest oversight in his paean of marital equality was his failure to entertain the possibilities that nurturing and caring for children might provide men with useful knowledge and experience, and that shared parenting would contribute to the friendship between spouses which he so ardently desired. Similarly, Mill had virtually nothing to say about the positive role which sex might play in marriage. The sharp language with which he condemned undesired sexual relations as the execution of "an animal function" was nowhere supplemented by an appreciation of the possible enhancement which sexuality might add to marital friendship. One of the striking features of Montaigne's lyrical praise of friendship was that it was devoid of sensuality, for Montaigne abhorred "the Grecian license," and he was adamant that women were incapable of the highest forms of friendship. Mill's notion of spousal friendship suggested the possibility of a friendship which partook of both a true union of minds and of a physical expression of the delight in one's companion, a friendship which involved all of the human faculties. It was an opportunity which (undoubtedly to the relief of those such as James Fitzjames Stephen) Mill himself was not disposed to use, but which was nonetheless implicit in his praise of spousal friendship.[38]

One cannot ask Mill or any other theorist to "jump over Rhodes" and address issues not put forward by conditions and concerns of his own society.[39] Nevertheless, even leaving aside an analysis of the oppression inherent in the class structure (an omission which would have to be rectified in a full analysis of liberation), time has made it clear that Mill's prescriptions alone will not destroy the master-slave relationship which he so detested. Women's aspirations for equality will not be met by insuring equal civic rights and equal access to jobs outside the home. To accomplish that end would require a transformation of economic and public structures which would allow wives and husbands to share those domestic tasks which Mill assigned exclusively to women. Some forms of publicly supported day-care, parental as well as maternity leaves, flexible work schedules, extensive and rapid public transportation, health and retirement benefits for part-time employment are among commonly proposed measures which would make the choice of Mill's ideal of marriage between equals possible. In their absence it is as foolish to talk about couples choosing the traditional division of labor in marriage as it was in Mill's day to talk about women choosing marriage: both are Hobson's choices, there are no suitable alternatives save at enormous costs to the individuals involved.

Mill's feminist vision, however, transcends his own immediate prescriptions for reform. *The Subjection of Women* is not only one of liberalism's most incisive arguments for equal opportunity, but it embodies as well a belief in the importance of friendship for human development and progress. The recognition of individual right is important in Mill's view because it provides part of the groundwork for more important human relationships of trust, mutuality and reciprocity. Mill's plea for an end to the subjection of women is not made, as critics such as Gertrude Himmelfarb assert, in the name of "the absolute primacy of the individual," but in the name of the need of both men and women for community. Mill's essay is valuable both for its devastating critique of the corruption of marital inequality, and for its argument, however incomplete, that one of the aims of a liberal polity should be to promote the conditions which will allow friendship, in marriage and elsewhere, to take root and flourish.

NOTES

AUTHOR'S NOTE: I wish to thank Nannerl O. Keohane, Dennis F. Thompson, Eileen Sullivan, Ann Congleton, and Francis G. Hutchins for helpful comments on an earlier version of this article.

1. Contemporary authors who criticize Mill's analysis of equal opportunity for women as not far-reaching enough are Julia Annas, "Mill and the Subjection of Women," *Philosophy* 52 (1977), 179–194; Leslie F. Goldstein, "Marx and

Mill on the Equality of Women," paper presented at the Midwest Political Science Association Convention, Chicago, April 1978; Richard Krouse, "Patriarchal Liberalism and Beyond: From John Stuart Mill to Harriet Taylor," unpublished manuscript, Williamstown, MA; Susan Moller Okin, *Women in Western Political Thought* (Princeton: Princeton University Press, 1979). From a different perspective, Gertrude Himmelfarb, *On Liberty and Liberalism: the Case of John Stuart Mill* (New York: Alfred Knopf, 1974) criticizes Mill's doctrine of equality as being too absolute and particularly takes issue with modern feminist applications of his theory.

2. J. S. Mill, *The Subjection of Women* (1869) in Alice Rossi, ed., *Essays on Sex Equality* (Chicago: University of Chicago Press, 1970), ch. 2, p. 173. All references to *The Subjection of Women* will be to this edition and will be given in the body of the text using chapter and page, i.e., (2: 173).

3. Hansard, *Parliamentary Debates*, series 3, v. 189 (May 20, 1867), p. 820.

4. Letter to Auguste Comte, October, 1843, *The Collected Works of John Stuart Mill* (hereafter *C. W.*), v. XIII, *The Earlier Letters*, ed. Francis C. Mineka (Toronto: University of Toronto Press, 1963), p. 609, my translation.

5. Mill's analysis of women's choice of marriage as a state of life reminds one of Hobbes' discussion of some defeated soldier giving his consent to the rule of a conquering sovereign. Women, it is true, could decide which among several men to marry, while Hobbes' defeated yeoman had no choice of master. But what could either do but join the only protective association available to each?

6. A brief account of the struggle to provide for women's higher education in England can be found in Ray Strachey, *The Cause* (London: G. Bell, 1928), pp. 124–165.

7. Hansard, v. 189 (May 20, 1867).

8. *Idem.* In the United States, one well-documented case in which a woman was prohibited from practicing law was *Bradwell v. Illinois* 83 U.S. (16 Wall) 130 (1873).

9. *The Principles of Political Economy* (1848) in *C. W.* II, p. 394 and III, pp. 765–766.

10. Tobias Hobson, a Cambridge carrier commemorated by Milton in two Epigraphs, would only hire out the horse nearest the door of his stable, even if a client wanted another. *Oxford English Dictionary*, II, pp. 369.

11. William Blackstone, *Commentaries on the Laws of England* 4 vols. (Oxford: Clarendon Pres, 1765–1769), Book I, ch. XV, p. 430. The consequences of the doctrine of spousal unity were various: a man could not make a contract with his wife since "to covenant with her would be to covenant with himself"; a wife could not sue without her husband's concurrence; a husband was bound to "provide his wife with necessaries . . . as much as himself"; a husband was re-

sponsible for certain criminal acts of his wife committed in his presence; and, as a husband was responsible for his wife's acts, he "might give his wife moderate correction . . . in the same moderation that (he is) allowed to correct his apprentices or children."

12. The rich found ways around the common law's insistence that the management and use of any income belong to a woman's husband, by setting up trusts which were governed by the laws and courts of equity. A succinct explanation of the law of property as it affected married women in the nineteenth century is found in Erna Reiss, *Rights and Duties of Englishwomen* (Manchester, 1934), pp. 20–34.

13. Hansard, v. 192 (June 10, 1867), p. 1371. Several Married Women's Property Bills, which would have given married women possession of their earnings were presented in Parliament beginning in 1857, but none was successful until 1870.

14. *Ibid.*, v. 189 (May 20, 1867), p. 826.

15. Mill's outrage at women's lack of recourse in the face of domestic violence is reminiscent of the protests in the United States during the civil rights movement at token sentences pronounced by white juries against whites accused of assaulting Blacks in Southern states, and of Susan Brownmiller's argument in *Against Our Will: Men, Women and Rape*, that the desultory prosecution of rapists is itself a manifestation of violence against women.

16. John Ruskin, "Of Queen's Gardens," in *Works*, ed. E. T. Cook and A. D. C. Wedderburn, 39 vols. (London: G. Allen, 1902–1912), XVIII, p. 122.

17. Walter E. Houghton, *The Victorian Frame of Mind* (New Haven: Yale University Press, 1957), p. 344.

18. James Fitzjames Stephen, *Liberty, Equality, Fraternity* (New York: Henry Holt, n. d.), p. 206.

19. On the relationship between John Stuart Mill and Harriet Taylor see F. A. Hayek, *John Stuart Mill and Harriet Taylor: Their Correspondence and Subsequent Marriage* (Chicago: University of Chicago Press, 1951); Michael St. John Packe, *The Life of John Stuart Mill* (New York: Macmillan, 1954); Alice Rossi, "Sentiment and Intellect" in *Essays on Sex Equality* (Chicago: University of Chicago Press, 1970); and Gertrude Himmelfarb, pp. 187–238.

20. The Matrimonial Causes Act of 1857, as the divorce measure was known, allowed men to divorce their wives for adultery, but women had to establish that their husbands were guilty of either cruelty or desertion in addition to adultery in order to obtain a separation. Mill was reluctant to say what he thought the terms of divorce should be in a rightly ordered society (see note 31), but he was adamant that the double standard was wrong in policy and unjust in principle.

Mill also spoke out sharply against that sexual double standard in his testimony before the Commission studying the repeal of the Contagious Diseases

Act, an act which allowed for the arrest and forced hospitalization of prostitutes with venereal disease, but made no provision for the arrest of their clients. "The Evidence of John Stuart Mill taken before the Royal Commission of 1870 on the Administration and Operation of the Contagious Diseases Acts of 1866 and 1869" (London, 1871).

21. For a discussion of Mill's views on equality generally, see Dennis Thompson, *John Stuart Mill and Representative Government* (Princeton: Princeton University Press, 1976), pp. 158–173.

22. See, for example, Dorothy Dinnerstein, *The Mermaid and the Minotaur: Sexual Arrangements and Human Malaise* (New York: Harper and Row, 1976); Nancy Chodorow, *The Reproduction of Mothering: Psychoanalysis and the Sociology of Gender* (Berkeley: University of California Press, 1978); and Philip Slater, *The Glory of Hera* (Boston: Beacon Press, 1971) and the references therein.

23. See also Mill's *Considerations on Representative Government* (1861) where he lambasted benevolent despotism because it encouraged "passivity" and "abdication of [one's] own energies," and his praise of the Athenian dicastry and ecclesia. *C. W.*, XIX, pp. 399–400, 411. During his speech on the Reform Bill of 1867, Mill argued that giving women the vote would provide "that stimulus to their faculties . . . which the suffrage seldom fails to produce." Hansard, v. 189 (May 20, 1867), 824.

24. Mill's insight was like that which Virginia Woolf used in *A Room of One's Own*. Woolf, trying to explain the source of men's anger at independent women, stated that such anger could not be "merely the cry of wounded vanity"; it had to be "a protest against some infringement of his power to believe in himself." Women have served throughout history as "looking glasses possessing the magic and delicious power of reflecting the figure of a man at twice its natural size." Mill also argued that in order to create such a mirror, men had distorted women by education and had warped the reflection which women showed to men. Virginia Woolf, *A Room of One's* Own (New York: Harcourt Brace and World, 1929), p. 35.

25. G. W. F. Hegel, *The Phenomenology of Mind*, trans. J. B. Baillie (New York: Harper and Row, 1969). This paragraph is indebted to the excellent study of the *Phenomenology* by Judith N. Shklar, *Freedom and Independence* (Cambridge: Cambridge University Press, 1976), from which the quote is taken, p. 61. Mill's analysis also calls to mind Simone de Beauvoir's discussion of "the Other" and its role in human consciousness in *The Second Sex*, trans. H. M. Parshley (New York: Random House, Vintage Books, 1974), pp. xix ff.

26. Mill argued in addition that men's injustices to women created habits which encouraged them to act unjustly towards others. In *The Subjection of Women* Mill asserted that the habits of domination are acquired in and fostered by the family, which is often, as respects its chief, "a school of willfulness, over-

bearingness, unbounded self-indulgence, and a double-dyed and idealized self-ishness" (2: 165). Virtue, for Mill, was not simply action taken in accordance with a calculus of pleasure and pain, but was habitual behavior. In *Considerations on Representative Government*, he lamented the effects "fostered by the possession of power" by "a man, or a class of men" who "finding themselves worshipped by others . . . become worshipers of themselves." *C. W.* XIX, p. 445.

27. For excellent studies of each of these authors' views on women (except for Grotius) see Okin. Grotius' views can be found in his *De Juri Belli ac Pacis Libri Tres* [*On the Law of War and Peace.*] (1625), trans. Francis W. Kelsey (Oxford: Clarendon Press, 1925), Bk. II, ch. V, sec. i, p. 231.

28. Montaigne's essay, "Of Friendship" in *The Complete Works of Montaigne*, trans. Donald M. Rame (Stanford: Stanford University Press, 1948), pp. 135–144.

29. Letter to Thomas Carlyle, October 5, 1833, *C. W.* XII, *Earlier Letters*, p. 184.

30. Letter to John Nichol, August 1869, *C. W.* XVII, *The Later Letters*, ed. Francis C. Mineka and Dwight N. Lindley (Toronto: University of Toronto Press, 1972), p. 1634.

31. *C. W.*, XVIII, 300. Elsewhere Mill wrote, "My opinion on Divorce is that . . . nothing ought to be rested in, short of entire freedom on both sides to dissolve this like any other partnership." Letter to an unidentified correspondent, November 1855, *C. W.* XIV, *Later Letters*, p. 500. But against this letter was the passage from *On Liberty*, and his letter to Henry Rusden of July 1870 in which he abjured making any final judgments about what a proper divorce law would be "until women have an equal voice in making it." He denied that he advocated that marriage should be dissoluble "at the will of either party," and stated that no well-grounded opinion could be put forward until women first achieved equality under the laws and in married life. *C. W.*, XVII, *Later Letters*, pp. 1750–1751.

32. *C. W.*, XVIII, p. 301.

33. Annas, 189.

34. Goldstein, p. 8. Susan Okin makes a similar point, stating that "Mill never questioned or objected to the maintenance of traditional sex roles within the family, but expressly considered them to be suitable and desirable" (Okin, p. 237). Okin's reading of Mill is basically sound and sympathetic, but does not recognize the theoretical priority of Mill's commitment to marital equality and friendship.

35. Of recent writers on Mill, only Richard Krouse seems sensitive to the inherent tension in Mill's thought about women in the household. Mill's own "ideal of a reformed family life, based upon a full nonpartriarchal marriage bond," Krouse points out, requires "on the logic of his own analysis . . . [the] rejection of the traditional division of labor between the sexes" (Krouse, p. 39).

36. *Considerations on Representative Government, C. W.*, XIX, pp. 399–403.

37. *Chapters on Socialism* (1879), *C. W.*, V, p. 736.

38. Throughout his writings Mill displayed a tendency to dismiss or depre-cate the erotic dimension of life. In his *Autobiography* he wrote approvingly that his father looked forward to an increase in freedom in relations between the sexes, freedom which would be devoid of any sensuality "either of a theoretical or of a practical kind." His own twenty-year friendship with Harriet Taylor be-fore their marriage was "one of strong affection and confidential intimacy only." *Autobiography of John Stuart Mill* (New York: Columbia University Press, 1944), pp. 75, 161. In *The Principles of Political Economy* Mill remarked that in his own day "the animal instinct" occupied a "disproportionate preponderance in human life," *C. W.*, III, p. 766.

39. G. W. F. Hegel, *The Philosophy of Right*, ed. T. M. Knox (London: Oxford University Press, 1952), p. 11, quoted in Krouse, p. 40.

Mary Lyndon Shanley is Assistant Professor of Political Science at Vassar College. She has published articles in Social Science Quarterly, Polity, Western Political Quarterly, *and* Signs. *Her current research deals with nineteenth-century English laws regarding women and the family.*

8

The Marriage of True Minds

The Ideal of Marriage in the Philosophy of John Stuart Mill

Susan Mendus

Mendus argues that The Subjection of Women is not only a political tract, but a moral one, inextricably tied to Mill's views on the human good. Mendus's account of Mill's ideal of marriage is critically different from Lyndon Shanley's. Mendus contends that Mill viewed marriage as an intellectual union and that his focus on marriage as a locus of perfectibility betrays a deeply problematic, because distorted, conception of human sexuality as "lower" and "animal." On Mendus's interpretation, Mill's commitment to replacing barbarism with civilization in marriage is a commitment to replacing sexuality with intellectual and spiritual perfection. What renders The Subjection of Women "radical" from one perspective renders it, overall, "morally depressing." Yet this depressing intellectualism, in Mendus's view, is not limited to his views on marriage but a feature of Mill's liberalism generally.

TRUE TO MY WELSH BAPTIST UPBRINGING, I begin with the text—taken from 'the crudest and most illogical' work which the Victorian age produced; a work that rests upon 'an unsound view of history, an unsound view of morals, and a grotesquely distorted view of facts'; a work whose 'practical application would be as injurious as its theory is false'; a work 'unpleasant in the direction of indecorum'; a work, finally, of 'rank moral and social anarchy'.[1] The work is John Stuart Mill's *The Subjection of Women*, and the text is this:

> what marriage may be in the case of two persons of cultivated faculties, identical in opinions and purposes, between whom there exists that best

kind of equality, similarity of powers and capacities with reciprocal supe-riority in them—so that each can enjoy the luxury of looking up to the other, and can have alternately the pleasure of leading and of being led in the path of development—I will not attempt to describe. To those who can conceive it, there is no need; to those who cannot, it would appear the dream of an enthusiast. But I maintain, with the profoundest conviction, that this, and this only, is the ideal of marriage, and that all opinions, cus-toms and institutions which favour any other notion of it, or turn the con-ceptions and aspirations connected with it into any other direction, by whatever pretences they may be coloured, are relics of primitive bar-barism.[2]

Resounding as anything ever uttered from a Welsh pulpit, this is Mill's positive thesis in *The Subjection of Women*: that marriage, properly un-derstood, is the marriage of minds and not of flesh. Throughout the book his main task is a negative one—to deny the prevailing view of women as naturally unequal and inferior to men—and it is this attempt to argue against the legal inequality of women which generated such high emotion in Mill's own day and which accounts for the greater part of modern interest in the book. In this paper I shall not add to the growing literature on Mill's views on legal inequality between the sexes; it is clear what Mill is *against*. He is against the requirement, embodied in Victo-rian law, that women renounce independence on marriage and submit to the domination of the husband. The scope and extent of women's de-pendence on their husbands in nineteenth-century Britain cannot easily be exaggerated. Legally, women did not count as persons and were not possessors of property. In her book, *Wives and Property*, Lee Holcombe tells how Millicent Garrett Fawcett had her purse snatched by a young thief in London. When she appeared to testify against him, she heard the youth charged with 'stealing from the person of Millicent Fawcett a purse containing £1 18s. 6d., the property of Henry Fawcett.' Long afterwards she recalled, 'I felt as if I had been charged with theft myself'.[3] The legal requirements governing the situation of married women—their inability to possess property, to vote, to obtain divorce except in the most extreme cases—served to make a woman, in Mill's words, 'the bond-servant' of her husband. She became his slave, except that by contrast with other slaves, 'no amount of ill-usage, without adultery superadded, will free her from her tormentor'.[4] Mill's impassioned invective against Victorian marriage and property laws as they relate to women is important and timely, but it often serves to disguise the fact that *The Subjection of Women* also suggests a positive thesis of what marriage ideally should be. What I wish to do here is to concentrate on this positive thesis. I shall suggest that *The Subjection of Women* is not only a political, legal, and social tract, but also a profoundly *moral* one, central to which are evaluative theses about human nature and the life worth living. My argument will be that Mill is not only the rejecter of Victorian images of women, he is also the creator of an alternative image, and I shall argue that the image he creates is a deeply depressing and distorted one. In brief, my claim will be that Mill employs his text both to object to the legal subordination of women in nineteenth-century Britain, and also to display his own deep-rooted prejudices on the subject of sexuality.

The Status of the Text

In her highly influential article, 'Mill and the subjection of women', Julia Annas remarks on the fact that philosophical commentaries tend to give Mill's essay rather short measure. She attributes this to the belief that the essay is almost exclusively concerned with women's legal disabilities in Victorian Britain. Taking such commentators to task, Annas points out that legal disabilities reflect social and economic inequalities, and she argues that

> while today there are few ways in which women are under legal disabilities compared with men (though it would be a mistake to think there are none) women are still subject to economic and social discrimination in a variety of ways, and it is extraordinary to think that Mill's essay no longer contains anything interesting or controversial just because there have been a few changes in the law.[5]

This is an important and much-neglected point, but it disguises a curious feature shared both by Annas's article and by the works of the commentators she criticizes: throughout there is an insistence on treating the essay as *sui generis*, relevant no doubt to Mill's activities as a politician and social reformer, but largely unconnected to the wider concerns of his moral philosophy. The impression is of a man with a substantive political belief (that existing sexual inequalities were unjustifiable) and in search of an argument to support that belief.

There is, however, no suggestion that Mill's positive thesis about marriage coheres with the moral doctrines he expounds elsewhere. Thus Annas concludes her piece with the clam that Mill, 'anxious to do justice to all sides of a question he sees to be complex and important, and unwilling to commit himself definitively to one simple line of thought, qualifies an originally bold and straightforward theory to the point of inconsistency.'[6] What is implied here is that Mill simply chose the wrong arguments, but that he could have chosen the right ones. It seems to me, however, that Mill can do no other than he does: if his account is confused and contradictory, then that verdict will have consequences for the whole of his philosophy, and it is simply untrue that he might have got it right if only he had thought more carefully. Where Annas insists that *The Subjection of Women* is not merely an account of legal disabilities, but a piece of social philosophy, I want to insist that it is not merely a piece of social philosophy, but a moral text which coheres in a disturbing manner with Mill's other moral writings. If the argument against legal inequality is central to his political thought, the argument for the ideal of marriage as a marriage of true minds is central to his moral thought and is the inevitable consequence of pursuing that thought to its logical conclusion.

The Ideal of Marriage in Mill's Philosophy

The first move is to establish exactly what Mill's ideal of marriage is. The ideal is stated explicitly in the passage quoted from chapter 4 of *The Subjection of Women*, and what I wish to draw attention to in that passage are the references to the 'path of development' and 'reciprocal superiority.' These terms obviously express Mill's hostility to the Victorian conception of marriage as a partnership based on inequality. However, it seems to me that this is not its only, nor its most significant, import: in addition to objecting to the Victorian requirement that, on marrying, the woman give up her independence and submit to the domination of her husband, Mill is also here proposing an alternative, moral ideal according to which marriage is a route to moral perfection. In the passage immediately following the one quoted at the beginning of the paper, Mill declares that justice under law is required in the interests of moral regeneration. The reason for insisting on legal equality is that this is a necessary precondition of moral improvement, and it is the possibility of moral improvement which really interests Mill. Central to his vision are two notions, explicit in the passage quoted earlier and, I shall argue, fundamental to his moral thought: these are the notions of perfectibility and of complementarity.

Perfectibility

The notion of perfectibility, and its role in Mill's philosophical thought, may be approached via a discussion of two related problems—the problem of two Mills, and the problem of the interpretation of Mill's account of freedom. Each of these has a bearing on Mill's concept of perfectibility, and each indicates how central that concept is to his moral philosophy. I begin, therefore, with the problem of two Mills.

The Problem of Two Mills

The story of Mill's early life and education, his rigorous drilling in Greek, Latin, logic, and history, is well known and does not need repeating here: Mill himself says, 'I never was a boy, never played at cricket: it is better to let nature have her way.'[7] Some have suggested that nature did, after all, have her way, for when he was in his early twenties Mill suffered a 'mental crisis', as a result of which he says: 'I found the fabric of my old and taught opinions giving way in many places, and I never allowed it to fall to pieces, but was incessantly occupied in weaving it anew.'[8]

Here are the seeds of the problem of two Mills. To what extent may the later writings be construed as a rejection of his early, Benthamite utilitarian teaching, and to what extent may they be viewed merely as revisions and refinements of the early works? Mill himself appears to be in no doubt. His references to weaving anew the old fabric, and his claim that he never allowed the old to fail to pieces, suggest quite strongly that he saw himself as remolding Benthamite utilitarianism, but never rejecting it. However, some commentators have denied that this can in fact be done, and they claim that the later writings, particularly those written under the influence of Harriet Taylor, are simply incompatible with the earlier Benthamite doctrines. There are, in other words, two Mills. I shall not here discuss the relative merits of the two Mills thesis, nor shall I spend time counting the number of Mills present in the texts. All that matters for my purposes is that there are, on any account, differences between the earlier and the later doctrines. Mill himself admits as much, and it is, I think, instructive to consider the nature and extent of these differences, since they bear upon the problem of perfectibility which is the immediate topic of concern here.

Three aspects of the distinction between Benthamite utilitarianism and Mill's mature moral and political philosophy are relevant:

1. his explicit objections to Bentham, as given in his essay on Bentham;
2. his distinction between higher and lower pleasures, as stated in *Utilitarianism*;
3. his distinction between animal and human characteristics, described in *A System of Logic*.

In his essay on Bentham, Mill tells us that for Bentham 'man is never recognised . . . as a being capable of pursuing spiritual perfection as an end; of desiring for its own sake the conformity of his own character to his standard of excellence'.[9] Against this, Mill insists that morality consists of two parts—the regulation of outward action, and the individual's own training of himself, his own character, affections, and will. In this latter department, Mill says, Bentham's system is a complete blank. Indeed, he goes further and suggests that even the regulation of outward actions will be imperfect and halting without consideration of excellence of character. Thus he concludes:

> A moralist on Bentham's principles may get as far as this, that he ought not to slay, burn or steal; but what will be his qualifications for regulating the nicer shades of human behaviour, or for laying down even the greater moralities as to those facts of human life which are liable to influence the depths of the character quite independently of any influence on worldly circumstances—such, for instance, as the sexual relations, or those of family in general, or any other social and sympathetic connexions of an intimate kind? The moralities on these questions depend essentially on considerations which Bentham never so much as took into the account; and when he happened to be in the right, it was always, and necessarily, on wrong or insufficient grounds.[10]

The message here is perfectly clear: Bentham's shortcoming lies in his persistent reference only to external actions—to what are basically police matters. On questions of human excellence and of human character, his philosophy is bankrupt. The fact that he simply took desires as brute—to be satisfied wherever possible, but never to be improved, refined, or made more noble—is, according to Mill, the great defect of his moral philosophy. Mill talks of Bentham as a man with only one eye: he saw a certain part of the truth, and is to be commended for that part which he saw. However, this fact should not blind us to the omissions in Bentham's writings, which render his account inadequate. It is important to note here that the areas in which Bentham is held to be particularly culpable are those of sexual relations and the family. What is crucial about these aspects of life is that they are areas where public action is not necessarily or normally in evidence, yet at the same time they are precisely the areas where excellence of character may be found and developed. Here, then, in the essay on Bentham, we find an indication of the differences between the early and the later Mill. Where Benthamite utilitarianism differs from Mill's own favoured version it is in the failure of the former to make reference to that perfectibility of character essential to the latter.

References to the notion of perfectibility are scattered throughout Mill's writings. For example, *Utilitarianism* contains references to a now notorious distinction between higher and lower pleasures: mindful of the criticism that utilitarianism is the philosophy of swine, Mill urges that this criticism is well founded only if we assume that the pleasures of men are indistinguishable from the pleasures of swine. This, he declares, is not so: it is, famously,

> better to be a human being dissatisfied than a pig satisfied; better to be Socrates dissatisfied than a fool satisfied. And if the fool, or the pig, are of a different opinion, it is because they only know their own side of the question. The other party to the comparison knows both sides.[11]

In the passage immediately following the one just quoted, Mill goes on to warn that 'capacity for the nobler feelings is in most natures a very tender plant, easily killed, not only by hostile influences, but by mere want of sustenance.'[12] Here, the teleological imputations of Mill's thought are clear: human nature may flourish if properly nurtured, but otherwise will wither away and die. Part of the purpose of moral philosophy—the part almost wholly ignored by Bentham—is to say something about the proper conditions for human flourishing and the development of excellence. We must not suppose that morality consists exclusively in the satisfaction of wants, for want may be better or worse, higher or lower, and utilitarianism will indeed degenerate into the philosophy of swine if we forget the requirements of perfectibility and the cultivation of excellence. If all this is borne in mind, the question which now arises is 'In what does human excellence consist?' We have seen that Mills is concerned to argue for the importance of moral excellence and the development of nobler feelings. How, then, are we to judge which are the nobler feelings and which the baser?

An indication of the response to this question is provided in *A System of Logic*, where Mill makes two points crucial to the present discussion. First, he claims that man is a natural kind separated from the kind animal by the specific determinants of rationality and having a certain external form. Natural kinds which reflect specific distinctions in this way are, says Mill, 'parted off from one another by an unfathomable chasm, instead of a mere ordinary ditch with a visible bottom'.[13] Of course, man shares characteristics with animals, but in respect of that which makes man mankind, these characteristics (rationality and having a certain external form) are central. The second crucial point which concerns us is Mill's insistence in *A System of Logic* that the sciences of human nature and society are distinguished by the fact that their subject-matter is changeable:

> The circumstances in which mankind are placed, operating according to their own laws and to the laws of human nature, form the characters of the human beings; but the human beings, in their turn, mould and shape the circumstances for themselves and for those who come after them.[14]

Putting these two together, we might expect Mill to argue that human progress and perfectibility will consist in the development of the human (as against the animal) characteristics. Having made the distinction between what is merely animal and what is essentially human, and having urged that the central feature of the science of human nature is that it deals with a pliable subject-matter, Mill is well placed to argue that the perfectibility of character ignored by Bentham consists precisely in fostering and encouraging the human, while minimizing the animal. And this is indeed his claim. In *Principles of Political Economy* he goes so far as to assert that 'Civilisation in very one of its aspects is a struggle against the animal instincts' and that 'society is possible precisely because man is not necessarily a brute'.[15] What, then, are these animal instincts and brutish impulses which must be guarded against if civilization is to advance? Chief among them is the sexual impulse, and time and again we find Mill speaking of this as 'brutish', 'swinish', 'lower'. Referring to his relationship with Harriet Taylor, Mill remarks:

> we disdained, as every person not a slave of the animal appetites must do, the abject notion that the strongest and tenderest friendship cannot exist between a man and a woman without a sensual relation, or that any impulse of that lower character cannot be put aside without regard for the feelings of others, or even when only prudence and personal dignity require it.[16]

His references to sexuality as 'lower' and 'animal' are, however, not confined to the rather personal (and understandably defensive) passages in which he discusses his relationship with Mrs. Taylor. In a letter to Lord Amberley he declares that the possibility of progress depends upon the reduction of sexuality, and that no great improvement in human life can be looked for so long as 'the animal instinct of sex occupies the absurdly disproportionate place it does therein'.[17] Likewise, in *Principles of Political Economy* he speaks of sex as 'a degrading slavery to a brute instinct' and calls upon the existence of impulses 'superior to mere animal instincts' to ensure that men do not 'propagate like swine'.[18] In all these cases Mill urges that there is a distinction between human and animal characteristics and suggests that man's animality is lower than his humanity, and that his animality can and should be suppressed. It is important to note here that, in urging the suppression of the sexual impulse, Mill is not merely appealing to Benthamite considerations such as that too large a population will flood the market with labour and result in poverty: consequentialist arguments of that sort do not require that sexuality be considered 'lower', or 'swinish', or 'brutish', yet what is central to Mill's case is precisely the claim that the sexually incontinent not only harm others, by flooding the market with labour, but also harm their own characters, much as the drunkard harms his own character quite independently of any consequentialist harm he visits on others.[19]

I began by asking how we can know what, for Mill, constitutes the better, higher, or nobler. The answer is that the distinction between the higher and the lower is premised on a distinction between human and animal characteristics, with sexual impulses and instincts firmly consigned to the latter category. This distinction is set against the background of Mill's objections to Bentham as neglecting considerations of spiritual perfection and self-education. Mill's post-Benthamite moral philosophy may thus be read as an extended argument for self-improvement and the rejection of what is purely animal—in particular, the suppression of all that is sexual or physical. Since the animal characteristics simply are what they are, and are incapable of being refined or developed in any way, it follows that Mill's rejection of sex is a natural and unavoidable consequence of his philosophical thought. His conception of marriage is properly the path of development, the route by which capacities may be refined and the nobler feelings cultivated, is characteristic of and essential to all his thought.

So far, I have said something about the problem of two Mills—about the ways in which Mill's moral philosophy differs from Bentham's, and about the consequences that appears to have for Mill's view of marriage—but earlier in the paper I said that the notion of perfectibility was associated with two problems in Mill's philosophy. The first of these is the problem of the distinctions and differences between Mill's earlier and later thought. The second, associated, problem is that of the compatibility between the notion of perfection, or moral self-education, and Mill's championship of the cause of liberty in his essay *On Liberty*. I turn now, therefore, to this second problem.

Freedom

Mill's commitment to the possibility of human development and self-improvement is not an unmixed blessing. While it might serve to distinguish his moral philosophy from 'the philosophy of swine', it also carries with it the implication that freedom is merely an instrumental good, to be allowed when and in so far as it will contribute to human advancement. The passage from *The Subjection of Women*, quoted at the beginning of the paper, reinforces the suspicion that Mill's commitment is simply to freedom as an instrumental good, for he tells us there that ideals of marriage distinct from his own are 'relics of primitive barbarism', and this suggests quite strongly that he believes that ultimately barbarism will give way to civilization and sexuality will yield to intellect. However, if this is Mill's view in *The Subjection of Women*, then it appears to be quite at odds with his stated position in his essay *On Liberty*. *On Liberty* is standardly seen as Mill's *tour de force* against the tyranny of the majority and in favour of unbridled individuality, even eccentricity. The motto of the essay is Wilhelm von Humboldt's statement that 'the grand, leading principle towards which every argument unfolded in these pages directly converges, is the absolute and essential importance of human development *in its richest diversity*'.

Appeal to diversity is omnipresent in the pages of *On Liberty*; again and again Mill inveighs against the tyranny of public opinion, against the despotism of custom, and against 'the Chinese ideal of making all people alike'.[20] Yet, we may ask, would he not himself make all people alike by insisting on this one true ideal of marriage and by dismissing as barbaric all other ideals? Crudely put, Mill's problem is this: if he thinks freedom an intrinsic good—a good in itself—then he must allow that people may express their freedom by subscribing to ideals of marriage contrary to his own. (They may, for example, genuinely believe that marriage is an institution whose purpose is to ensure regular and reliable sexual gratification. Far from leading them to reject this ideal, freedom may simply serve to encourage it.) On the other hand, if Mill thinks that freedom is an instrumental good, justified by its contribution to human advancement and improvement, then he must allow that certain freedoms are impermissible, namely those freedoms which do not in fact contribute to human advancement and improvement. One thing seems certain—he cannot have it both ways. Or can he? Two preliminary points need to be made here.

First, the earlier discussion has shown only Mill's belief in human development, and, as the quote from von Humboldt illustrates, nothing in that entails commitment to uniformity. Indeed, in *On Liberty*, Mill implies quite the reverse when he says:

> there is no reason at all that human existence should be constructed on some one or some small number of patterns. If a person possesses any tolerable amount of common sense and experience, his own mode of laying out his existence is best, not because it is the best in itself, but because it is his own mode. Human beings are not like sheep, and even sheep are not indistinguishably alike.[21]

So from the belief in human development nothing follows about conformity or uniformity. The analogy between human flourishing and the flourishing of plants in nature is instructive here. There may be no more reason why two different persons should flourish in the same moral climate than why the daffodil and the orchid should flourish in the same physical climate. (I shall return to this point later.)

Second, even if Mill is in fact (though not in logic) committed to a single ideal of marriage, he need not be committed to the diminution of freedom involved in the forcible imposition of that ideal: marriage for the purpose of sexual gratification is indeed ignoble, base, and dehumanizing, but barbarians must be allowed to wallow in their own barbarism.

So Mill's belief in development does not entail a single ideal, and even if he in fact subscribes to a single ideal he is not thereby committed to the legitimacy of forcibly imposing the ideal. However, even if his thesis does not lead him to a single ideal, it does nevertheless rule out a substantial number of ideals. In particular, his distinction between higher and lower pleasures, based on the contrast between human and animal characteristics, rules out the possibility of construing marriage as primarily a sexual relationship. Perhaps we are not compelled to think of marriage as the marriage of intellects, but we must not think of it as the marriage of bodies. Anyone who did think of it in this way would be like the fool who prefers pushpin to poetry or like the pig satisfied with his swinish pleasures. Of this Mill is in no doubt, and he tells us that 'one of the deepest seated and most pervading evils in the human mind is the perversion of the imagination and feelings resulting from dwelling on the physical relation and its adjuncts.'[22] But this is a problematic conclusion for Mill: if there is a correct ideal of marriage (as he clearly thinks there is), and if failure to embrace this ideal constitutes a pervading evil and a perversion (as he clearly thinks it does), then why freedom? For it is hard to see what the positive value of freedom could be where freedom is only freedom to submit to one's animal instincts. Mill may think that barbarians should be allowed to wallow in their barbarism, but it could hardly be a virtue to allow them to do so. In brief, what justifies construing freedom as a virtue is Mill's optimism. Throughout the whole of his writings he displays a touching faith in the propensity of individuals to seek their own self-development and improvement. Hence his claim that 'the only unfailing and permanent source of improvement is liberty, since by it there are as many possible independent centres of improvement as there are individuals.'[23] Commitment to human perfectibility is commonly associated not with liberal political theories of the sort Mill espoused, but with authoritarian, even totalitarian, theories according to which any amount of interference with individual liberty is justified simply by appealing to subsequent gratitude for improvement. Mill escapes the authoritarian implications of his own writings only by coupling a belief in human perfectibility with optimism about human nature. This is most clearly seen in his views on population policy, where he envisages that men and women (but particularly men) will gradually refine their feelings to a point where affinity of intellect and taste will replace sexual passion as the main impulse to marriage. Population policy will not be needed, as people will come to see for themselves that abstinence is superior to sex, just as the wise man sees that poetry is superior to pushpin. As Geoffrey Smith puts it in a recent article:

> Mill simply takes it for granted most of the time that—at least in the long run and for the great majority of people—a policy of tolerance, encouragement of social variety and concerned, non-coercive intervention will trigger, not any arbitrary range of self-regarding desires, but a very specific desire: that for individual self-improvement.[24]

In the case of marriage, the desire for self-improvement will issue in the recognition of the true ideal of marriage as a marriage of minds. For there can be no self-improvement without the recognition of this, but only a slow decline into animality and sensuality.

I began by pointing to a tension between Mill's belief in individual freedom and his belief in perfectibility, and I asked whether he could have it both ways. The burden of the preceding discussion is to suggest that, in a sense, Mill can have it both ways: he can resist the authoritarian implications of the belief in human improvement and cling on to the ideal of freedom as an intrinsic good if, and only if, he is willing to adopt an optimistic view of human nature, according to which freedom and perfectibility are inextricably linked. And he is (in general) prepared to adopt such a view, stating that 'the only unfailing and permanent source of improvement is liberty'. But, even if Mill can reconcile the apparently conflicting claims of freedom and perfectibility, he is still left with the problem of diversity. Von Humboldt had advocated the essential importance of human development *in all its richest diversity*. But, if freedom and development can be made to march together, then they appear to march not towards diversity but towards uniformity—towards a single ideal of marriage which is intellectual, refined, and largely asexual. If there is human development, and if people are free, then, Mill implies, they will freely choose a single ideal, but how much room for diversity is allowed by this single ideal? The answer lies, I think, in the second of the two notions mentioned in the original quotation from *The Subjection of Women*, the notion of complementarity, and I turn now to that.

Complementarity

Mill's essay on Bentham, mentioned earlier in discussing the differences between Benthamite utilitarianism and Mill's utilitarianism, was published shortly before his essay on the poet Coleridge. Mill speaks of Bentham and Coleridge as 'the two great seminal minds of England in their age', and his aim in the essays is to draw attention to the differences and similarities between the two, the ways in which they complement one another, the ways in which, for example, Coleridge may make good the defects and omissions in Bentham and vice versa. He remarks:

> For among the truths long recognised by Continental philosophers, but which very few Englishmen have yet arrived at, one is, the importance, in the present imperfect state of mental and social science, of antagonistic modes of thought: which it will one day be felt are as necessary to one another in speculation, as mutually checking powers are in a political constitution.[25]

Mill's belief in the importance of complementarity goes back to his early mental crisis. In the *Autobiography* he tells us that he was released from depression partly by reading the poems of Wordsworth, which appealed powerfully to his emotions and expressed 'not mere outward beauty, but states of feeling and of thought coloured by feeling, under the excitement of beauty'.[26] His emergence from the mental crisis brought with it a reluctance to place total faith in powers of analysis and intellect. He searched now for people—poets, writers, artists—who could make up the deficits in his own character and early education by providing emotion and intuition to complement his own rationality. He turned first to Carlyle: 'the good his writings did was not as philosophy to instruct, but as poetry to animate'.[27]

I did not deem myself a competent judge of Carlyle. I felt that he was a poet, and that I was not; that he was a man of intuition, which I was not, and that as such he not only saw many things before me, which I could only, when they were pointed out to me, hobble after and prove, but that it was highly probable he could see many things which were not visible to me even after they were pointed out. I knew that I could not see round him, and could never be certain that I saw over him; and I never presumed to judge him with any definiteness until he was interpreted to me by one greatly superior to us both—who was more a poet than he, more a thinker than I—whose own mind and nature included his and infinitely more.[28]

Of course, the one greater than them both was Harriet Taylor and, in speaking of her, Mill again refers to the notion of complementarity; what was important about Harriet (as about Carlyle) was that she was able to make good the defects in Mill's character with respect to feeling, emotion, intuition. She was a poet, where Mill was only a thinker. It is in these references to complementarity that room is made for diversity within the single ideal of marriage. Mill's ideal of marriage is unswervingly the ideal of a marriage of true minds. The diversity he recommends is not the diversity of lower as against higher, or animal as against human characteristics. Rather, proper diversity is to be found in the marriage between the poet and the thinker, the emotional and the rational, the intuitive and the intellectual. Moral self-development will best be effected by the joining of equal but complementary partners, who may thus inform and educate one another. Just as Bentham had only one eye without the insights of Coleridge, so Mill had only one eye without the insights of Harriet (or so he thought). Remarking on the actual (as against the supposed) relationship between Mill and Mrs. Taylor, Phyllis Rose says:

> I speak with great trepidation about 'facts' in such matters, but, speaking loosely, the facts in the Mills' case—that a woman of strong and uncomplicated will dominated a guilt ridden man—were less important than their shared imaginative view of the facts, that their marriage fitted their shared ideal of a marriage of equals.[29]

What Mill saw in his relationship with Harriet Taylor was a complementarity of powers and talents which fitted her to lead him in the path of development. The diversity between them thus effected a move to moral and spiritual perfection. This is the true and only genuine diversity allowed for by Mill's ideal of marriage—the diversity of complementary characters who may lead one another towards truth and towards individual self-fulfillment. Indeed, I would go so far as to say that this is the only diversity allowed for in society either: Mill's dream of a world of individuals and eccentrics is really a dream only that the world will contain Coleridge as well as Bentham, Carlyle as well as himself—not a dream that the world will contain Barry Manilow or Samantha Fox or any of the darker, lower, and less acceptable examples of individuality. Of course, this is not wholly wrong: I do not myself subscribe to the view that the world is a richer place for the presence in it of diversity of all and any sort. The world we live in may well be more diverse if it contains racists and fascists, but I cannot myself see that it is the richer or better for that diversity. Nevertheless, we may wonder whether there is in Mill's account sufficient room for diversity. Even if we do not want the diversity which racism and fascism bring with them, we may understandably want something more than merely the choice between Coleridge and Bentham.

The question of exactly how much diversity Mill's theory allows is a complex and controversial one: at one level, a great deal of diversity is to be tolerated. Mill recognizes that we are not yet far progressed on the road to moral improvement, and insists that we cannot forcibly impose any ideal on the unwilling. So the diversity he actually countenances in the actual world is great, even if the ideal amount of diversity in the ideal world would be much smaller. For the purposes of this paper, however, I wish simply to draw attention to an important and, I think, ironic feature of Mill's doctrine. This is the way in which his complementarity thesis informs his view of women generally and makes *The Subjection of Women* a more radical and a less attractive text than is normally allowed.

Complementarity and the 'Woman Question'

Earlier in the paper I made reference to Julia Annas's discussion of Mill's *The Subjection of Women* and her claim that the book is important for its recognition of the social and economic inequalities in Victorian society, as well as for its objections to women's legal disabilities. Annas argues that Mill goes badly wrong in vacillating between different kinds of argument against inequality: in particular, she says, Mill is never clear whether he is adopting a reformist approach, according to which women are in fact rendered miserable and wretched by their inequality, or whether he is adopting a radical approach, according to which the very fact that women are not miserable and wretched is proof positive that changes must be made. This latter argument is akin to the claim that, where slaves do not object to servitude, that fact itself shows what is wrong with slavery. And Mill himself appeals to this analogy in *The Subjection of Women.* In his more radical moods, Mill insists that woman's true nature cannot really be known, so deformed is it by prevailing social standards and expectations. Yet, apparently forgetful of his own earlier claims, he goes on in chapter 3, to tell us that women are (by nature) capable of intuitive perception of situations, they have a natural bent towards the practical, and they can bring 'rapid and correct insight into present fact'.[30] Annas is appalled:

> Here is the oldest cliché in the book: women are intuitive while men reason. If any cliché has done most harm to the acceptance by men of women as intellectual equals, it is this, and it is distressing to see Mill come out with it. It is even more distressing to find him patronizingly recommending to any man working in a speculative subject the great value of an intuitive woman to keep him down to earth.[31]

However, this seems to me not the only nor the most plausible explanation of what Mill was about in the relevant passages of *The Subjection of Women.* We have seen that the distinction between intellect and emotion, rationality and intuition, thought and poetry, is not a simple male/female one in his philosophy. The argument about complementarity applies quite generally, and it is a consequence of this that when Mill appeals to it he need not be construed as always placing women on the emotion side of the dichotomy, nor that, when he does so place women, it is in any patronizing or disreputable fashion. The mistake in Annas's interpretation of Mill lies in her failure to see that the complementarity thesis pervades his thought, and is not simply a feature of *The Subjection of Women.* What Mill finds lacking in Bentham and in his own earlier thinking is precisely a sense of the importance of something other than analysis and intellect. In fact, this defect was made good for Mill by his association with Harriet Taylor, but, before he ever met Harriet, the defect was partway to being remedied by his friendship with Carlyle and his reading of Wordsworth. It is a contingent fact of Mill's life that the emotional and intuitive facets were provided for him by a woman but they might just as well have been provided by a man and would have been none the better or worse for that. (See, for example, the cooling of the relationship between Carlyle and Mill after the latter's meeting with Harriet Taylor. Mrs. Taylor took over the function which Carlyle had been performing, much to the dissatisfaction of both Thomas and Jane Carlyle.)[32]

If the mistake of Annas's interpretation lies in her failure to see that the reason/emotion dichotomy is not to be understood as a male/female one, the irony of her interpretation lies in the fact that Mill's complementarity thesis in a sense foreshadows radical feminist accounts of the inadequacy of 'male' conceptions of reason and its powers. In *The Dialectic of Sex* the radical feminist writer, Shulamith Firestone, concedes that women are indeed intuitive rather than rational, emotional rather than logical. Yet, she insists, what is often wrong with science is precisely that it ignores the emotions. She advocates 'emotional science' as a corrective of the overvaluing of technology and its powers, much as Mill praised the corrective influence of the poet in Carlyle, and subsequently in Harriet Taylor.[33] As Alison Jaggar puts it:

> Radical feminists glorify women precisely for the same reasons that men have scorned and sometimes feared them; in so doing they give special value to the psychological characteristics that have distinguished women and men. By grasping the nettle so firmly, radical feminists intend not only to crush the sting, but even to produce some celebratory wine.[34]

Similarly, I think, in Mill. The appeal to women's nature as emotional and intuitive is far from patronizing; it is (rightly or wrongly) eulogistic.

In conclusion, I want to use some of the points made earlier to suggest that there is a misperception in our present-day assessment of Mill's *The Subjection of Women*. At the very beginning of this paper I quoted some Victorian critics of Mill: the objection that his text rests upon 'an unsound view of morals' and that it is a work of 'rank moral and social anarchy'. By contrast with this nineteenth-century assessment, modern commentators frequently praise Mill as being ahead of his time and attribute the original unpopularity of *The Subjection of Women* to the fact that it was too radical for its day. I have mentioned one way in which the text is indeed radical, but the overwhelming impression left by it is, I think, morally depressing. In this sense, Mill's contemporaries were more nearly right in their judgment than are twentieth-century feminists. They were right to construe *The Subjection of Women* as essentially a moral tract—not merely a legal one, nor even a social and political one—for embedded in it is commitment to a particular positive ideal of the marriage relationship, which we ignore to our peril. If the weakness of Mill's contemporaries lay in their refusal to countenance the relationship of marriage as a relationship between legal equals, their strength lies in their insistence on seeing it as something other than a legal relationship of any sort. By contrast, modern commentators are so impressed by Mill's objections to legal, social, and economic inequalities that they fail to see the moral ideal by reference to which his objections are voiced. Briefly, the point is this: Mill is so concerned to emphasize the inequality in Victorian marriage contracts that he never stops to ask whether marriage as an ideal is a contract at all, but simply assumes that it is so. His claim is that it must be a contract between equals, and legally this is surely right. Yet in his enthusiasm for this notion he forgets the social and economic circumstances which meant that it could be no such thing for the vast majority of Victorian women, and he also forgets that questions about legality are distinct from questions about ideals. Mill's contemporary, James Fitzjames Stephen, saw this clearly when he pointed out the consequences of taking literally Mill's view that divorce should be freely available. 'If this were the law,' he says, 'it would make women the slaves of their husbands.'[35] And so it would have done in Victorian Britain. If not coupled with extensive social and economic changes, mere changes in the law of divorce would have been disastrous for women, and it is a sign of Mill's persistent unworldliness that he fails to see this. This failure is positively bizarre when considered in its contemporary context: other writers were insistent on the need to open up new professions to women, and the consequences of women's containment in the domestic sphere wee constantly pointed out to Mill by feminists of the day. Yet he remains curiously silent on the issue.[36]

More important, however, than Mill's unworldliness about the actual situation of women in Victorian Britain is his genuine belief in the lower, animal nature of the sexuality and his commitment to substituting the intellectual for the physical. This feature of his account (also favoured by some modern feminists) found some support among feminists of the day, but Victorian feminists were also often worried by the ways in which sex thwarted women's independence and advancement: for women, sex meant children—lots of children—and inevitably children meant loss of independence, frequently loss of health, and almost certainly containment in the home. By contrast, what concerned Mill was sex itself. He construed it as animal, ignoble, debasing, dehumanizing, and to be avoided wherever possible. In his 1832 *Essay on Marriage and Divorce* he declared the marriage laws to be made 'by sensualists, for sensualists, to bind sensualists'.[37] And it was this sensualism which was the target of Mill's real attack. The marriage laws were objected to primarily because they made women sexual slaves. If the disease is sex, the cure is certainly abstinence, and Mill embraced the cure with all the zeal at his disposal. Of course, this dephysicalizing of human nature fits in well with liberalism generally. It is a curious and troublesome feature of liberalism, often remarked upon by its critics, that it fails to take serious account of the practical circumstances of people's lives, construing these as merely contingent factors, unassociated with one's essential nature as a rational agent. Mill adopts this view in spades: not only does he ignore the practical circumstances of women's lives, which were such that mere changes in law (about the franchise or about divorce) would be at best irrelevant and at worst catastrophic; he also presents an ideal of marriage which sometimes appears to aim at the complete denial of the physical—as though sexuality were an unfortunate by-product of our animal nature, to be avoided and discouraged wherever possible. Freud referred to Mill's *Autobiography* as 'so prudish or so ethereal that one could never gather from it that human beings consist of men and women, and that this distinction is the most significant one that exists.'[38] The ethereal quality pervades much of Mill's writing and informs the greater part of his moral thought. His ideal of marriage is not only deeply depressing; it is also dangerous: to set one's faith on a great day when there will be no more sensualism, and to behave as though that day might be tomorrow (or, at any rate, next week), is to display a view of human nature just as impoverished as Bentham's and much less realistic.

Notes

An earlier draft of this paper was presented to the Women's Studies Workshop and to the Political Theory Workshop, both at the University of York. I am grateful to all who participated in those meetings for their helpful and incisive comments. My thanks also go to the Trustees of the C. and J. B. Morrell Trust, which funded my research during the academic years 1985–7.

1. References are to contemporary criticism of Mill's *The Subjection of Women*, and as quoted in M. St John Packe, *The Life of John Stuart Mill*, London, Secker & Warburg, 1954, 495ff.

2. John Stuart Mill, *The Subjection of Women*, London, Virago 1983, 177.

3. Lee Holcombe, *Wives and Property*, Oxford, Martin Robertson, 1983, 3.

4. Mill, *The Subjection of Women*, 59.

5. Julia Annas, 'Mill and the subjection of women', *Philosophy*, 52, 1977, 179.

6. Ibid., 194.

7. As quoted in William Thomas, *Mill*, Oxford, Oxford University Press, 1985, 5.

8. John Stuart Mill, *Autobiography*, ed. J. Stillinger, Oxford, Oxford University Press, 1969, 94.

9. *Mill on Bentham and Coleridge*, ed. F. R. Leavis, Cambridge, Cambridge University Press, 1980, 6.

10. Ibid., 71.

11. John Stuart Mill, *Utilitarianism*, ed. Mary Warnock, Glasgow, Fontana, 1962, 260.

12. Ibid., 261.

13. John Stuart Mill, *A System of Logic*, in *Collected Works*, vol. 7, Toronto, University of Toronto Press, 1973, 123.

14. Ibid, vol. 8, 913.

15. Mill, *Collected Works*, vol. 2, 367. Mill's distinction between humanity and animality is discussed in some detail in John M. Robson, 'Rational animals and others', in John M. Robson and Michael Laine (eds.), *James and John Stuart Mill: Papers of the Centenary Conference*, Toronto, University of Toronto Press, 1976, 143–60.

16. *The Early Draft of Mill's Autobiography*, ed. J. Stillinger, Champaign, University of Illinois Press, 1961, 171.

17. As quoted by L. S. Feuer, 'John Stuart Mill as a sociologist' in Robson and Laine (eds.), op. cit., 101.

18. Mill, *Collected Works*, vol. 2, 157; see also 156–8, 352, 358.

19. Ibid., vol. 2, 368. See also G. W. Smith, 'J. S. Mill on freedom,' in Z. Pelczynski and J. Gray (eds.), *Conceptions of Liberty in Political Philosophy*, London, Athlone Press, 1984, 210.

20. Mill, *On Liberty*, Harmondsworth, Penguin, 1974, 138.

21. Ibid., 133.

22. *Autobiography*, 65.

23. Mill, *On Liberty*, 136.

24. Smith, op. cit., 197.

25. *Mill on Bentham and Coleridge*, 9.

26. *Autobiography*, 89.

27. Ibid., 105.

28. Ibid., 106.

29. Phyllis Rose, *Parallel Lives: Five Victorian Marriages*, Harmondsworth, Penguin, 1985, 15.

30. Annas, op. cit., 184.

31. Annas, op. cit., 184.

32. Rose, op. cit., 117.

33. Shulamith Firestone, *The Dialectic of Sex: The Case for Feminist Revolution*, New York, William Morrow, 1970.

34. Alison Jaggar, *Feminist Politics and Human Nature*, Brighton, Harvester, 1983, 97.

35. James Fitzjames Stephen, *Liberty, Equality and Fraternity*, ed. R. J. White, Cambridge, Cambridge University Press, 1967, 195.

36. See Jane Rendall, *The Origins of Modern Feminism: Women in Britain, France and the United States, 1780–1860*, Basingstoke, Macmillan, 1985, 284–291.

37. In Alice Rossi (ed.), *Essays on Sex Equality*, Chicago, University of Chicago Press, 1970, 70.

38. As quoted in Feuer, op. cit., 101.

9

John Stuart Mill on Androgyny and Ideal Marriage

Nadia Urbinati

In stark contrast to Mendus's analysis, Urbinati argues that Mill's ideal of marriage rests on a fundamental challenge to the dichotomies between reason and intellect on the one hand and sentiment and physicality on the other. Urbinati maintains that central to The Subjection of Women *is the refusal to ascribe to psychology a physiological foundation, that is, to ascribe to gender a foundation in sex. In breaking the gender-sex connection, and appropriating the language of Androgyne, Mill liberated women from the rigid distinctions imposed by sex-roles. In endorsing an ideal of marriage based on friendship and equality, Mill not only denounced the model of family life as "dominion," but also actually strengthened his case for a democratic polity generally. Urbinati underscores the lasting potential of an ideal of marital friendship based on androgyny actually to overthrow the traditional domestic division of labor.*

JOHN STUART MILL NEVER EMPLOYED the term "androgyny" or "androgyne." Nonetheless, he contemplated the possibility of "abolish[ing] the distinction between characters." In this essay, I argue that androgyny forms the philosophical foundation for Mill's vision of civil and political equality between men and women and of his belief in the free development of individuality. His concern with the question of the "identity" of masculine and feminine is both the outcome of his own personal experience—particularly his reaction to the abstract rationalism of his father and the Benthamists—and of his acquaintance with

English romanticism and the French St. Simonians. His commitment to overcoming the artificial dichotomy between feminine and masculine character leads him to theorize a new type of family life grounded in the classical notion of friendship as a relation between equals and not on hierarchy and domination. Mill wanted the family to become a school of moral and civic education—a modern adaptation of the ideal of the ancient *polis*.

I

The image of the Androgyne in Mill's thought appears overtly in a discussion of "masculine" and "feminine" character that he had with Thomas Carlyle in fall 1833. In a letter to Mill, Carlyle spoke of *Madame Roland* as "a most remarkable woman; one of the clearest, bravest, perhaps as you say *best* of her sex and country; tho' (as indeed her time prescribed) almost rather a man than a woman."[1] In his reply, Mill attempted to clarify his friend's assertion, and the fact that he chose to do so at the end of his letter leads us to assume that he wished to give it particular emphasis:

> There was one thing in what you said of Madame Roland which I did not quite like—it was, that she was almost rather a man than a woman: I believe that I quite agree in all that you really meant, but *is* there really any distinction between the highest masculine and the highest feminine character?[2]

Mill proceeded to make an interesting distinction between physical ("mechanical *acquirements*") and psychological qualities in order to explain the meaning he intended for the word "identity." Finally, he concluded his letter to Carlyle by saying that if "masculine" and "feminine" characters appeared opposite and incompatible it was because the contemporary organization of society, education, and family life impeded a normal evolution of women's and men's mental potential. As proof of this, Mill cited cases (even if rare) of the "highest women," where it was impossible to see any kind of difference between them and men.[3] "Something feminine—not *effeminate*—is discoverable in the countenances of all men of genius," Coleridge had written a year before.[4]

Particularly interesting in this regard are Mill's comments on George Grote's terminology in the preface to his *History of Greece*. In speaking of the "Greek mind," Grote had labeled the "inclination" to "the religious and poetical view" as "feminine," while attributing the term "masculine" to "powers of acting, organizing, judging, and speculating." Significantly,

Mill replied to Grote by repeating what he had written to Carlyle more than ten years before: Only the external circumstances made for a "difference in the understandings." Such circumstances aside, man and woman "are both precisely alike."[5]

Commenting on Mill's severity, J. M. Robson noted in the 1836 article on *Civilisation* that Mill himself employed this "untenable distinction," attributing to "the refined classes" a "moral effeminacy, an inaptitude for every kind of struggle."[6] Because this passage reveals that Mill too had some uncertainties, one could find here a confirmation of Harriet Taylor's decisive role in convincing him to address the problem of feminine and masculine identity. There is no need to enter into the old problem of Mill's and Taylor's psychological and intellectual relationship, the discussion of which is so frequently tainted by the sympathy or antipathy that scholars personally felt and feel toward Harriet Taylor and the roles she succeeded in playing in Mill's intellectual life.[7] The earlier quotation from the essay on *Civilisation* reveals, however, how difficult it was for Mill, too, to resist his epoch's inveterate attitudes, at least its linguistic ones. Mill's insistence may have been above all an attempt to convince himself that the contrast between masculine and feminine needed to be overcome. As Sigmund Freud wrote years later, referring to the translation he had made of some works of Mill, "He was perhaps the man of the century who best managed to free himself from the domination of customary prejudices." But it is very curious that Freud himself disagreed with Mill on what has to be considered a "customary prejudice." And if Mill tried to do his best in avoiding any preconceived distinction between men and women, Freud judged this attitude a sign of Mill's misunderstanding of the relationship between the sexes.[8]

Whatever can be said about the prudery and moralism contained in Mill's view of women, it is nonetheless quite difficult to share Freud's opinion about the *natural destiny* of women, of which Mill would have certainly spoken as the remnants of dated prejudice. Any citation of Freud's comment to emphasize Mill's incapacity to recognize "the deep human emotions at work in our most intimate relations,"[9] should also add Freud's next statement, where he proposes his own contrasting idea of women:

> I believe that all reforming action in law and education would break down in front of the fact that, long before the age at which a man can earn a position in society, Nature has determined woman's destiny through beauty, charm, and sweetness. Law and custom have much to give women that has been withheld from them, but the position of women will surely be what it is: in youth an adored darling and in mature years a loved wife.

In rejection the segregation of feminine and masculine, Mill explicitly gestured toward the unity of human beings beyond sexual difference. To emphasize this concept, he placed the sexual moment among the "mechanical" or pure physical factors. In doing so, Mill introduced the distinction between what we call today sex and gender, that is, between biological (female and male) and social (feminine and masculine) spheres. Assuming that biological sexuality was an "accidental" factor, he implied that psychological qualities are not linked to sexual determinations and that, properly speaking, "masculine" and "feminine" do not exist, or, if they do, only as cultural and social products. This conclusion appears to be the result of Mill's polemical confrontation with the "scientific" argument for biological diversity. Mill's refusal to ascribe to psychology a physiological foundation was one of the main characteristics that distinguished him from the positivist thinkers of his time (from Auguste Comte and his belief in phrenology, for instance, and from Herbert Spencer's biological determinism).[10] The refutation of the idea that feminine and masculine qualities were dichotomous because dependent on natural and biological differences took a central role in *The Subjection of Women*. As we know, Mill based his critique on the argument that science's present state leaves us totally ignorant as to what constitutes human nature and tells us little about the influences that determine the character of individuals.[11]

According to the Freudian classification of theories of sexuality, Mill could be considered a "sociologist" because he thought that pure masculinity and femininity could not be defined in a biological sense: Everyone displays a mixture of qualities of character conventionally associated with his own and the other sex.[12] By insisting on the psychological dimension and accepting the androgynous metaphor, Mill could easily make a case for the individual as *persona*, with respect to which masculine and feminine merge, because everyone combines in her- or himself all virtues or qualities that can make a complete personality.[13] This means that what is called "feminine" and "masculine" involves the existence of qualities that would be good for everyone to possess in order to develop their character in the best way. Hence what people commonly call feminine and masculine are not incompatible properties at all. Rather, they are *human* attributes that for social and historical reasons are distributed separately among men and women and misleadingly called "feminine" and "masculine."[14]

Mill's protest was against the "narrow and degrading" attitude to confine the individual into borderlines settled by cultural tradition and imposed by social conformism.[15] He insisted on pluralism of the human potentials, not on their dichotomy. Reason and emotion, activity and passively, strength and docility were different components of the individual character of men and women alike. Speaking, for instance, about the qualities connected with the "intellect" and with "sentiment," Mill did not contest that they were different nor did he deny that individuals could develop these qualities to different degrees. However, he firmly combated the belief that they were mutually exclusive. In other words, he challenged the common opinion which held that reason is masculine and sentiment is feminine and that the latter is inferior to the former. Defending the unity of the human mind, Mill argued that an individual lacking in one or the other quality is not a complete but a one-dimensional person. As Margaret Fuller wrote in 1848 about the "harmony of mind," there is "one thought, but various ways of treating it."[16]

Mill was convinced that the opposition between reason and feeling was one of the worst theoretical mistakes produced by abstract rationalism. Indeed, this point of view prevented an understanding of human activity in all its aspects. Mill's critique of Bentham can help us to appreciate his perspective better. Focusing only on individual interests, Bentham provided "half truths" and ignored the multitude of components that made actions possible, above all, the sentiments which Mill conceived of as the foundation of human opinions and social institutions. In a Homeric image derived from Coleridge, Mill described Bentham as a cyclops, a "one-eyed man" whose sight was as acute as it was partial.[17] He saw in Bentham's limited analysis of the human mind an example of what happened when one took mental qualities as opposites and antithetical. Thus when he contested the distinction between masculine and feminine, Mill was arguing against both a philosophical perspective and its main consequence: the habit of underestimating the role of the sentiment in human life and ranking women in an inferior state as a result. For this reason, what I call psychological androgyny is for Mill more than an ideal value in support of a political proposal but, rather, a coherent consequence of his larger philosophical critique of abstract rationalism:[18]

Thought and feeling in their lower degrees antagonize, in their higher harmonise. Much thought and little feeling make a mental voluptuary who wastes life in intellectual exercise for its own sake. Much feeling and little thought are the common material of a bigot and fanatic. Much feeling and much thought make the hero and the heroine.[19]

Here, Mill presents a hierarchy of four types. Between the "inferior natures"—which needed to be improved—and the "superior" ones, Mill included two other transitional forms, both insufficient and lacking: the person who pursues mental pleasure, and the person who seeks great feelings.[20] The importance of this hierarchy emerged even more clearly in connection with his own experience and with his characterizations of Thomas Carlyle and Harriet Taylor.

It is not necessary to go into the real or supposed causes of his "mental crisis."[21] For our purposes, we must accept what Mill himself said about his breakdown and his contemplation of suicide. After some failed attempts at recovery, Mill wrote that he finally found comfort in reading Wordsworth, whose poems provided him with "a medicine for my state of mind." This medicine allowed him to diagnose his illness: "They [the poems] seemed to be the very culture of the feelings, which I was in quest of."[22] He realized that his spiritual suffering was the consequence of his father's passionless system of education and perceived that thought and sentiment together constituted the unity of the human mind. Indeed, if thought permitted the distinction between goals and means, only emotion and sentiment could provide the *desire* to achieve such goals and support the sacrifices necessary to achieve them.

In his *Autobiography* and in his *Diary*, Mill described himself as a person whose existential unity was broken. He was only half an individual, a divided person like Aristophanes' creatures after the god's punishment, a "mental voluptuary who wastes life in intellectual exercise for its own sake," who has "much thought and little feeling." Considering that Mill used the word "thought" to signify the acquisition and the implementation of exact principles by experience and logical equipment, his description of Carlyle can help to clarify another kind of unhappy duality', that of the person who has "much feeling and little thought." He considered Carlyle not a thinker but a poet.[23] As a thinker, Carlyle seemed to him the representative of "German metaphysics," an expression used by Mill to signify that which he considered not a philosophy at all. Indeed, Mill ended his description of Carlyle by saying that "the good his writings did me, was not as philosophy to instruct, but as poetry to animate." In his opinion, both he and Carlyle were, again, two incomplete beings because each of them manifested either feeling or thought. Carlyle was a mirror-like image of himself. Mill's encounter and long relationship with Harriet Taylor continues and completes his typology. She represented the highest level of his human typology because she had "much feeling and much thought." She was the example of a human being beyond any gender distinction; she was an *equal*:

> I had always wished for a friend whom I could admire wholly, without reservation and restriction, and I had now found one. To render this possible, it was necessary that the object of my admiration should be of a type very different from my own; should be a character preeminently of feeling, combined however as I had not in any other instance known it to be, with a vigorous and bold speculative intellect.[24]

Through union with such a person, Mill believed it was possible to overcome his own "loneliness" and look forward to a time when most individuals would integrate what were usually identified as feminine and masculine traits and characters—now a privileged condition of a well-educated minority.[25]

Mill understood earlier and more clearly than his contemporaries that biological sex should not be the criterion for attributing gender characteristics. He transformed the androgynous metaphor into a universal value in keeping with his idea of liberty. Sexual equality became for him a precondition of individual free choice and self-determination. In breaking the connection between sex and gender, Mill liberated human beings—women, above all—from the rigid distinctions imposed by sex roles. He claimed that men and women could construct their lives according to their own capacity and competence. Women's emancipation was at the same time a condition and a result of liberal principles.[26]

In this regard, one should remember that Mill's plan to write *On Liberty* (1855) proceeded along with his thoughts on marriage as a relationship between *equals*. Both his *Diary* (1854) and his letters to Harriet Taylor from Italy (1855) show very clearly the connection between his reflection on the equality of sexes and his elaboration of the idea of individuality as a good per se. And certainly *On Liberty* (published in 1859) can be read as related to his long-standing concern with the problem of feminine and masculine identity and as an introduction to *The Subjection of Women* (written in 1861). This radical approach would have offered him the possibility of denying any inherent psychological difference based on sex, and it anticipated the theory of political equality. Properly speaking, his androgyne was the Individual, the human being's exemplary, the subject of what in *On Liberty* he called *individuality*. It was the sexually blended type that he developed in discussions with his wife transferred into the ethical and political fields. In this light, Mill's insistence on attributing the ideas of *On Liberty* to both himself and his wife is more than understandable.

II

Mill's insistence on the necessity of combining the human psychological attitudes can help us to revise several partial interpretations about his presumed "idolatry" and "apotheosis of Reason." The entire body of his philosophical research shows an untiring effort to combat "geometrical deductivism" in the human sciences. If it is true that Mill was disturbed by the presence of instincts in human nature, it is therefore not correct to conclude, as does Jean Elshtain, that Mill also excluded sentiment and desire if only because Mill did not confuse instinct and desire.[27] Along the same lines, according to Julia Annas, Mill's rationalism would not allow him to understand the importance of "re-educating people's desires"; and because of his individualism, he would have been "disturbed" by the eventuality of reforming the school system.[28]

In fact, however, Mill was actually deeply aware of the role of sentiment in the development and consolidation of opinions. *The Subjection of Women* took inspiration from this awareness. In 1833, comparing William Bridges Adams to the "narrow-minded" radical social reformers, Mill underscored the futility of expecting the emancipation of mankind to be achieved "exclusively by the cultivation" of the "*reasoning* faculty," and asserted that "even supposing perfect knowledge to be attained, no good will come of it, unless the *ends*, to which the means have been pointed out, are *desired*."[29]

Because of their devotion to the image of Mill as the "Saint of Rationalism," the aforementioned interpretations assume that, after splitting reason and sentiment, Mill merely repeated the stale idea that opposed feminine intuition and sentimentality to masculine rationality.[30] Such criticisms reach this conclusion because they do not consider the historical context within which Mill developed his thought and because they set the woman question apart from the rest of his work. In doing so, they disregard Mill's contention that the primary error lay in identifying philosophy with some "one-eyed" system, whether rationalist or romantic.[31] Such objections neglect to appreciate the role that Mill assigned to sentiment in mental life and the meaning of his hostility toward the stereotyped use of the distinction between feminine and masculine. Both of these arguments—which are strictly connected to one another—call into question Mill's dialogue with English Romanticism.

The most important suggestions that Mill received from Coleridge were the eclectic attitude toward philosophical systems and the belief in the unity of the human mind. It was Coleridge, after all, who said, "The truth is, a great mind must be androgynous."[32] In a similar way, Mill developed an idea of equality between men and women which was far more complex than what one critic calls a simple reproduction of "the Helvetius doctrine of the natural equality of human being in regard of capacity."[33] It is correct to claim that, in keeping with his liberalism, Mill does not prescribe any kind of ideal model of life. However, there is no error in speaking of Mill's espousal of androgyny as a basis for his principle of equality and justice in human relationships,[34] if one specifies that Mill accepted the concept of androgyny circulating in the intellectual life of the time.

The interest in the Androgyne, after all, was very widespread in the nineteenth century.[35] As an interpretation of a myth, it was employed both by the Romantics and by the early French Positivists (especially the St. Simonians). Through it, the poets and philosophers expressed their hopes for a cultural and moral regeneration of mankind: the former insisted primarily on the spiritual and psychological aspects of androgynism, the latter on its social and political implications.[36] In *Epipsychidion*, for example, Shelley stated that only the encouragement of an androgynous culture could save humanity. In Coleridge this image implied a vindication of the completeness of character. In Mill, finally, it involved the idea of sexual equality.

But the Androgyne also served to formulate a philosophy of history based on the ideas that humanity has been corrupted by immoral passions and that the "highest characters" have the *duty* to regenerate society by reeducating individuals and reforming social institutions. The St. Simonians, for instance, used this metaphor to illustrate their "religion of humanity" and to present the "Humanity" as "*l'Homme en général, l'Homme universel*" without internal differences.[37] They showed that it was possible to give an image of what the philosophers called the Individual, an abstract and general name capable of signifying both sexes and all races. *Androgyne* was synonymous with *Humanity* or *Human Being* and transcended any sort of historical or physical distinctions. It expressed the idea of mankind's unity in time and space and communicated a strong sentiment of political and social justice toward all who were oppressed for prejudicial and "accidental" reasons, such as sex or skin color.[38] It was in light of this perceived unity that the reformers placed women and black slaves together in their campaigns for emancipation. Such a perspective also characterized Mill's thought, though without the cosmogonic philosophical framework. Thus even after his break with Comte, Mill did not cease to proclaim his adherents to *le culte de l'humanité* as a "sentiment of fraternity with all our fellow beings, past, present, and to come."[39] The sentiment was, in addition, perfectly coherent with his love as "a Greece-intoxicated man" for classical humanism.[40]

Apart from its cultural significance, one must pay particular attention to the role played by the Androgyne in the women question. In this regard, it is undeniable tht Mill shared the ideas expressed by those in his time who dissented from orthodox rationalism. His debt is even more evident if one considers the crucial years between 1828 and 1832. In this epoch, before his personal acquaintance with Harriet Taylor (1830) and Carlyle (1831), Mill began to familiarize himself with the poetry and literature of English Romantics. In the same period, he encountered the St. Simonians and Unitarians. In 1829, Mill started his correspondence with Gustave D'Eichthal whom he had met a year before in England; shortly after, he withdrew from the London Debating Society and distanced himself from his old Benthamite friends in favor of Coleridge's circle, above all John Sterling, who became his closest companion.

Alice S. Rossi has shown very well the role played by the Unitarians in Mill's personal and intellectual biography.[41] Similar arguments could be made about the role of the St. Simonians, whose influence extended beyond Fox's club. Even if his *esprit critique* made him incapable of being a St. Simonian, Mill nonetheless showed much sympathy toward their beliefs: "Although I am not a St. Simonist nor at all likely to become one, *je tiens bureau de St. Simonisme chez moi.*"[42] Even when he became very critical of the illiberal consequences of French positivism, he continued to recognize the importance of the St. Simonian contribution to sexual equality. In 1855, writing from Rome, Mill suggested that his wife read *Eugéne* by Emile Barrault, a St. Simonian "*missionaire.*"[43] The novel was a kind of fresco of the dichotomous universe of contemporary society, but it contained also the message of a new world built on the Androgyne. Man and woman could join together because they were equals, and they were equals because they were creatures of a god who was "*mâle et femelle.*"[44] Barrault presented marriage as the place where "*la force morale*" does not know sex, where tenderness and sympathy unify "*les deux moitiés du monde.*" The metamorphosis from wife-slave to wife-person was equivalent to the restoration of moral integrity of society.[45] As Mill had written some years before reviewing Ware's *Letters from Palmyra* (1838), this was the true message of Christianity:

> to abolish the distinction between the two characters, by teaching that neither of them can be really admirable without the qualities supposed to be distinctive of the other, and by exhibiting, in the person of its Divine Founder, an equally perfect model of both.[46]

Between the Platonic and Christian interpretations of the androgynous mythology, the latter was more popular in the Victorian era. Where the former emphasized the egocentric value of self-realization, the latter focused more on love and on the life of the couple.[47] Proceeding toward the secularization of Christian principles, French thinkers and English Romantics assigned a privileged position to marriage.[48] Their vision of ideal marriage functioned as a critique of the present state of society and as a model for the future. It helped to define a philosophy of history based on the antithesis between "moral" and "immoral" passions. In Mill's and Harriet Taylor's writings, as in Robert Owen's, *sensuality* and *chastity* expressed two opposing models of life: force, tyranny, and selfishness, on one hand, and tendenees, friendship, and sympathy, on the other.[49] Mill did not, therefore, merely oppose the passions; rather, he insisted on distinguishing between moral and immoral passions. As he wrote in *The Subjection of Women*, marriage was based on fear, and fear springs up from the power exercised by force.[50] Force and fear imply an unequal relationship between individuals and stimulate the pleasure of possession and the sentiment of hostility. On the contrary, only sympathy, because it is settled on a mutual reciprocity, can promote a just and a good society. Mill based his denunciation of the condition of women in marriage on the phenomenology of these two "sensual passions." Then, he transformed it into a political critique by employing the language of ancient philosophy, using the concept of "dominium" or "tyranny."

III

By insisting on the role of the family, Mill did not intend to justify woman's traditional role, although it might appear so at first glance. Indeed, his claim for an equality of rights amounted to a critique of the philosophy of abnegation which formed the basis for women's education.[51] If he emphasized domestic life it was because of his awareness of the peculiar character of the modern age. Comparing ancient and modern society, Mill perceived that while in the classical world the life in the city was the main instrument for moral education, in the present time this role was assumed by the family:

> Citizenship, in free countries, is partly a school of society in equality; but citizenship fills only a small place in modern life, and does not come near the daily habits or inmost sentiments. The family, justly constituted, would be the real school of the virtues of freedom.[52]

Because of its preponderant position, the family should assume the role taken by the *polis* in the past in the formation of the citizens. This is one of the main concepts in *The Subjection of Women*. It allows us to understand both Mill's critique of marriage legislation and customs and his idea of *true marriage* as friendship. In addition, it enables us to assess the role of marriage in his notion of emancipation.

Mill's critical argument was a historical one. However, he did not simply use historical episodes but instead constructed a kind of philosophy of history employing an empirical strategy within a deductive framework. Mill viewed the history of Western society in terms of two cycles, each with an internal autonomous evolution, but both moving in the same direction: from "sensualism" to "chastity," from the realm of "animal passions" to the free exercise of spiritual passions. The ancient republics succeeded in supplanting a social order based on force and fear with one based on justice and equality. After the barbarian invasions, the task of humanity throughout modern history has been to return to the level of the ancient republics. The path of progress again leads toward a society of justice and equality. Nonetheless, between these two cycles of historical movement, there was only a partial identity. Christianity, indeed, allowed for the extension of equality to all human beings without distinction. For this reason the modern era can raise humanity to a higher condition.[53] Through this cyclical and progressive scheme, Mill was able to present his ideal society as a *new* polis, and "true marriage" as a *micro* polis. The modern world had no need to create anything new;[54] it had to restore the principle of a society of equals based on civic virtues and enriched by enlightened sympathy. Mill's political vision was the sum of a classical inheritance and Christian universalism.[55]

The future perspective, together with the criterion of the link between social and political institutions, strengthened his critique of the contemporary domestic system. According to Mill, the world was moving toward democracy. However, the dominant school of moral and social sentiments was still organized as a tyranny. Where society had need of citizens, the family provided only tyrants and subjects. Because experience was the principal means for the education of sentiment, family roles needed to be changed.[56]

Mill equated married life in his time with despotism and slavery in both the ancient and the modern worlds—in any case, women's ends were external to themselves.[57] In presenting the comparison between family and slavery and in defining the husband as a master and *despot*, Mill revived the Platonic and Aristotelian representations of *oikos* as an example of political tyranny in order to reinforce the value of civic government. Given these premises, Mill concluded that both private and political despotism were perverse because each brought forth the worst aspects of human nature, both the tyrant and his subjects.[58] The similarity between Mill's and Hegel's words on this subject is striking—all the more so since it is unlikely that Mill knew Hegel's *Phenomenology of the Mind*, and especially since Hegel did not conceive of the family as a tyranny at all.[59] To find the historical roots of Mill's phenomenology of tyranny, one would do better to examine his deep love for the philosophy and political life of the ancient republics (above all, of Athens) and his appreciation of St. Simonian and Owenist ideas. Both of these sources contained a forceful description of the consequences of tyranny on its subjects. Above all, before Hegel, Plato, Aristotle, and Cicero had insisted that the tyrant, like his slaves, was alone and not free because his relations were with unfree men.

By focusing on his debt to the classics, one can understand the comparison that Mill made between the polis and ideal marriage: Both of these societies need equality, justice, and friendship in order to be a school of freedom. In this regard, he was a modern interpreter of ancient political thought, and by attributing moral virtues to women, he universalized the notion of *equal* and of *friend*. This allowed him to consider marriage as a kind of friendship. Nonetheless, Mill did not simply "adopt" the classic language of friendship;[60] rather, he assumed that marriage and friendship were exactly the same:

> The constant partaking in the same things, assisted by their sympathy, draws out the latent capacities of each for being interested in the things which were at first interesting only to the other. This often happens between two friends of the same sex, who are much associated in their daily life.[61]

This statement is particularly important because it confirms Mill's belief in the equality of man and woman. In *The Subjection of Women*, he employed the same words used many years before in confiding to Sterling his sentiment of friendship in terms of having found "one fellow traveller, or one fellow soldier," a companion "in the pursuit of a common object."[62] By this description, Mill expressed his vision of life as intellectual search ("travel") and as engagement with goals that transcended the individual sphere ("war").[63] Travel and war need companionship, and "the feeling of being engaged in the pursuit of a common object, and of mutually cheering one another on, and helping one another in an arduous undertaking."[64] Above all, mutuality and sharing of responsibilities require an equal partnership, identical values, and a unity of complementary strengths. All these are crucial characteristics, also because they are connected with the idea of the Androgyne, and help to understand Mill's predilection for the ancient language of friendship. In Mill's view, similarity excluded any kind of egocentric perspective because it entailed *idem sentire de republicâ*, to share "all the great objects of life" without looking for another ego. Equality did not mean searching for one's "own double" but rather a quest for *reciprocal superiority*. Friendship for Mill was a kind of *friendly emulation*, enriching both the individuals and the couple;[65] it was a tie between two persons, one of whom "knows many things which the other knows not" and can do many things "which the other values but cannot himself do."[66] We can find exactly the same expressions in Mill's letters to his friends Sterling and Adams, in the *Autobiography* where he described his relationship with Harriet Taylor, and in *The Subjection of Women* where he opposed marital friendship to its tyrannical counterpart.

Given these premises on marriage and friendship, it was clear that both relations change the individuals involved to the point that they reach a "gradual assimilation" of tastes and characters with respect to "the great objects of life." This transformation is achieved "partly by the insensible modification of each, but more by a real enriching of the two natures."[67] The "true marriage" transforms the couple into a single being, more perfect than the two partners because it fulfills everyone's need of completeness. The criterion of "voluntary association"—which Mill opposed to the contemporary vision of, and legislation on, marriage—was the minimal condition for establishing a union capable of overcoming the stereotyped distinction between feminine and masculine qualities and of promoting the growth of individuality and civic attitudes.[68] Certainly, the notion of an ideal marriage, of a soul mate, was a *tópos* during Mill's epoch. But it was only Mill who transformed this notion into an instrument with which to denounce the reality of family life as it really was.

Mill's ideal also has important critical functions for our time. If one considers friendship as a criterion by which men and women can manage their lives on the basis of equality and dignity, then one certainly cannot ignore or underrate Mill's proposal. Marital friendship, based on conjugal androgyny, could also represent a great opportunity to overcome the traditional division of domestic roles. Mills' thoughts on mutual cooperation are illuminating:

> The association of men with women in daily life is much more complete than it ever was before. Men's life is more domestic. Formerly, their pleasures and chosen occupations were among men, and in men's company: their wives had but a fragment of their life.[69]

In this view, man and woman share duties and responsibilities not as the result of sexual roles but because of a renewed agreement between two free-willed and equal human beings. Any unequal relationship should be opposed—as Mill did—on the ground of the idea of mental communion. For this reason, one can consider the general ideas of solidarity and cooperation that arise from Mill's conception of conjugal friendship to be positive and universal values, untouched by the prevalent domestic dimension that he assigned to women.

IV

The question of the presumed contradictions in Mill's thought between womens' emancipation and their role in the family deserves more attention. Some critics insist that Mill's inability to overcome the family relationship stemmed from his faith in the value of the "bourgeois family."[70] Others link Mill's traditional view of marriage with his inability to develop an androgynous character.[71] The contradiction, however, is less severe than it appears. Our dissatisfaction with Mill's feminism is, in fact, a dissatisfaction with particular opinions that he expressed on specific problems rather than with his principles per se. In other words, Mill's critics are implicitly saying that he is not our contemporary and that there has been some progress since his time, at least concerning beliefs on women's roles inside and outside the family. As has been recently observed, his views on traditional family functions do not alter the value of his liberal feminism.[72] On more than one occasion, Mill himself confronted the tension between his principles and his mental habits. When this occurred, he was able to accept the social implications of his strong belief in free choice.

The critics often take as their departure point the last pages of the second chapter of *the Subjection of Women*, analyzing them in terms of internal coherence or contradiction. In so doing, they overemphasize the theoretical aspects of Mill's essay and ignore or neglect the concrete support that Mill gave for the movement of social and political emancipation of women. One should remember at least that he considered the exclusion of women from the functions of social life to be one of the worst contemporary *evils*.[73] In his public and political activity, he always adhered to this position.

As Mill himself wrote, a historical event has to be assessed not only by questioning its internal coherence but by asking "What is the meaning of it?"[74] Thus we should consider what *The Subjection of Women* was and what Mill wanted to pursue in writing it. Certainly, *The Subjection of Women* was a political essay, a *pamphlet* in support of the cause of sexual equality. A we know, it was written eight years before it was actually published. As with other political questions he addressed (such as religion and divorce), Mill was deeply aware of the proper time, and manner, in which to make political action most efficient and useful.[75] In writing the essay, his primary goal was to convince that cultivated minority most able to help his reforming project: "Such persons ought to support the principles here advocated" and work in favor of them.[76]

Moreover, Mill faced the issue of domestic roles after challenging the contemporary acceptance of legal intervention in adjudicating the "division of duties and functions" within the family. In his view, such issues could be better resolved by the actors themselves. Here, he not only employed an antipaternalist argument but asserted that the law's silence did not entail a subversion of the foundations of society.[77] Mill wanted to assure his Victorian readers that even without formal obligation, women would choose to raise a family, behaving "like a man when he chooses a profession."[78] This prudent strategy was very common among the early emancipationists and not only in England.[79]

The political caution argument, which is supported by his correspondence, does not prevent us from speculating that while Mill defended the principles of free choice and not those of socially imposed roles, he personally remained open to the possibility that the majority of women might choose to raise a family. Nonetheless, referring specifically to women's equal opportunities, he firmly denied that "the majority should give laws to the individual action of the minority"—in this case, the majority of women who devoted themselves to raising families.[80]

There is, finally, in Mill's thought another argument that we can use to support his belief "that all employments and positions should be open to women."[81] This is the link between the question of population and the *quality of life*.[82] Mill's concern was inspired by the belief that it was necessary to guarantee not simply the survival of mankind but a life that allows us to realize the minimal conditions in which to pursue material well-being and spiritual happiness.[83] For our purposes, it is important to pay attention to the means which Mill chose to control the "instinct of population."[84] The principal means was education, in particular a secular education of moral habits and attitudes.[85] Mill did not write in favor of an exclusive women's right to decide about procreation; nonetheless, he was aware of the inner connection between the condition of women and the question of population.[86] There are at least two examples of this awareness: his propensity to define ideal marriage independently from the presence of children and his desire to promote— not to restrain—the employment of women outside the family. On this latter question, both his correspondence and his essays are clear:

> On the present occasion I shall only indicate, among the probably consequences of the industrial and social independence of women, a great dimnution of the evil of overpopulation. It is by devoting one-half of the human species to that exclusive function, by making it fill the entire life of one sex, and interweave itself with almost all the objects of the other, that the animal instinct in question is nursed into the disproportionate preponderance which it has hitherto exercised in human life.

Mill then linked the question of population to the principle of women's free choice:

> Let women who prefer the occupation, adopt it; but that there should be no option, no other *carrière* possible for the great majority of women, except in the humbler departments of life, is a flagrant social injustice.[87]

The distinction that he made between life as a struggle for survival and as a way to improve our own and our fellow creatures' individuality also appears in *The Subjection of Women*, in which he writes on women's labor both inside and outside the family. Mill concluded the second chapter by distinguishing between labor as a necessity and labor as a means of self-realization. Whereas in the latter case, it is a question of free choice and personal abilities and desires, in the former, the opposite is true: Wife and husband *must* labor to support their family. Mill proclaimed as unjust that division of labor which compelled women to work both inside and outside the family. After all, if today, labor—even when done by necessity—is understood and felt to be a means of self-realization, it is because of its organization and legislation, which is very different from labor in Mill's age. This is perhaps another good reason why Mill condemned as unjust social and familial arrangements that imposed on women the necessity of working. When the goal of labor was not survival but personal gratification or, more simply, when it was a matter of free choice, Mill's attitude was certainly different.[88] The document he left on the occasion of his own marriage is perhaps, in this regard, a testimony of his most profound belief:

> And in the event of marriage between Mrs. Taylor and me I declare it to be my will and intention, and the condition of the engagement between us, that she retains in all respects whatever the same absolute freedom of action, and freedom of disposal of herself and of all that does or may at any time belong to her, as if no such marriage had taken place.[89]

Author's Note

This essay was made possible by a grant from the Italian National Council of Research (C.N.R.). I am very grateful to Professors Amy Gutmann, George Kateb, and Alan Ryan for their helpful comments and encouragement.

Notes

1. Carlyle to Mill, 24 September 1833 in *Letters of Thomas Carlyle to John Stuart Mill, John Sterling and Robert Browing*, edited by A. Carlyle (New York, Haskell, 1970), 71.

2. Mill to Carlyle, 5 October 1833, in *The Earlier Letters of John Stuart Mill 1812-1848*, vol. 12 of *Collected Works of John Stuart Mill* (Toronto: University of Toronto Press), 184 (Hereafter *CW*).

3. Ibid. Carlyle would have undoubtedly responded that this was his "woman-man" too, entirely subscribing to Mill's ideal (to Mill, October 1833, in *Letters of Thomas Carlyle*, 81). Nonetheless, Carlyle would have never subscribed to Mill's idea of marriage as relationship between equals: "'The man— he wrote—should bear rule in the house, and not the woman.' This is an eternal axiom, the law of nature, which I am not the head," quoted in M. St. J. Packe, *The Life of John Stuart Mill* (London: Secker & Warburg, 1954), 181.

4. S. T. Coleridge, *Specimens of the Table Talk*, 2d ed. (London: Murray, 1836), 152 (17 March 1832). "Few persons have exercised more influence over my thoughts and character than Coleridge has; not much by personal knowledge of him, but by his works and by the fact that several persons with whom I have been very intimate with completely trained in his school;" through them he had the chance to read "various unpublished manuscripts of his" (Mill to John Pringle Nichol, 15 April 1834, in *CW*, 12:221).

5. J. S. Mill, *Grote's History of Greece* (1846), in *CW* 11: 275–76 and n. 46.

6. John M. Robson, "'Feminine' and 'Masculine' Mill vs. Grote," *Mill Newsletter* 12 (1977): 21 n. 1.

7. On this controversial collaboration and its ambivalent interpretations, see Alice S. Rossi, "Sentiment and Intellect: The Story of John Stuart Mill and Harriet Taylor Mill," introduction to *Essays on Sex Equality*, by J. S. Mill and H. T. Mill (Chicago and London: University of Chicago Press, 1970) 31–45. On Mill's "subjection" to Harriet Taylor, see Phyllis Rose, "Harriet Taylor and John Stuart Mill, 1830–1858," in *Parallel Lives: Five Victorian Marriages* (New York: Alfred A. Knopf, 1984), 95–140, and as a response, Gertrude Himmelfarb, *Marriage and Morals among the Victorians* (New York: Alfred A Knopf, 1986), chap. 1.

8. "In his [Mill's] whole presentation it never emerges that women are different beings—we will not say lesser, rather the opposite—from men. He had simply forgotten all that, like everything else concerning the relationship between the sexes. That is altogether a point with Mill where one simply cannot find him human. His autobiography is so prudish or so ethereal that one could never gather from it that human beings consist of men and women and that this distinction is the most significant one that exists" in Ernest Jones, *The Life and Works of Sigmund Freud* (New York: Basic Books, 1953), 1:176.

9. Jean B. Elshtain, *Public Man, Private Woman: Women in Social and Political Thought* (Princeton, NJ: Princeton University Press, 1981), 141; but see also L. S. Feuer, "J. S. Mill as a Sociologist: The Unwritten Ethology," in *James and J. Stuart Mill: Papers of the Centenary Conference* (Toronto and Buffalo, NY: University of Toronto Press, 1976), 101; Susan Mendus, "The Marriage of True Minds: The

Ideal of Marriage in the Philosophy of John Stuart Mill, " in *Sexuality and Subordination: Interdisciplinary Studies of Gender in the Nineteenth Century*, edited by S.
Mendus and J. Rendal (London and New York: Routledge, 1989), 190.

10. See, for example, his letters to Comte in the years 1844 and 1845, in *CW*,
vol. 13.

11. J. S. Mill, *The Subjection of Women*, in *CW*, 21:276–77 Regarding this, see
Alan Soble, "The Epistemology of the Natural and the Social in Mill's *The Subjection of Women*," in *Mill Newsletter*, 16 (1981): 3–9 and n. 2. Mill's circum-
spect attitude toward psychobiological monism puts him in an uncertain position: He avoided the reductionism which resulted from the positivist
philosophy, but he also exaggerated the separation between body and mind,
falling into one of two main "theoretical errors" attributed to him by Alexander Bain: "I mean the disregard of the physical conditions of our mental life,"
in *John Stuart Mill: A Criticism with Personal Recollections* (London: Longmans,
Green 1882), 146–47. Certainly, Mill recognized that the associationists "have
passed without any attempt at explanation" the fact that "there is evidently in
all our emotions an animal part," but he did not press his critique further. His
rehabilitation of the emotions and passions was more likely a reaction to his father's rigidity than a result of philosophical meditation. He remained substantially faithful to associationism and to the idea that the analysis of the "animal
part" of the emotions "must evidently be the work of physiologists," in *Bain's
Psychology* (1859), in *CW*, 11:361–62. Associationism confirmed him in his rigorous moralism. This was fully resonant with his stoic ideal of virtue, and his
antipathy to any kind of "indulgence" which he inherited from his father (*Autobiography*, in *CW* 1:49–51). His admiration for neo-Platonic romantic poetry
reinforced this attitude, leading him to emphasize the role of spiritual faculties
in the individual character and to portray a view of woman like that of a modern Diotima.

12. Sigmund Freud, "Three Essays on the Theory of Sexuality" (1905), in *The
Standard Edition of the Complete Psychological Works of Sigund Freud*, vol. 7,
essay 3, sec. 4 (London: Hogarth, 1953), 219–20 and n. 1. Here, I assume the expression "sociologist" as synonymous with "environmentalist." As Gail Tulloch
says in speaking about Mill: "The suggestion that characteristics thought natural to women can be explained as being the result of environmental factors
raises the possibility that there are no characteristics which are natural," in
G. Tulloch, *Mill and Sexual Equality* (Boulder, CO: Lynne Rienner, 1989), 16.

13. See Joyce Treblicot, Two Forms of Androgynism," in *"Femininity." "Masculinity," and "Androgyny,"* edited by Mary Vetterling-Braggin (Totowa, NJ:
Rowman & Littlefield, 1982), 161–62, reprinted in *Feminism and Philosophy*, edited by M. Vetterling-Braggin, F. A. Elliston, and J. English (Totowa, NJ: Littlefield, Adams, 1989), where see also Ann Ferguson, "Androgyny as an Ideal for
Human Development," 45–46, 63.

14. "If they [man and woman] are still far from being equal, the hindrance is not now in the difference of physical strength, but in artificial feelings and prejudices," in J. S. Mill, *On Marriage* (1832), in *CW*, 21:42.

15. J. S. Mill, *Ware's Letters from Palmyra* (1832), in *CW*, 1:460.

16. Margaret Fuller, *Women in Nineteenth Century and Kindred Papers* (Boston: Jewett, 1855), 72.

17. J. S. Mill, *Bentham* (1832), in *CW*, 10:93–94. Coleridge wrote about "half the truth" in *Specimen of the Table Talk*, 139 (12 September 1831).

18. I borrow the expression "psychological androgyny" from Mary Anne Warren, "Is Androgyny the Answer to Sexual Stereotyping?" in *"Femininity."* *"Masculinity,"* and *"Androgyny,"* edited by Vetterling-Braggin esp. 170–73.

19. J. S. Mill, *Diary*, in *CW*, 27:660.

20. On "popular morality," see Mill, *On Marriage*, 3, 40.

21. Regarding this, see A. W. Levi, "The 'Mental Crisis' of John Stuart Mill," *Psychoanalytical Review* 31 (1945): 86–101 and n. 1, and more recently Ronald V. Sampson, *The Psychology of Power* (New York: Vintage, 1968).

22. Mill, *Autobiography*, 151.

23. "I felt that he was a poet, and that I was not; that he was a man of intuition, which I was not," *Autobiography*, 183. But see also his description of George Sand in an unpublished letter to *"Voix des femmes"* (1848), in *CW*, 25:1094–95.

24. J. S. Mill, Early Draft of the *Autobiography*, in *CW* 1:623. What Mary W. Shelley said about Percy B. Shelley ("Shelley possessed two brilliant qualities of intellect—a brilliant imagination and a logical exactness of reason"), Mill would have repeated about his wife: "But you are to me the type of Intellect—because you have all the faculties in equal perfection—you can both think, & impress the thought on others—& can both judge what ought to be done." On the other hand, Mill liked to compare his wife to Shelley. See Mary W. Shelley, *Note to The Revolt of Islam*, quoted by Newell F. Ford, "Introduction," in *The Poetical Works of Shelley* (Boston: Houghton Mifflin, 1975), J. S. Mill to Harriet Taylor (1850), in *CW*, 14:43; *Autobiography*, 195.

25. Mill spoke about his "loneliness" to John Sterling, 15 April 1829, in *CW* 12:29–30.

26. For this reason, he discussed it in much the same way that he discussed working-class emancipation. In both cases, it was a question of liberation from a "patriarchal or paternal system of government," in J. S. Mill, *Principles of Political Economy* (1848), in *CW*, 3:761–62.

27. Elshtain, *Public Man, Private Woman*, 135.

28. Julia Annas, "Mill and *The Subjection of Women*," *Philosophy* 52 (1977): 192; but see *The Subjection of Women*, 294.

29. J. S. Mill, *Writing of Julius Redivivus*, in *CW*, 1:375–76.

30. Elshtain, *Public Man, Private Woman*; Annas, "Mill," 185–87.

31. J. S. Mill, *Coleridge* (1840), in *CW*, 10:133.

32. *Specimens of the Table Talk,* 188 (1 September 1832). Shelley, Coleridge, and Wordsworth thought that feeling were the true engine of human actions. By acting on man's imagination, they believed to make the individual able to develop disinterested love and compassion. See D. Newsome, *Two Classes of Men: Platonism and English Romantic Thought* (London; Butler & Tanner, 1974), 46–47, 56; Ford, "Introduction," in *Poetical Works of Shelley,* xxiii; C, Turk, *Coleridge and Mill: A Study of Influence,* Averbury Series in Philosophy (Aldershot: Averbury, 1988), 189–97; Wolf Lepenies, *Between Literature and Science: The Rise of Sociology* (Cambridge: Cambridge University Press, 1988), 102–6.

33. Bain, *John Stuart Mill,* 84.

34. Elaine Spitz, "On Shanley 'Marital Slavery and Friendship,'" *Political Theory* 10 (1982): 461–63.

35. See C. G. Heilbrun, *Toward a Recognition of Androgyny,* 6th ed. (New York: Alfred A. Knopf, 1973); J. L. Busst, "The Image of the Androgyne in the Nineteenth Century," in *Romantic Mythologies,* edited by I. Fletcher (New York: Barnes Noble, 1967), 1–2, 12, 85.

36. See, for example, A. Comte, *Système de politique positive: Ou traité de sociologie, instituant la Religion de l'Humanité* (Paris: Chez l'Auteur et Dalmont, 1851–54), 4:16–17, 30–31, 37–41; F. Lammenais, *De la Société Première et de ses lois: Ou de la Religion,* 2d ed. (Paris: Garnier Frères, 1848), 11–17, 155–74; P. Janet, *Saint-Simon et le Saint-simonisme* (Paris: Baillière, 1878), 133–36.

37. See P. Leroux, *De l'Humanitê, de son principe, et de son avenir* (Paris: Perrotin, 1840), tome 2, livre 6ème: *De la tradition relativement à la vie future,* 509–26, 530–37, and the publication *Doctrine de Saint-Simon: Exposition Première année 1829,* edited by Le Bureau de l'Organisation (Paris, 1831), 6–6, 174, 179, 200–2, 268.

38. As Mill wrote in *Representative Government* (1861), these differences were "as entirely irrelevant to political rights, as differences in height, or in the color of the hair," in *CW,* 19:479.

39. Mill, *Diary,* 646 (24 January 1854).

40. Bain, *John Stuart Mill,* 94.

41. Rossi, "Sentiment and Intellect," 19–31. See also Francis E. Mineka, *The Dissidence of Dissent: "The Monthly Repository," 1806–1838* (Durham: University of North Carolina Press, 1944), chaps. 4–7.

42. Mill to G. D'Eichthal, 1 March 1831, in *CW,* 12:71. On the relationship between Mill and St. Simonians, see Richard K. P. Pankhurst, *The Saint Simonians Mill and Carlyle: A Preface to Modern Thought* (London: Lalibela, 1957), and Bernard Semmel, *John Stuat Mill and the Pursuit of Virtue* (New Haven, CT: Yale University Press, 1984), chap. 2.

43. "It is full of good things well said about marriage, divorce and the position of women. St. Simonians and Fourierists deserve eternal gratitude for what they have done on the subject." Mill to his wife, 18 January 1855, in *CW,* 14:298.

44. "*Sans doute, dans l'ordre de la justice éternelle, l'homme et la femme sont égaux, et Dieu, en pesant dans la même balance leurs fautes et leurs mérites, n'établit aucune différence entre les deux moitiés d'un même limon remontées devant son tribunal,*" in E. Barrault, *Eugéne,* 2 vols. (Paris: Desessart, 1842–43), 2:358.

45. Ibid., 2:364, 71–72; 1:173.

46. *Ware's Letters from Palmyra,* 461. Mill never confused Christ with the Christian churches. As he said in many occasions, he admired Christ and Socrates in a similar way (i.e., to F. Mistral, 6 October 1869, in *CW,* 17:1646).

47. William Veeder, *Mary Shelley and Frankenstein: The Fate of Androgyny* (Chicago and London: University of Chicago Press, 1986), 23–27.

48. See Jehan D'Ivray, *L'aventure Saint Simonienne et les femmes* (Paris: Alcan, 1928), 84; J. A. Notopoulos, *The Platonism of Shelley: A Study of Platonism and the Poetic Mind* (Durham, NC, Duke University Press, 1949), 289.

49. Mill, *On Marriage,* 38, 40–41. Regarding this subject, see Kate Millet, *Sexual Politics* (Garden City, NY: Doubleday, 1970), 103–6.

50. See R. Owen and A. Campbell, *Debate on the Evidence of Christianity: Containing an Examination of the "Social System"* (Bethany: Campbell, 1928), and J. S. Mill, *On Marriage,* 43. It is legitimate to see in his picture of women's subordination a sort of transfiguration of his past subjection. According o Sampson, *Psychology of Power,* 92-102, Mill developed this critical attitude through a reflection on his condition while under his father's tutelage and that from this experience of tyranny emerged his description of marriage. After all, if chronology has any value, one cannot forget that Mill began to write *On Liberty*—which was closely associated with his reflection on women's equality—at the same time that he began to compose his autobiography. In this regard, the Owenists and St. Simonians offered him the interpretive instruments for clothing his personal sentiments in theoretical dress.

51. Mill, *The Subjection of Women,* 293.

52. Ibid., 295. Concerning the connection between domestic life and political justice, see Susan M. Okin, *Justice, Gender, and the Family* (New York: Basic Books, 1989), 17–18; Mary L. Shanley, *Feminism, Marriage, and the Law in Victorian England, 1850–1895* (Princeton, NJ: Princeton University Press, 1989), 63–65, 193–95.

53. "We are entering into an order of things in which justice will again be the primary virtue; grounded as before on equal, but now also on sympathetic association; having its root no longer in the instinct of equals for self-protection, but in a cultivated sympathy between them; and no one being now left out, but an equal measure being extended to all," in Mill, *The Subjection of Women,* 295.

54. Ibid., 266.

55. "But the true virtue of human being is fitness to live together as equals; claiming nothing for themselves but what they freely concede to every one else; regarding command of any kind as an exceptional necessity, and in all cases a

temporary one; and preferring, whenever possible, the society of those with whom leading and following can be alternate and reciprocal," ibid., 294. Comparing Athens and modern civilization, Mill seemed to be very skeptical about the superiority of the latter. He acknowledged the unmatched greatness of the civic liberties of Periclean democracy, even if he also admitted that the "moderns" were able to improve in three fields: the invention of a representative system of government, economic organization capable of generating wealth without the use of slavery, and the progressive emancipation of women. See J. S. Mill, *Grote's History of Greece* (1853), in *CW*, 11:315–15.

56. Mill, *The Subjection of Women*, 294–95.

57. Ibid., 286–87, 268.

58. Ibid., 288.

59. Mary L. Shanley, "Marital Slavery and Friendship: John Stuart Mill's *The Subjection of Women*," *Political Theory* 9 (1981):237 n. 2. See also *Hegel's Philosphy of Right*, translated by T. M. Knox (Oxford: Oxford University Press, 1979), part 3, sec. 166 and addition. So Mill wrote Comte about German philosophy: "*Je ne suis pas peut-être en droit de donner là-dessus une opinion tres décidée, n'ayant moi-même lu ni Kant ni Hegel ni aucun autre des chefs de cette ecole, que je n'ai d'abord connue que par ses interprètes anglais et français*" in (*CW* 13:576). The English interpreters were Coleridge and Carlyle; the French one was Victor Cousin, "*qui présente les même idées tenébreuses avec une lucidité et un esprit de systématisation tout français*" in (*CW*, 13:509). From his letters to A. Bain and F. Brentano we know with certitude that Mill read Stirling's *The Secret of Hegel* (See *CW*, 16:1324) and perhaps Hegel's *Wissenschaft der Logik* (See *CW*, 17:1935).

60. Shanley, "Marital Slavery," 239.

61. Mill, *The Subjection of Women*, 334.

62. Mill to Sterling, 15 April 1829.

63. Bain, with a hint of irony, called Mill's heroic self-representation a "fixed idea," an obsession with living "not to serve himself but to serve his race," in *John Stuart Mill*, 159.

64. Mill to Sterling, 15 April 1829. It is interesting to see what Carlyle wrote about friendship as "communion of Soul with Soul" in antithesis with the utilitarian (that is, materialistic) tradition that made this one an obsolete statement: "Thus we, instead of Friends, are Dinner-guests," in *Sartor Resartus* (1831), in *Carlyle's Complete Works*, vol. 1 (New York: University Press), 162, 90–91, 175–76.

65. As he wrote in *On Liberty*, the relationship between different individuals makes each one better and improves society as well.

66. Mill to W. B. Adams, 20 October 1832, in *CW*, 12:123.

67. Mill, *The Subjection of Women*, 334.

68. Ibid., 290–91. Mill is so strongly devoted to this ideal union that sometimes, when he contemplates his own marriage, he leaves in the reader a kind of

disconcert. This is the case, for instance, when he wrote in his *Diary*: "But when I am nearest to feeling in myself some likeness to the one being who is all the world to me, then I am ready to kill myself for not being like her and worthy for her," p. 660 (12 March 1854).

69. Mill, *The Subjection of Women*, 335.

70. Regarding this argument, see, for example, Susan M. Okin, *Women in Western Political Thought* (Princeton, NJ: Princeton University Press, 1979), 226–28, and her more recent *Justice, Gender, and the Family*, 20–21; Leslie Goldstein, "Mill, Marx, and Women's Liberation," *Journal of the History of Philosophy* 18 (1980): 325–30; J. Ring, "Mill's *The Subjection of Women*: The Methodological Limits of Liberal Feminism" *Review of Politics* 47 (1985): 27–44, at n. 1.

71. "Since Mill favored a more androgynous character type in his ideal of human personality, one might here expect from him a frontal attack upon traditional sex role differentiation in the family. Mill in the end capitulates to the traditional sexual division of labor within the family," in Richard W. Krouse, "Patriarchal Liberalism and Beyond: From John Stuart Mill to Harriet Taylor," in *The Family in Political Thought*, edited by Jean B. Elshtain (Amherst: University of Massachusetts Press, 1982), 164.

72. Tulloch, *Mill and Sexual Equality*, 12–14.

73. Mill, *Diary*, 664 (26 March 1854).

74. Mill, *Coleridge*, 119.

75. "It is necessary on such a subject [women's equality] to be as far as possible invulnerable" (Mill to W. E. Hickson, May 1851, in *CW*, 14:66).

76. Mill, *The Subjection of Women*, 295.

77. Regarding this, see also his article, *Stability of Society* (1850), in *CW*, 25:1180–82.

78. Mill, *The Subjection of Women*, 298.

79. I have found the same argument among the first radical emancipationists in Italy. Examples include Anne Maria Mozzoni, who translated in 1870 Mill's essay on the subjection of women, and the writers of the first Italian feminist weekly, *La Donna*.

80. Mill to John Allen, 27 May 1867, in *CW*, 26:1273–74. This letter was used by Leslie Goldstein to prove that the "tactical stratagem" argument cannot be sustained (in "Mill, Marx," 329–30). But the letter does not prove Mill's predilection for the traditional view of the division of labor between wife and husband. On the Contrary, it says that "the adaptation of the work of each person" is not "a thing to be preappointed by society"—that is, it defends the principle of personal free choice and the rights of minorities.

81. Mill to Helen Taylor, 21 February 1860, in *CW*, 15:683.

82. On Mill's Malthusianism and its contradictory location in his thought on liberty, see Gertrude Himmelfarb, *On Liberty and Liberalism: The Case of John Stuart Mill* (New York: Alfred A. Knopf, 1974), 119–25; David Levy, "Libertarian,

Communism, Malthusians, and J. S. Mill Who Is Both," *Mill Newsletter* 14 (1980): 2–16, at n. 1.

83. "I confess I am not charmed with the ideal of life held out by those who think that the normal state of human beings is that of struggling to get on; that the trampling, crushing, elbowing, and treading on each other's heels, which form the existing type of social life, are the most disagreeable symptoms of one of the phases of industrial progress," in Mill, *The Principles of Political Ecomony*, in *CW*, 3:754.

84. Ibid., in *CW* 2:367–68. It is important to emphasize that among the characteristics of a good life that Mill contemplated was "solitude," to which he subordinated at times even scientific and industrial progress, ibid., in *CW*, 3:756.

85. Ibid., in *CW* 2:368–69.

86. But Mill upheld women's right to have "an equal voice with men in what concern that function," ibid., 373. See Eugenio Lecaldano, "John Stuart Mill e il diritto alla vita," *Rivista di filosofia* 74 (1983): 62–85.

87. Mill, *The Principles*, in *CW*, 3:765–66. But see also his letter to Lord Amberley, 2 February 1870, in *CW*, 17:1693.

88. Mill to Florence Nightingale, 31 December 1867, in *CW*, 16:1343.

89. F. A. Hayek, *John Stuart Mill and Harriet Taylor: Their Correspondence and Subsequent Marriage* (Chicago: University of Chicago Press, 1951), 168.

Selected Bibliography

Works by J. S. Mill

Autobiography. Collected Works of John Stuart Mill (hereafter "CW"). Edited by John M. Robson. Toronto: University of Toronto Press, 1963-1991. Vol. X, 261-386.

Chapters on Socialism. CW, Vol.V, 703-53.

"Nature." CW, Vol. X, 373-402.

On Liberty. CW, Vol. XVIII, 213-310.

"On Marriage." CW, Vol. XXI, 37-49.

Periodical Literature: Edinburgh Review. CW, Vol. I, 291-325.

Principles of Political Economy: With Some of Their Applications to Social Philosophy. CW, Vols. II and III.

Sexual Equality: Writings by John Stuart Mill, Harriet Taylor Mill, and Helen Taylor. Edited by Ann P. Robson and John M. Robson. Toronto: University of Toronto Press, 1994.

The Subjection of Women. CW, Vol. XXI, 261-340.

Utilitarianism. CW, Vol. X, 203-59.

Other Works

Baum, Bruce. *Rereading Power and Freedom in John Stuart Mill.* Toronto: University of Toronto Press, 2000.

Campos Boralevi, Lea. "Utilitarianism and Feminism." In *Women in Western Political Philosophy: Kant to Nietzsche*, edited by Ellen Kennedy and Susan Mendus. Hertfordshire, England: Wheatsheaf Books, 1987.

Di Stefano, Christine. "John Stuart Mill: The Heart of Liberalism." In *Configurations of Masculinity: A Feminist Perspective on Modern Political Theory*, edited by Christine Di Stefano. Ithaca: Cornell University Press, 1991.

Donner, Wendy. "A Millian Perspective on the Relations Between Persons and Their Bodies." In *Persons and Their Bodies: Rights, Responsibilities, Relationships*, edited by Mark J. Cherry and Thomas J. Bole III. Dodrecht: Kluwer Academic Publishers, 1999, 57-72.

Eisenstein, Zillah. *The Radical Future of Liberal Feminism*. Northeastern Series in Feminist Theory. Boston: Northeastern University Press, 1986.

Goldstein, Leslie. "Mill, Marx, and Women's Liberation." *Journal of the History of Philosophy*, 18 (1980).

Hekman, Susan. "John Stuart Mill's *The Subjection of Women*: The Foundations of Liberal Feminism." *History of European Ideas*, 15 (1992): 681-686.

Heyek, F. A. *John Stuart Mill and Harriet Taylor: Their Friendship and Subsequent Marriage*. London: Routledge and Kegan Paul, 1969.

Himmelfarb, Gertrude. *On Liberty and Liberalism: The Case of John Stuart Mill*. New York: Alfred A. Knopf, 1974.

Krouse, Richard. "Patriarchal Liberalism and Beyond: From John Stuart Mill to Harriet Taylor." In *The Family in Western Political Thought*, edited by Jean Bethke Elshtein. Amherst: University of Massachusetts Press, 1982.

Lyndon Shanley, Mary. *Feminism, Marriage, and the Law in Victorian England, 1850-1895*. Princeton: Princeton University Press, 1989.

Lyons, David. "Mill's Theory of Justice." In *Values and Morals: Essays in Honor of William Frankena, Charles Stevenson, and Richard Brandt*, edited by Alvin Goldman and Jaegwon Kim. Dordrecht: D. Reidel, 1978, pp. 1-20.

Mendus, Susan. "John Stuart Mill and Harriet Taylor on Women and Marriage." *Utilitas*, 6 (1994).

Morales, Maria H. *Perfect Equality: John Stuart Mill on Well-Constituted Communities*. Lanham, MD: Rowman & Littlefield Publishers, Inc., 1996.

Okin, Susan Moller. "John Stuart Mill, Liberal Feminist." In *Women in Western Political Thought*. Princeton: Princeton University Press, 1979, chap. 9.

Packe, Michael St. John. *The Life of John Stuart Mill*. New York: Macmillan Co., 1954.

Rees, John. "The Thesis of the Two Mills." *Political Studies*, 15 (1977): 368-82.

Rossi, Alice. "Sentiment and Intellect: The Story of John Stuart Mill and Harriet Taylor Mill." In *Essays on Sex Equality*. Chicago: The University of Chicago Press, 1970, pp. 3-63.

Stephen, James Fitzjames. *Liberty, Equality, Fraternity*. London: Smith Elden, 1873.

Stove, David. "The Subjection of John Stuart Mill." *Philosophy* 68 (1993).

Tulloch, Gail. "Mill's Epistemology in Practice in His Liberal Feminism." *Educational Philosophy and Theory*, 21 (1989).

Tulloch, Gail. *Mill on Sexual Equality*. Hertfordshire, England: Harvester Wheatsheaf, 1989.

Index

About the Contributors

Julia Annas is the Regents professor of philosophy at the University of Arizona. She specializes in ancient Greek philosophy, especially psychology, epistemology, and Platonic ethics. She is the author of *An Introduction to Plato's Republic* (Oxford, 1981), *Hellenistic Philosophy of Mind* (University of California Press, 1992), *The Morality of* Happiness (Oxford, 1993), and *Platonic Ethics, Old and New* (Cornell University Press, 1999).

Keith Burgess-Jackson is associate professor of philosophy at the University of Texas, Arlington. His areas of specialization are moral, social, political, and legal philosophy. He is the author of *Rape: A Philosophical Investigation* (Dartmouth Publishing Company, 1996), and "Our Millian Constitution: The Supreme Court's Repudiation of Immorality as a Ground of Criminal Punishment," *Notre Dame Journal of Law, Ethics and Public Policy* 18 (2004, in press).

Wendy Donner is professor of philosophy at Carleton University. Her areas of specialization include the philosophy of John Stuart Mill, ethical theory, environmental philosophy, political philosophy, and philosophy of feminism. She is the author of *The Liberal Self: John Stuart Mill's Moral and Political Philosophy* (Cornell University Press, 1991) and "Utilitarianism" in the *Cambridge Companion to Mill*, ed. John Skorupski (Cambridge University Press, 1997).

John Howes is president of Learningguild, an education and social movement based in Melbourne, Australia. He was lecturer and senior lecturer in philosophy at the University of Melbourne, and professor and head of philosophy at Cape Town, where he lectured on Mill's *On Liberty* and wrote against apartheid and for an open society. His work includes articles on Mill and on Plato.

Mary Lyndon Shanley is professor of political science on the Margaret Stiles Halleck Chair at Vassar College. Her work in political theory has focused on historical and contemporary issues of gender. She is the author of *Feminism, Marriage and the Law in Victorian England* (Princeton University Press, 1989) and "The Subjection of Women" in the *Cambridge Companion to Mill*, ed. John Skorupski (Cambridge University Press, 1997). She has co-edited *Feminist Interpretations and Political Theory* (Polity Press and Penn State Press, 1990) and *Reconstructing Political Theory: Feminist Essays* (Polity Press, 1997).

Susan Mendus is professor of politics at the University of York. Her work in historical and contemporary problems in political philosophy has been informed by feminism. She is the author, most recently, of *Feminism and Emotion* (Macmillan 2000), as well as of numerous papers on such issues as toleration, impartiality, and pluralism. She has co-edited *Women in Western Political Philosophy: Kant to Nietzsche* (Wheatsheaf Books, 1987).

Maria H. Morales is associate professor of philosophy at Florida State University. Her areas of specialization are the British utilitarians, especially John Stuart Mill, social and political philosophy, and philosophy of feminism. She is the author of *Perfect Equality: John Stuart Mill on Well-Constituted Communities* (Rowman and Littlefield Publishers, Inc., 1996).

Susan Moller Okin was Marta Sutton Weeks professor of ethics in society and professor of political science at Stanford University. At the time of her untimely death on 3 March 2004, she held the Marta S. Horner Distinguished Visiting Professorship at the Radcliffe Institute for Advanced Study. It has been said of her that she "invented the study of gender and political theory." Okin's work focused on the exclusion of women from most Western political thought, historical and contemporary. She made notable contributions to the understanding of the politics and economics of work and family. Recently, she was expanding on her work on gender, economic development, and women's rights in the late twentieth-century. Three of her most famous works are *Women in Western Political Thought* (Princeton, 1979), *Justice, Gender, and the Family* (Basic Books, 1989), and co-authored with others *Is Multiculturalism Bad for Women?* (Princeton, 1999). Her influence has been such that it has become difficult, if not impossible, to write about political theory regarding the position of women without taking the domestic sphere and the economic impact of "private" life into account.

Nadia Urbinati is associate professor of political science at Columbia University. A political theorist, her areas of specialization are in democratic political philosophy, modern political thought, and theories of political representation. She is the author of *Mill on Democracy: From the Athenian Polis to Representative Government* (The University of Chicago Press, 2002).